T0302052

Examining the Role of National Promotional Banks in the European Economy:

Emerging Research and Opportunities

Iustina Alina Boitan
Bucharest University of Economic Studies, Romania

A volume in the Advances in Finance, Accounting, and Economics (AFAE) Book Series

DISSEMINATOR OF KNOWLEDGE

www.igi-global.com

Published in the United States of America by
    IGI Global
    Business Science Reference (an imprint of IGI Global)
    701 E. Chocolate Avenue
    Hershey PA 17033
    Tel: 717-533-8845
    Fax: 717-533-8661
    E-mail: cust@igi-global.com
    Web site: http://www.igi-global.com

Copyright © 2017 by IGI Global. All rights reserved. No part of this publication may be reproduced, stored or distributed in any form or by any means, electronic or mechanical, including photocopying, without written permission from the publisher.
Product or company names used in this set are for identification purposes only. Inclusion of the names of the products or companies does not indicate a claim of ownership by IGI Global of the trademark or registered trademark.

Library of Congress Cataloging-in-Publication Data

Names: Boitan, Iustina Alina, author.
Title: Examining the role of national promotional banks in the European
  economy : emerging research and opportunities / by Iustina Alina Boitan.
Description: Hershey, PA : Business Science Reference, [2017]
Identifiers: LCCN 2016046845| ISBN 9781522518457 (hardcover) | ISBN
  9781522518464 (ebook)
Subjects: LCSH: Development banks--Europe. | Financial institutions--Europe.
  | Economic development--Europe. | Public welfare--Europe.
Classification: LCC HG1976.E85 B65 2017 | DDC 332.2/8094--dc23 LC record available at
https://lccn.loc.gov/2016046845

This book is published in the IGI Global book series Advances in Finance, Accounting, and Economics (AFAE) (ISSN: 2327-5677; eISSN: 2327-5685)

British Cataloguing in Publication Data
A Cataloguing in Publication record for this book is available from the British Library.

All work contributed to this book is new, previously-unpublished material. The views expressed in this book are those of the authors, but not necessarily of the publisher.

Advances in Finance, Accounting, and Economics (AFAE) Book Series

ISSN:2327-5677
EISSN:2327-5685

Editor-in-Chief: Ahmed Driouchi, Al Akhawayn University, Morocco

Mission

In our changing economic and business environment, it is important to consider the financial changes occurring internationally as well as within individual organizations and business environments. Understanding these changes as well as the factors that influence them is crucial in preparing for our financial future and ensuring economic sustainability and growth.

The **Advances in Finance, Accounting, and Economics (AFAE)** book series aims to publish comprehensive and informative titles in all areas of economics and economic theory, finance, and accounting to assist in advancing the available knowledge and providing for further research development in these dynamic fields.

Coverage

- Public Finance
- Economic Downturn
- Auditing
- Entrepreneurship in Accounting and Finance
- Evidence-Based Studies
- Statistical Analysis
- Banking
- Applied Accounting
- Economic Policy
- Economics of Innovation and Knowledge

IGI Global is currently accepting manuscripts for publication within this series. To submit a proposal for a volume in this series, please contact our Acquisition Editors at Acquisitions@igi-global.com or visit: http://www.igi-global.com/publish/.

The Advances in Finance, Accounting, and Economics (AFAE) Book Series (ISSN 2327-5677) is published by IGI Global, 701 E. Chocolate Avenue, Hershey, PA 17033-1240, USA, www.igi-global.com. This series is composed of titles available for purchase individually; each title is edited to be contextually exclusive from any other title within the series. For pricing and ordering information please visit http://www.igi-global.com/book-series/advances-finance-accounting-economics/73685. Postmaster: Send all address changes to above address. Copyright © 2017 IGI Global. All rights, including translation in other languages reserved by the publisher. No part of this series may be reproduced or used in any form or by any means – graphics, electronic, or mechanical, including photocopying, recording, taping, or information and retrieval systems – without written permission from the publisher, except for non commercial, educational use, including classroom teaching purposes. The views expressed in this series are those of the authors, but not necessarily of IGI Global.

Titles in this Series

www.igi-global.com

701 East Chocolate Avenue, Hershey, PA 17033, USA
Tel: 717-533-8845 x100 • Fax: 717-533-8661
E-Mail: cust@igi-global.com • www.igi-global.com

Table of Contents

Preface

The topic of the book gravitates around the concept of national development banks in Europe, also known as promotional banks (although the two terms can be used interchangeably, European legislation typically refers to "promotional" entities).

National promotional banks (NPBs) came back in the spotlight after the onset of the 2008 financial crisis, when they proved the ability to restore the functioning of the credit market and channel liquidity towards real economy. At present they are gaining momentum, especially at European level, being increasingly perceived as key financial institutions within the broader EU policy framework meant to enhance investment, growth and employment. Thus, once the financial turmoil had been overcome, NPBs returned to their basic mission, namely to provide support for structural change in national economies through a smarter use of national and European public financial resources.

National promotional banks are a natural complement of mainstream banking, due to their broad expertise and knowledge of the local business and investor communities as well as of national development strategies and to the capacity to mobilize both national and European funding and catalyze long-term finance.

Consequently, a topical issue on the European Commission's agenda is represented by national promotional banks and practical manners they could actively get involved in supporting structural change in economies. In a European Commission communication launched in July 2015 it is strongly outlined their role in providing financing to different key sectors where market failures have been identified and which are underserved by commercial banks. In this respect, it is envisaged the role that NPBs have to play in providing financing through the new financial instruments designed by EC (such as ESIF, COSME and InnovFin, NCFF and PF4EE under the LIFE programme, Creative Europe), in order to support the Investment Plan for Europe launched by European Commission in November 2014. It is also proposed a flexible definition of NPBs, meant to expand the coverage area of the more traditional one, which included only the national development banks. This relaxation of the conceptual framework opens the debate related to the typology of financial intermediaries that should fall under the scope of the flexible definition. The European Association of Public Banks acknowledges the high degree of diversity and complexity which characterizes the business models of promotional banks and other financial institutions and argues that these coexisting highly specialized financial institutions are able to best serve the different financing needs in a national economy.

National promotional banks across Europe are a trending and timely topic to be further investigated, the more so as in February 2016 the Committee on Budgets within EC launched a call for proposals for a briefing on new financial instruments and the role to be played by national promotional banks for the benefit of Small and Medium Sized Enterprises.

The book aims to provide a comprehensive overview of European NPBs business model specificity, as well as a manifold perspective on its financial performance, by employing both qualitative and empirical (mathematic and statistical) approaches. The theme developed in this publication aims at filling a major gap in the research literature devoted to promotional banks and is expected to exert an impact especially among decision makers, financial institutions, professionals and academics interested in this topic. To the best of my knowledge this research approach distinguishes from existing working papers due to several novel, unique features, namely:

1. Comprehensiveness of the sample of banks, by relying on all the national promotional banks operating at present in Europe;
2. A time span that relies on the most recent available data (years 2011 - 2014);
3. The use of real data taken from NPBs annual financial statements;
4. An interdisciplinary nature, bringing together the financial markets with social sciences (economy), mathematical and statistical methods;
5. A gradual presentation and succession of arguments, from conceptual ones, to case studies and empirical analyses, all focusing on the 18 NPS considered.

The first chapter explains the context that triggered the revival of national promotional banks' concept and emphasizes the market failures that can be successfully addressed. It has been described the traditional acceptation on national development/promotional banks launched by international organizations, financial institutions and academia, as well as the newer, flexible definition proposed by European Commission. Further, it has been outlined their business model specificity in terms of promotional mandate, ownership structure, the features of their funding mechanisms, the allocation of financial resources on destinations and the specific sources of risk. It has been performed a case study approach, by analyzing the 18 European national promotional banks included in the sample against each business model feature.

The second chapter discusses the contribution exerted by national promotional banks to economic and social welfare. The chapter follows a three-tier structure in order to discriminate between the views expressed by policymakers and market participants (financial institutions, consultancy firms and practitioners in the financial sector), by academia/research centers and by the historical data. Information and analyses in this chapter depict a practical nature and are strongly connected to current realities, as they:

1. Clearly state the European countries comprising a NPB or having recently launched one and explain the reasons a country decides to set up a NPB;
2. Outline the NPBs involvement in implementing EC's financial instruments by receiving funding under the various EC's financial programs;
3. Assess the contribution of NPBs activity to increasing a country's welfare, measured through several financial, economic and social indicators within the resident country.

The third chapter provides an exploratory approach, in order to identify resembling NPBs, in terms of:

1. Several financial indicators related to profitability, capital adequacy and size, and
2. Financial structure indicators.

It has been employed the Cluster Analysis method as it is best suited for assessing the proximity between banks, for identifying the homogenous ones and establishing optimal group membership. The algorithms at the core of Cluster Analysis divided the initial sample of 18 NPBs into distinct, meaningful groups, by relying on several financial indicators in such a manner that the degree of similarity between two NPBs is maximal if they are included in the same cluster or minimal otherwise. This method is a valuable statistical tool for uncovering latent, hidden structures existing in the sample considered and for performing an operational classification of promotional banks into more manageable, meaningful clusters. It helps at investigating whether

NPBs across EU countries have aligned their business practices and balance sheets structure, or on the contrary, there is evidence of heterogeneity across financial positions and financial indicators. The research direction developed in this chapter hasn't been addressed by any other study devoted to national promotional banks, being the first screening exercise of the European NPBs.

The fourth chapter develops another so far unexplored research direction as it investigates the financial performance recorded by NPBs, by relying on the concepts of efficiency and productivity. To estimate the relative degree of efficiency recorded by each national promotional bank in the sample, it has been employed the Data Envelopment Analysis nonparametric technique. At the core of this method is the solving of several linear programming problems, the final outcome being the computation of efficiency scores for each NPB and the construction of a best practice or efficiency frontier. These findings allow us to discriminate between efficient and inefficient banks and make a ranking, to understand how each NPB performs relative to others in the sample, which are its closest peers and how it can improve its performance to become efficient. DEA analysis has been run distinctly for each year in the time span 2011 – 2014. It has been tested an output-oriented DEA model, with variable returns to scale and single-input single-output specification, in the assumption of a financial intermediation approach, because the role of NPBs is to act as mediators between the demand of money, represented by small and medium sized enterprises, and the offer of money, comprising both national and European sources. Further, to gain a complementary and dynamic picture, it has been computed a DEA-type Malmquist index of total factor productivity to measure the productivity changes over time for each NPB in the sample. This technique also allows the identification of the main sources of changes in total productivity levels, in terms of catch-up effect (technical efficiency change) and technological progress (developments of banking activity driven by new information technology). The Malmquist index is constructed by relying on Data Envelopment Analysis' distance functions and a panel data that reconciles the 18 European NPBs and all the 4 years considered.

The last chapter of the book has its roots in several recent debates which have raised the question on the opportunity to expand the coverage of the promotional banks' main definition so as to include other types of non-banking financial institutions that could also exert a significant influence within the process for the implementation of the Investment Plan for Europe. Consequently, the chapter launches several proposals for widening the coverage of NPBs typologies, according to European Commission's flexible definition. It has been performed a radiography of the diverse, coexisting typology of financial intermediaries that depict the potential for operating as NPBs, due to their public commitment for making a valuable contribution for pursuing and achieving medium and long-term economic, environmental and social goals. The financial intermediaries envisaged are represented by cooperative banks, ethical/social banks, and sustainable/socially responsible banks, because their business models imply holding specific knowledge on the economic and financial territorial realities, and in addition comply with the criteria defined by the European Commission in its flexible definition of promotional banks. It has been performed an incursion into the definition and peculiarities of each financial institution's business model by following an in-depth documentation and data collection strategy. Moreover, to reveal the territorial spread across European countries of each type of financial institution identified as operating according to the principles of NPBs, it has been created a geographical map. Further, the chapter has investigated whether these types of financial institutions have applied for obtaining European funding from EU or the European Investment Bank. It has been detailed the EU sources of finance, the type of financing provided and the typologies of customers benefitting from it.

Throughout the book it has been adopted both a practical and empirical strategy for addressing this subject from multiple perspectives, as it is in the spotlight of European and national decision makers, financial institutions, academia and research centers. To date, existing research on this particular topic takes the form of working papers or policy research papers published by financial institutions' research departments or academia. Their emphasis is on discussing the importance of NPBs both in crisis and non-crisis periods, issues related to their business model, regulatory and supervisory practices, pros and cons of establishing a new NPB. However, they all lack a quantitative assessment of NPBs activity or impact on national economies, being preponderantly related to a theoretical approach.

This publication aims at bringing a fresh, topical and comprehensive analysis of NPBs already established in EU countries, as well as the survey of the most recent incentives in this regard. The practical approach brought by the first two chapters (the review of the mandate they have in each EU country, the status of their application for receiving funding under the newly launched EC's financial programs, past involvement in channeling EU funding to national SMEs, the impact their activity had on macroeconomic fundamentals in the country of residence) is complemented with an empirical assessment of their business model's resemblance, their efficiency in performing their financial intermediation function, the productivity change one year from another and the drivers of these changes.

The book is appropriate for the use of multiple audiences, from European and national decision makers, to professional associations and financial institutions (World Bank, United Nations, Deutsche Bank Research department, the European Central Bank, the European Association of Public Banks, the Network of European Financial Institutions for Small and Medium Sized Enterprises, the Long-term Investors Club).

It also might be of importance for academia, research centers within universities and for the use of under-graduate and graduate students. In this respect, there are envisaged the faculties/universities providing lectures on Credit Institutions or Banking/Financial Systems which might devote several hours to the study of NPBs.

Chapter 1
National Promotional Banks in European Union:
Definition and Business Models' Peculiarity

INTRODUCTION

Short after the acute phase of the 2008 financial crisis has been overcome, national and international regulatory bodies, financial institutions as well as researchers have initiated a wide search for the financial turmoil's triggers and for vulnerabilities to be further monitored and addressed. A large strand of literature has investigated, both qualitatively and empirically, the weak points at banks' individual level, at the macro level of the financial system but also of the regulatory frameworks in place at that moment.

Another strand of literature has put emphasis on the large scale and diverse range of effects financial crisis has generated, namely: erosion of public confidence in the financial system, particularly in banks; financial system and real economy disruption; cross-border contagion; clear proofs of market and regulatory frameworks failures. In respect of the latter, the European Union has witnessed a broad reconfiguration of its regulatory and supervisory institutional architecture, has designed and implemented proper frameworks for the recovery and resolution of failing banks, for addressing the pro-cyclicality of previous capital adequacy framework, has outlined the need for broader use of quantitative early warning systems for prudential supervision purposes and shifted the focus of surveillance policies and tools to macro-prudential supervision, in order to best address issues related to systemic risk and contagion among financial markets.

DOI: 10.4018/978-1-5225-1845-7.ch001

Copyright ©2017, IGI Global. Copying or distributing in print or electronic forms without written permission of IGI Global is prohibited.

The fundamental, growing role to be played by national promotional banks (NPBs) emerged against a background characterized by tight constraints for small and medium-sized enterprises (SMEs) and companies to access bank or capital market long-term finance. Policy-makers have become aware on the increased potential of national promotional banks to provide counter-cyclical funding in times of financial and economic distress.

NATIONAL PROMOTIONAL BANKS' ROLE AND DEFINITION

Deutsche Bank (2015, p.1) argues that NPBs have gained a key place in the economic policy toolkit for over-coming cyclical and structural difficulties, in completing financial systems' functioning. It expects that promotional banks will continue exerting an important role in the next years, due to their genuine mission focused on supporting structural economic changes and mitigating market failures. The European Association of Public Banks (2015a, p.4) observes that, in times of recession or financial and economic distress, promotional banks perform a beneficial lender of last resort function for the SMEs and companies.

A report launched by United Nations (2005, p.13) enumerates some issues which can be successfully addressed by NPBs when solving various forms of market failures, as follows: creating inclusive financial markets, boosting the development of financial system, acting as a catalyst for all the players in the business sector and private sources of capital, diminishing a country's economic volatility. Griffith-Jones (2015, p.4), adds that NPBs help alleviating another form of market failure, represented by banks' unwillingness to finance complex or expensive sectors of activity or investment projects due to their potential uncertainty regarding the future success rate and financial returns to be obtained. According to Svilan (2016, p.2), promotional banks, as a special segment of the broad financial sector, have been established with the fundamental aim of covering the market gaps which can be the result of asymmetric information, externalities and weak competition, by operating complementarily with other financial intermediaries and catalyzing long-term finance.

In a similar fashion, United Nations (2012, p.1) perceives NPBs as a viable alternative to commercial banks, as they target long-term social and economic welfare while the latter depict pro-cyclical lending patterns and a financial behavior oriented on short-term profitability.

The European Committee of the Regions (2016, p.4) concludes that promotional banks are valuable instruments for implementing the economic, structural and social policy of a country, but stresses that, for alleviating structural weaknesses in markets functioning, it is necessary a long-term, wide-ranging definition and interpretation of the market failures.

The concept of promotional bank[1] is often used interchangeably with the terms development bank or policy bank, but they all share the same mandate of promoting economic development. In the following there is a brief overview of the NPBs conceptual acceptations and scope.

World Bank defines them as "a bank or financial institution with at least 30% state-owned equity that has been given an explicit mandate to reach socioeconomic goals in a region, sector or particular market segment (De Luna Martinez, Vicente 2012, p.4)."

According to the United Nations (2005, pp. 10-11), they are "government owned financial institutions set up to foster economic development, often taking into account objectives of social development and regional integration, mainly by providing long-term financing to, or facilitating the financing of projects generating positive externalities".

In the view of Deutsche Bank (2015, p.2), NPBs "are a particular type of public financial institution with a dedicated promotional mission. They are instruments for implementing economic policy goals". In addition, it is proposed three criteria for best describing the features and scope of NPBs, namely: an official development mandate set out by law, state ownership and competitive neutrality in regard of financial intermediaries.

The particularities of promotional banks' financial activities reside from their dual purpose, which reconciles in a complementary fashion a public function with banking specific features. NPBs are acting as instruments of public policy, due to their state-ownership which obliges them to a firm commitment in supporting state's economic and social objectives and performing a public function, and on the other hand are governed, regulated and supervised similar to a credit institution (Association of German Public Banks, 2014, p.6).

Smallridge et al. (2013, p. 15) point the mobilizing role played by NPBs, which derives from active collaborations with national or cross-country financial intermediaries in order to provide end-customers appropriate financial and non-financial products and services. The authors outline that "it is typically not in the nature of NPBs to compete", as their business rationale is to valuably complement, not crowding out private financial intermediaries.

NPBs are assimilated to "institutional instruments of public policy whose performance is measured more in terms of social benefits generated" (Bruck, 2009, p.62).

Dalberg (2010, p.4) describes NPBs as "government-controlled institutions that invest in sustainable private sector projects with the twofold objective of spurring development in developing countries while themselves remaining financially viable".

These generally agreed traditional acceptations on national development/promotional banks presented above have to be complemented with a newer, more flexible definition proposed by European Commission (2015) in its Communication on the key role NPBs have to exert in supporting and implementing the Investment Plan for Europe. Accordingly, NPBs "are defined as legal entities carrying out financial activities on a professional basis which are given a mandate by a Member State or a Member State's entity at central, regional or local level, to carry out development or promotional activities" (EC, 2015, p. 3). This definition aims at expanding the range of financial institutions that depict the potential for providing promotional products and services and opens the field for new debates regarding the specific financial intermediaries' typologies that might fall under the scope of NPBs flexible definition.

Specificities of the Promotional Banks' Business Model

Although NPBs have to mandatory depict some specific features, in terms of ownership and mission (policy mandate), at European level the promotional landscape appears to be fragmented and heterogeneous, due to idiosyncratic features of their business models (Deutsche Bank 2015, p.6). The remaining of the chapter provides a comprehensive examination on NPBs' business models' peculiarities. It has to be mentioned that throughout the entire book the sample of national promotional banks considered for qualitative and quantitative analyses comprises all the 18 NPBs which depict a track record of at least 10 years of activity. The newly launched ones (since 2012) cannot make the subject of the analysis due to their small track record, and hence low data availability for comparative assessments. The 18 NPBs and their country of origin are: Bulgarian Development Bank (Bulgaria), Eximbank (Romania), Českomoravská záruční a rozvojová banka (CMZRB - Czech Republic), Landwirtschaftliche Rentenbank (Germany), KfW (Germany), Instituto de Crédito Oficial (Spain), Hrvatska Banka (HBOR - Croatia), Cassa Depositi e Prestiti (Italy), Societe Nationale de Credit et d'Investissement (Luxembourg), MFB Hungarian Development Bank (Hungary), OeEB

(Austria), Bank Gospodarstwa Krajowego (Poland), SID Bank (Slovenia), Slovenská záručná a rozvojová banka (Slovakia), Municipality Finance (Finland), Finnvera (Finland), KredEx (Estonia) and BNG Bank (Netherlands).

Policy or Promotional Mandates

These may be classified as *general*, and *specific*, meant to promote particular economic sectors or activities. At international level, the distribution between general and specialized mandates is about even (Deutsche Bank 2015, p.3). Similarly, de Luna-Martinez and Vicente (2012, p. 11) have identified two types of mandates, namely: a narrow, specific one, which explicitly presents the economic sectors, activities and type of customers to be supported by the NPB, and a broad mandate which is formulated in general terms without reference to a given sector or activity. The authors also discuss the strengths and weaknesses of each mandate-type. Narrow mandates allow NPBs specialization, sound monitoring and performance evaluation, but lack the flexibility of shifting the targeted sectors or customers. On the other hand, the broad mandates benefit from increased flexibility in financing a wide range of key sectors and activities, but are more prone to lose focus and effectiveness.

Both international organizations and researchers have outlined several activities and sectors that the mandate of a NPB should commit to.

United Nations (2012, p.2) emphasize the fundamental role that NPBs may play in catalyzing the expansion of social and economic infrastructure (education, health, energy, transport, sanitation, housing), in the development of strategic importance sectors such as R&D and innovation, in the internalization of strategically important production chains, in increasing the export competitiveness of domestic firms, local community or regional development.

A report financed by the Federal Ministry of Finance of Germany and elaborated by Berlin Economics (2014, p.2), a consulting firm in Germany, enumerates several recommendations derived from international best practice, that have to be implemented in the mandate of a NPB, namely:

a broad and flexible definition of potential sectors to be promoted, since government priorities can change over time; a limitation of allowed activities, in order to avoid unfair competition with commercial banks; and provisions to ensure long-term financial sustainability, to make sure the bank is solvent under any circumstances.

It is also clearly stated those sectors to whom NPBs should focus: SME development, innovation, export promotion, energy efficiency, investment in housing or municipalities infrastructure, deepening of commercial banks' activities, development of the local government bond market.

Bassanini, Pennisi, and Reviglio (2015, p.8) claim that the major distinction between mainstream banking and NPBs resides in the latter's aim "of providing medium and long-term capital for productive investment, often accompanied by technical assistance". In authors' opinion, productive investment projects are those in infrastructure, the industrial sector, agriculture, education and health. The identification and selection of this type of projects has to be based on two criteria: employment increase and productivity of the production factors increase.

Griffith-Jones (2015, p.5) adds a new perspective, by claiming that the mandate of a NPB has to include also the funding of sectors and activities highly exposed to environmental externalities, in which social returns are usually higher than market returns.

In practice[2], the European NPBs depict various types of mandates, either general or specialized ones, in line with the status of development, constraints and needs within their national financial and economic environment, as follows:

- Bank Gospodarstwa Krajowego (Poland) mission is to support social and economic growth of the country and the public finance sector. It finances investment projects from selected industries (housing infrastructure, energy efficiency, public utilities), and provides guarantees to SMEs.
- Bulgarian Development Bank (Bulgaria) supports with priority the activity of domestic SMEs: pre-export and export lending, crediting through local banks or directly the activity of SME, guarantees for participation in tenders, good performance bonds, advance payment bonds, guarantees for repayment of exporter loans, consultancy relating mainly to preparation of projects and application for utilization of funds/subsidies from European Union funds, consultancy regarding SME capital structure.
- Cassa Depositi e Prestiti (Italy) finances investments and promotes the leveraging of the real estate assets, social housing, infrastructure, and assists businesses of all sizes, in the export and internationalization process.
- Českomoravská záruční a rozvojová banka (CMZRB - Czech Republic) has a primary goal the broad provision of assistance to SMEs on various topics (access to financial capital, business risk management, support tools as bank guarantees, preferential loans and financial subsidies). In addition, it implements the Government nation-wide eco-

nomic strategy and the individual regions policy related to economic sectors, finances projects related to regional technical infrastructure and housing.

- Croatian Bank for Reconstruction and Development (HBOR, Croatia) finances the reconstruction and development of the Croatian economy, infrastructure, promotes exports, supports the development of SME, promotes environmental protection, insures export transactions against political and commercial risks, issues guarantees and provides business advice.
- KredEx (Estonia) provides financial support to enterprises, manages credit risks connected with export activities, and offers loans with particular focus on housing and energy-efficiency.
- Kreditanstalt für Wiederaufbau (KfW, Germany) finances activities in the areas of SME and start-up finance, risk capital, innovation, technical progress, housing, environmental and climate protection, infrastructure, municipal finance, measures for the promotion of education, development cooperation.
- Landwirtschaftliche Rentenbank (Germany) grants promotional loans for agribusiness and rural areas.
- Instituto de Crédito Oficial (Spain) supports the economic activities that contribute to the growth and balanced distribution of national wealth, with particular focus on social, cultural, innovating or environmental activities.
- MFB Hungarian Development Bank (Hungary) finances micro, small and medium-sized enterprises, pharmacists, agricultural producers and family farmers, investments in infrastructure.
- Municipality Finance Plc – MuniFin (Finland), is specialized in the financing of the Finnish public sector, by providing loans exclusively to Finnish municipalities, their majority-owned companies, and non-profit housing companies.
- Finnvera (Finland) – provides financing for start-ups and SMEs, in order to support their growth, export activities and internationalization.
- OeEB (Development Bank of Austria) has the public mandate to work for better living conditions in developing countries, by providing long-term loans for investments and by acquiring a financial interest in companies in developing countries and emerging markets.
- SID Bank (Slovenia) has the mission to develop and promote long-term financial services designed to supplement financial markets for the sustainable development of Slovenia. Its specific focus is to complement the activities performed by the domestic financial market.

- Slovenská záručná a rozvojová banka (Slovakia) focuses primarily on the development of SMEs, agricultural entities, the funding of cities, towns and municipalities and housing reconstruction.
- Societe Nationale de Credit et d'Investissement (Luxembourg) grants start-up/transmission loans to newly incorporated or inherited domestic SMEs, finances investments of Luxembourg companies abroad.
- Bank Nederlandse - BNG Bank (Netherlands) focuses exclusively on providing financing for the public sector, represented by local authorities, public sector housing, healthcare and educational institutions and public utilities, the goal being to minimize their financing costs.

Ownership Structure

A report issued by United Nations (2012) explains that the significant discrepancy across NPBs has its roots in the ownership models. Some promotional banks are fully state-owned, while others depict mixed ownership. The research performed by Deutsche Bank (2015, p.3) subscribes to the view above mentioned, stating that NPBs around the globe depict very different patterns and sizes. In terms of ownership, the partial public ownership is complemented with a mix of private national, foreign, and multilateral ownership. De Luna-Martinez and Vicente (2012, p.9) argue that NPBs are typically the largest state-owned and controlled financial institutions. Irrespective the extent of state-ownership, government is in charge with establishing the strategic direction of the NPB, as well as its senior management and board members. In cases when private sector is a minority shareholder, it has the right to own part of NPB's capital, while the control of the institution is exerted by Government.

Berlin Economics (2014, p.3) puts more emphasis on the role that policy makers should play in the governance of a NPB. They should involve in defining the mission and general strategy of the NPB and in supervising its activities, but not interfere in the regular conduct of business or the decision-making process. Moreover, governance has to secure the NPBs long-term financial sustainability.

By analyzing the 18 most important NPBs in Europe in terms of ownership structure, it has been found that 6 out of 18 NPBs are partially owned by the state (state is their main shareholder), while the wide majority of promotional banks are fully state-owned.

Českomoravská záruční a rozvojová banka (CMZRB) is 72% owned by the State, as well as some major Czech banks. Czech Republic is the bank's main shareholder, being represented by three ministries: Ministry of Indus-

Figure 1. Type of ownership
Source: author

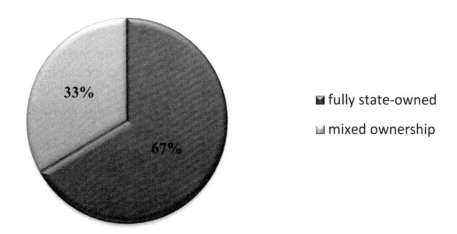

try and Trade, Ministry of Regional Development and Ministry of Finance. KfW is 80% owned by the Federal Government, while the remaining 20% is held by Germany's regional states. The Romanian state, through the Public Finance Ministry, is the main shareholder of Eximbank (95.37%) while the remaining is hold by several financial investment companies. Municipality Finance Plc (MuniFin) is owned by the Finnish public sector, comprising the municipalities, the government of Finland and a public sector pension fund. Cassa Depositi e Prestiti (Italy) is majority owned by the state, through the Ministry for the Economy and Finance which holds 80.1% of share capital, with the remainder being held by 64 different banking foundations regulated by the central government. BNG Bank (Netherlands) share capital is held in proportion of 50% by the State of the Netherlands and the other half by municipal authorities, provincial authorities and a water board.

Funding Mechanisms

United Nations (2012, p.3) observes that globally many NPBs are capitalized through tax revenues, in complementing other additional sources of funding such as low-cost foreign loans and aid. The sources of funding, in terms of maturity and stability, help NPBs to strengthen their financial autonomy and to decrease the exposure to liquidity risk, which is the risk that due to ample maturity mismatches the lending capacity of a NPB be seriously limited.

A World Bank research report summarizes the different options NPBs in various geographic areas may use and combine for collecting financial resources, such as:

(i) taking savings and deposits from the public, (ii) borrowing from other financial institutions, (iii) raising money in the domestic or international capital markets, (iv) using their own equity, and (v) receiving budget allocations from the government (De Luna-Martinez and Vicente, 2012, p.10).

It is also mentioned that almost half of the NPBs in the sample are deposit-takers, while the others do not resort at all to raising deposits from general public.

Deutsche Bank (2015, p.11) noticed the similarities between European NPBs and their global peers in terms of the mixed funding base. However, European NPBs are not encouraged to take retail deposits, although they may take deposits from other banks.

In the following, it has been performed an in-depth review of European NPBs funding mechanisms, to shed light on their intrinsic peculiarities. It has been considered 18 NPBs, for which data on annual reports have been available. Generally, the items in the liability side of their balance sheet are represented by:

- Deposits from banks;
- Deposits from customers (corporate and/or retail clients) represented by current accounts, term deposits, guarantee deposits;
- Borrowings from regional, European or international financial institutions and multilateral organizations. It consists of long-term loans obtained mainly from European Investment Bank, Council of Europe Development Bank, European Investment Fund, Nordic Investment Bank, Black Sea Trade and Development Bank, Japan Bank for International Cooperation, China Development Bank, International Investment bank;
- Debt securities issued on the capital market, consisting of bonds;
- Financial liabilities held for trading.

A major finding of this case study approach resides in classifying NPBs in two groups, namely deposit taking and non-deposit taking institutions (see Figure 2). NPBs that do not raise deposits are KredEx in Estonia, Municipality Finance and Finnvera in Finland, Landwirtschaftliche Rentenbank and KfW in Germany, Cassa Depositi e Prestiti in Italy, Societe Nationale de Credit et d'Investissement located in Luxembourg, BNG Bank in Netherlands, SID Bank in Slovenia and Instituto de Crédito Oficial in Spain. These 10 promotional banks have replaced the funds to be obtained through deposits by the item liabilities to banks and customers, which comprises money-market transactions, repurchase agreements, credit-linked notes (as in Luxembourg, German and Spanish NPBs), or by postal passbook accounts and postal bonds (as is the case for Italian NPBs). In addition, Landwirtschaftliche Rentenbank employs also securitized liabilities, which might include medium-term notes, global bonds, Euro commercial papers, or bearer bonds while KfW relies also on certificated liabilities, consisting of money-market issues, bonds and notes.

Bank Gospodarstwa Krajowego in Poland is a hybrid between the two types of funding, as it removed from its liability portfolio, since 2012, the deposits collected from individuals but still maintains the deposits attracted from corporate sector and banks. The remaining 7 NPBs act as deposit-taking institutions, both from financial institutions and customers.

By analyzing the structure of the funding mechanisms, it has been noticed that NPBs in the sample heavily use at least two instruments for raising financing from the national or international markets and that they resort on diverse maturities, amounts and reimbursement patterns for their borrowings. The Italian NPB is the only that puts most emphasis on 3 types of liabilities for obtaining financing, namely liabilities to customers, borrowings from international institutions and debt securities issuance. At the opposite are several NPBs with the less diversified structure of funding, as they raise most of their financing mainly by a single instrument (deposits from customers at

Figure 2. Deposit taking versus non-deposit taking NPBs
Source: author

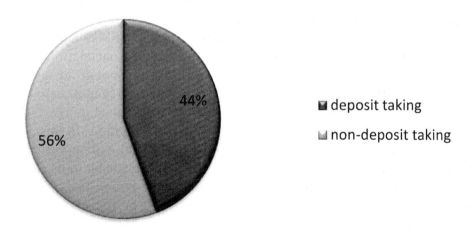

Českomoravská záruční a rozvojová banka – CMZRB from Czech Republic, debt securities issuance at Finnvera from Finland, securitized liabilities at Rentenbank and certificated liabilities at KfW both located in Germany, liabilities to customers at Societe Nationale de Credit et d'Investissement in Luxembourg), the other liability items recording low amounts.

Eight out of 18 NPBs obtain funding by relying on borrowings from central banks and international financial institutions, as follows: Bulgarian Development Bank (Bulgaria), Instituto de Crédito Oficial in Spain, Hrvatska Banka (HBOR - Croatia), KredEx (Estonia), Cassa Depositi e Prestiti (Italy), MFB Hungarian Development Bank (Hungary), SID Bank (Slovenia) and Slovenská záručná a rozvojová banka (Slovakia). From these, banks in Croatia, Hungary, Italy and Slovenia place the higher weight on this particular liability item.

Issuance of debt securities is mostly used by 12 out of 18 NPBs, as follows: OeEB (Austria), Municipality Finance and Finnvera (Finland), Rentenbank and KfW (Germany), Hrvatska Banka (HBOR - Croatia), Cassa Depositi e Prestiti (Italy), MFB Hungarian Development Bank (Hungary), BNG Bank (Netherlands), Bank Gospodarstwa Krajowego (Poland), SID Bank (Slovenia), Instituto de Crédito Oficial (Spain). NPBs in Finland, Germany, Hungary and Spain put the stronger emphasis on this liability item for obtaining funding for their promotional activities. Consequently, debt securities issued hold the highest share in total liabilities.

Deposits represent the main source of financing for only 3 NPBs, namely Českomoravská záruční a rozvojová banka – CMZRB from Czech Republic (deposits from customers), OeEB from Austria (deposits from banks), and Bank Gospodarstwa Krajowego from Poland (deposits from the state).

The case of Eximbank from Romania is quite apart, as its highest amounts of funding have the source in three state funds, namely the guarantee fund, the financing fund and the insurance fund. Consequently, the bank acts as a financial intermediary between the state and the real economy. The financing, guarantees or insurance services provided by the bank to SMEs and companies from these state funds are granted on behalf of the Romanian state and cannot be used by the bank in order to obtain further economic advantages for it. The NPB also relies on deposits from customers to fund its activity.

Apart from the traditional sources of funding described above, NPBs may apply for obtaining funding from EU financial programs. In this case, European NPBs act as intermediaries between EU and end customers in their countries, their role being to distribute the EU financing to particular sectors of activity or investment projects in several pre-established fields. As Deutsche Bank (2015, p.11) observed, usually NPBs in weaker economies (e.g. Hungary, Bulgaria) tend to be more reliant on EU financial support for their operation. In this regard, it is notable to mention the big step ahead made by European Commission (2015) which emphasized the increased role that NPBs will have to play in providing financing through the new financial instruments designed by EC, in order to actively support the Investment Plan for Europe launched by EC in November 2014.

More practical details related to NPBs which applied for receiving funding under the EC's financial programs and their involvement in channeling EU funding to national SMEs in various sectors of activity is provided in chapter 2.

Allocation of Financial Resources on Destinations

The asset side of NPBs balance sheet provides information on the financial and non-financial products and services offered to customers. It worth to be mentioned that the specific activities performed by NPBs require good knowledge about financial markets, capital market, financial intermediation, financial transactions, human resources, marketing, technical assistance (Bruck, 2009, p.62).

The report published by United Nations (2012, p.2) comprehensively synthesizes the broad range of financial and non-financial operations NPBs could perform, as follows:

a. *Project appraisal and technical assistance to key sectors and strategic projects, taking into account social rather than private rates of return;*
b. *Pooling of small private or public sector (e.g. municipality) loans into negotiable packages;*
c. *Purchase of equity positions (shares or options) to signal state support for specific projects, and to catalyze private sector credit for strategic ventures;*
d. *Provision of export-import credit for local firms, helping to overcome the chronic scarcity of commercial credit due to information costs and risks involved in export-import banking;*
e. *Provision of credit guarantees, especially for small and medium enterprises;*
f. *Provision of long-term loans and credit guarantees for infrastructure projects;*
g. *Creation of new mechanisms and markets for long-term lending, fostering competition in financial markets, supporting financial sector develop-ment (banks, securities companies and the stock market) and leading to allocation improvements even in the private segments of the market.*

An interesting observation has been provided by a World Bank report (de Luna-Martinez & Vicente, 2012, p. 16). Its survey found that over 70% of global NPBs rely on the provision of loan guarantees, the rationale for heavily using it being to stimulate private commercial banks and other financial intermediaries in lending with their own financial resources to the same clients and economic sectors targeted also by NPBs.

Deutsche Bank (2015, p.4) argues that apart from traditional loans and guarantees products, NPBs are becoming increasingly more active in the area of long-term, strategic investment. In this respect, Griffith-Jones (2015, p.4) observes that NPBs often channel financing to highly complex and expensive sectors / investment projects as in their decision making put greater emphasis on positive impacts to be exerted by the loan applicant across the economy (positive externalities) or on cases in which social returns to be generated by the project exceed financial returns. Dalberg (2010, p.5) explains that European NPBs use to perform a screening of the private investment projects to be further financed, in terms of both economic development impact and financial viability. The author also enumerates several principles of good-practice that are guiding the selection process, namely: "the need to be additional (going where other investors don't), catalytic (paving the way for others to follow) and sustainable (making sure that investments have long-term viability)". To sum up, a key feature of NPBs activity is to critically evaluate investment projects from a two-fold perspective, namely their ability to generate financial returns and at the same time positive economic and social impacts, reason for which they are also called hybrid financial institutions (Sobreira and Zendron, 2011).

A particular attention is paid to a characteristic of NPBs lending models, known as first-tier (retail) lending and second-tier (wholesale) lending. Promotional banks implement a first-tier lending model when they envisage a direct provision of financing to end-customers. It is also relied on in cases when the territorial spread of traditional banking network is scarce and dispersed, being the risk that some local communities can't be reached (Deutsche Bank, 2015, p.4). Second-tier lending implies cooperation between NPBs and banking system, in which the former provides financing to other financial institutions which subsequently re-direct this funding to end-customers and handle all the application and loan monitoring process. As second-tier NPBs do not lend directly to customers, they neither collect funds by means of retail deposits. Deutsche Bank (2015, p.11) appreciates that "second-tier lending tends to be particularly dominant in countries where relationship banking is strong".

The study of De Luna-Martinez and Vicente (2012, p.14) found out that globally, more than half of NPBs surveyed lend through a combination of first and second-tier, 36% lend only through first-tier and the remaining of 12% employ only second-tier lending. Berlin Economics (2014, p.3) draws attention on the potential risk for banks' crowding-out and recommends that NPBs should use mainly the commercial bank channel for financing end-customers (second-tier model).

The previous analysis of the 18 European NPBs financial position has been completed in the following with an in-depth study of their asset side configuration. Generally, the items in the asset side of NPBs balance sheet are represented by:

- Cash and balances with central Bank (current accounts, deposits);
- Loans provided to banks;
- Loans provided to customers;
- Financial assets held for trading;
- Financial assets held to maturity;
- Financial assets available for sale.

A major classification of NBPs can be performed in terms of their lending models (first-tier vs. second-tier). Three out of 18 NPBs exclusively use second-tier lending for financing real economy sectors, namely Rentenbank and KfW (Germany) and Instituto de Crédito Oficial (Spain). Other promotional banks provide financing by relying on both lending models, although the second-tier structure is more pronounced and holds a higher amount than first-tier. It is the case of OeEB in Austria, Bulgarian Development Bank in Bulgaria, Hrvatska Banka in Croatia, Societe Nationale de Credit et d'Investissement in Luxembourg, and SID Bank in Slovenia. There are also several NPBs that still rely heavily on first-tier lending approach, as follows: Českomoravská záruční a rozvojová banka in Czech Republic, KredEx in Estonia, Municipality Finance and Finnvera in Finland, MFB Hungarian Development Bank in Hungary, Cassa Depositi e Prestiti in Italy, BNG Bank in Netherlands, Bank Gospodarstwa Krajowego in Poland, Eximbank in Romania, and Slovenská záručná a rozvojová banka in Slovakia.

Another classification can be performed in terms of the size and composition of their financial assets portfolio. The majority of NPBs in the sample (14 out of 18) follow a prudent, precautionary approach, explained by the fact that they place higher weight on financial assets held to maturity (Rentenbank and KfW in Germany, Cassa Depositi e Prestiti in Italy, Bank Gospodarstwa Krajowego in Poland, Slovenská záručná a rozvojová banka in Slovakia, Instituto de Crédito Oficial in Spain) or financial assets available for sale (Bulgarian Development Bank in Bulgaria, Českomoravská záruční a rozvojová banka in Czech Republic, Hrvatska Banka in Croatia, KredEx in Estonia, Municipality Finance and Finnvera in Finland, BNG Bank in Netherlands, SID Bank in Slovenia, Slovenská záručná a rozvojová banka in Slovakia). Financial assets held to maturity represent a stable financial resource of the promotional bank as they regularly generate interest income, but in addition they can be used as collateral, for guaranteeing the financing obtained by a NPB from the central bank or other financial institutions.

There are also two promotional banks (OeEB in Austria and Eximbank in Romania) whose portfolio of financial instruments comprises a large share of assets held for trading. The rationale for this type of financial assets is to be held in banks' portfolio for short periods of time and to make the subject of successive sells and acquisitions, conditioned by the market price of the financial assets at a given moment in time. In other words, NPBs relying mostly on financial assets held for trading depict a speculative behavior, as they aim at obtaining profits from frequent, price advantageous trading.

Risk Management

Promotional banks' unique features reside from pooling together different but complementing tasks. They all follow a public mission that has to reconcile clear public goals established at regional, national or supra-national level with the real needs of local communities and SMEs and a commercial business strategy, without distorting the proper functioning of the financial system and altering competition. The specific risks NPBs are exposed to represent a natural consequence of this mix of activities. Many of the traditional financial risks commercial banks deal with are also present in the regular activity of a NPB, namely credit risk, market risk, liquidity risk or capital adequacy requirements.

A necessary delineation between the promotional activities performed by NPBs and their operational side has been introduced by European Commission (2015, p.5). The range of promotional activities to be effectuated by a NPB are usually subject to approval by the supervisory board, which comprises government representatives, while the operational part is exempted from political influence being left to professional management. Consequently, the existence of "sound risk management and internal control procedures prevent NPB boards from taking hazardous financial and organizational decisions".

Deutsche Bank (2015, p.16) outlines the strong emphasis NPBs should put on sound and reliable risk management procedures and provides several reasons in this respect, namely:

1. Regular activities are performed in areas where uncertainty and risks are higher;
2. They often depict concentrated exposures to particular economic sectors, geographical regions or categories of debtors;
3. The typology of risks they deal with is more difficult to anticipate, due to the specificity of their projects financed (e.g. projects with a long-term focus in economic, social or environmental fields, investments in infrastructure).

A comprehensive study performed by World Bank (De Luna-Martinez and Vicente, 2012) on a sample of global promotional banks found that over 70% of respondent NPBs perceive as a major challenge the improvement of risk management capacity, followed by the need to become financially self-sustainable (almost 60%) and improving corporate governance and transparency (around 50%).

An interesting viewpoint pertains to Sobreira and Zendron (2011), which argue that the range of risks NPBs currently deal with have been already pre-established when governments have defined the scope of promotional banks as being related to financing activities susceptible to generate positive externalities, to provide long-term lending and support start-ups and new sectors of activity. All these types of activities determine NPBs to take on risks that financial intermediaries are not willing to bear due to increased uncertainty regarding projects' rate of success.

Another source of increased risks relates to the mere financial environment NPBs operate. In times of financial distress, when traditional banks' risk aversion increases being followed by a significant decline of the amount of lending directed to real economy sectors, promotional banks have to step in and act countercyclical. The financing they provide alleviates the financing constraints of SMEs, defreeze the lending channel and prevents the national economy enters in recession. Nevertheless, NPBs shouldn't lose sight of their public role and capacity constraints, in terms of maintaining good capital adequacy, own financial viability and balanced risk profile.

Deutsche Bank (2015, p.17) argues that NPBs' countercyclical activities contribute to a supplementary risk expansion in terms of scale and scope and greater uncertainty in assessing the creditworthiness of a borrower or the success of an investment project, hence requiring the intensification of risk-management procedures.

The German Development Institute (2015, pp. 2-3) explains that, when NPBs decide to extend their lending activity, they have to be aware of the existing tradeoff between the loan portfolio's pace of growth and its quality.

Although it is ascertained that the scale of lending operations is important, especially in bad times, the priority has to be always the high quality loans. Good quality loans, which can be fully reimbursed at maturity and do not expose the promotional bank to the default risk, are important not only from the standpoint of improving NPBs' credit rating, but also they can be converted into profit and then reinvested in further sustainable loans.

The credit risk to be incurred by NPBs also depends heavily on the lending models implemented, namely first-tier and/or second-tier. If the NPB provides loans through a first-tier structure, then it will deal with the entire credit risk of the project financed, as it acts like a commercial bank and offers loans directly to the applicant. In cases when the NBP relies mostly on second-tier lending, it provides loans to a financial intermediary who will redirect them to end-customers. In other words, the promotional bank acts as a refinancing tool for local commercial banks; it establishes the terms and the conditions for granting the loan, but project selection, risk assessment procedures and further loan monitoring are delegated to other private banks (Schmit, Gheeraert, Denuit, & Warny, 2011, p.86).

Consequently, the NPB will take the credit risk of the financial intermediary, while the latter will be exposed to project's credit risk (Smallridge et al., 2013, p. 17). Gutierrez, Rudolph, Homa, and Beneit (2011, p. 21) agree that risk-management procedures implemented by second-tier promotional banks need not be as sophisticated as in first-tier ones, because NPBs have only to assess the risk and risk management skills of the commercial bank through which they lend to reach the end-customer. The task of analyzing project's risk and outcomes belongs to the commercial bank, which from authors' standpoint adds objectivity to the credit allocation due to limiting political interference for financing unsustainable projects.

Apart from being subject of general banking regulation and central bank's prudential monitoring, it would be indicated that NPBs obtain credit ratings from reputable agencies too, to gain a more comprehensive assessment of their activity (Berlin Economics 2014, p.3).

The European Association of Public Banks (2015a) has performed a comprehensive analysis on the impact to be exerted by the new prudential supervisory requirements on NPBs financing capacity and operational costs. It is outlined the imperative need for European Central Bank and national regulators to adopt a proportional approach in respect of promotional banks' regulation and supervision, by taking into account several criteria such as balance sheet size, systemic importance, complexity of activities and interconnectedness with financial sector entities. The reason relies in the very low or virtually non-existent level of complexity and interconnectedness, due to their public mandate which implies low risk business model, limited geographical scope and specialized, narrow field of activities.

In addition to financial risks, promotional banks are also greatly exposed to reputational risk due to their positioning as a binder between the state and the market. As their prevailing ownership model is the full state-ownership, a particular attention should be paid on the fulfillment of ethical principles in conducting the business, transparency of decision making and funds allocation, non-involvement in speculative financial activities. Any failure in achieving their public commitments will propagate directly to impairing the trust in the state authorities, because they are those that have established the governance structure of the NPB, its business strategy and public mission. According to European Commission (2015, p.5), the key drivers of NPBs' reputation are the promotion of high standards of transparency and accountability, professional management, the maintaining of a necessary degree of independence from policymakers and prudential supervision exercised independently by a monetary policy authority.

The risk of strategy is also of particular importance, as the governing board of the NPBs has to define and implement a clear balance between promotional activity and operating in a competitive environment with other financial intermediaries. As Deutsche Bank (2015, p.21) observes, "risks lie with potential overburdening of development banks and setting expectations too high for what they can achieve".

Unlike the traditional banking system, promotional banks are less exposed to operational risk arising from the use of information communications technology (ITC). The explanation resides in their mere object of activity, which is focused on providing financial resources to entrepreneurs and companies, with little or very low interaction with natural persons. Consequently, they do not provide internet or mobile banking services through which individuals could perform by their own various financial transactions (online payments through their current account, interrogation of their current account balance, creation of a deposit). Promotional banks rely only on an internet platform or website to transparently advertise and disclose their operations and financial reports. On the contrary, banks are increasingly benefiting from connectivity enhancement (such as high-speed internet, increased number of mobile subscribers, electronic banking services) in order to attract new customers, expand their territorial spread (both urban and rural customers) and increase the number and volume of online transactions performed by customers. According to World Bank's (2016) economists, ICT is becoming the largest distribution platform for providing market information, financial education and financial services to millions of people in urban, rural and poor areas.

Griffith-Jones (2015, p.6) advocates for the beneficial effects of having a more diversified financial system, comprising various complementing types of financial institutions with different strengths and mutual synergies on achieving inclusive, sustainable and dynamic growth. However, the author stresses that the vices of one sector (short-term thinking, focus on profit optimization, excessive financial risk-taking) shouldn't be transmitted to the promotional banks. Their genuine scope and mission is to deal with economic risks residing from the uncertainty specific to new projects, new sectors of activity or entrance on new markets, rather than assuming purely financial risks and mimicking the financial behavior of their private commercial bank peers.

REFERENCES

Association of German Public Banks. (2014). *Promotional Banks in Germany: Acting in the public interest.* Author.

Bassanini, F., Pennisi, G., & Reviglio, E. (2015). *The Development/Promotional Banks: From the Financial and Economic Crisis to Sustainable and Inclusive Development.* Retrieved from http://www.bassanini.it/wp-content/uploads/2015/02/Bassanini_Pennisi_Reviglio_CDP-developmentbanks-FINALE-n.-207-numero-142014.pdf

Berlin Economics GmbH (2014). *Establishment of a Promotional Bank in Ukraine, Analysis and Recommendations.* Final report financed by the Federal Ministry of Finance of Germany.

Bruck, N. (2009). *The role of development banks in the twenty-first century.* Retrieved from http://www.adfiap.org/wp-content/uploads/2009/10/the-role-of-development-banks-in-the-twenty-first-century.pdf

Dalberg Global Development Advisors. (2010). The Growing Role of Development Finance Institutions in International Development Policy. Author.

De Luna-Martínez, J., & Vicente, C. L. (2012). *Global Survey of Development Banks.* World Bank Policy Research Working Paper No.5969.

Deutsche Bank Research (2015). *Promoting investment and growth: the role of development banks in Europe.* EU Monitor Global Financial Markets.

European Association of Public Banks. (2015a). *EAPB Annual Report 2014-2015.* Author.

European Commission. (2015). Working together for jobs and growth: The role of National Promotional Banks (NPBs) in supporting the Investment Plan for Europe. Communication from the Commission to the European Parliament and the Council.

European Committee of the Regions. (2016). *Opinion - Working together for jobs and growth: The role of National and Regional Promotional Banks (NPBs) in supporting the Investment Plan for Europe.* Communication from the Commission to the European Parliament and the Council, COM (2015) 361 final, 117th plenary session.

German Development Institute. (2015). *Financing Global Development: The BRICS New Development Bank.* Briefing paper, no.13/2015. Author.

Griffith-Jones, S. (2015). *The case and role for development banks: The European example.* Retrieved from http://policydialogue.org/files/events/Stephany_Paper.pdf

Gutierrez, E., Rudolph, H. P., Homa, T., & Beneit, E. B. (2011). *Development Banks, Role and Mechanisms to Increase their Efficiency.* World Bank Policy Research paper no. 5729.

Schmit M., Gheeraert L., Denuit T., & Warny C. (2011). *Public Financial Institutions in Europe.* European Association of Public Banks.

Smallridge, D., Buchner, B., Trabacchi, C., Netto, M., Gomes Lorenzo, J. J., & Serra, L. (2013). *The Role of National Development Banks in Catalyzing International Climate Finance.* Inter-American Development Bank.

Sobreira, R., & Zendron, P. (2011). Implications of Basel II for National Development Banks. In *Credit, Money and Macroeconomic Policy: A Post-Keynesian Approach.* Cheltenham, UK: Edward Elgar Publishing. doi:10.4337/9781849808729.00018

Svilan, S. (2016). The role of national promotional – investment banks. Info day CEF.

United Nations. (2005). *Rethinking the Role of National Development Banks. Background document.* New York: Department for Economic and Social Affairs, United Nations.

United Nations. (2012). *The Continuing Relevance of Development Banks.* UN Conference on Trade And Development, Policy Brief no. 04/April 2012.

World Bank. (n.d.). *Information Communications Technology for Development*. Accessed on September 25, 2016, http://live.worldbank.org/information-communications-technology-development

ENDNOTES

[1]   As the European legislation typically uses the term "promotional" (Deutsche Bank 2015, p.6) and the present book comprehensively investigates the business model and financial position of national development banks located in EU countries, it will be further employed only the term promotional.

[2]   Information on each NPB mandate has been collected from their websites.

Chapter 2

National Promotional Banks' Contributions to European Union Countries' Economic and Social Welfare

INTRODUCTION

To better delineate between the official, academic/research and historical record perspectives on European national promotional banks' economic and social involvement, the chapter follows a three-tier structure. The first part is devoted to underlining NPBs contribution to national economy, as documented by policymakers and market participants (financial institutions, consultancy firms and practitioners in the financial sector). It has been depicted the further role NPBs have to play in implementing the new financial instruments launched by European Commission and it has been synthesized the most active European national promotional banks that have applied for EC's funding instruments. The second part reviews existing qualitative and empirical research literature to assess academia's research premises and findings on the impact exerted by NPBs on financial and economic fundamentals. The last part investigates the relationship between NPBs size, in terms of total assets amount, and several financial, economic and social indicators within the resident country, in a comparative fashion. In addition, there are explained the reasons a country decides to set up a NPB and are presented the most recently established ones.

DOI: 10.4018/978-1-5225-1845-7.ch002

Copyright ©2017, IGI Global. Copying or distributing in print or electronic forms without written permission of IGI Global is prohibited.

POLICY-MAKERS' VIEW ON NPBS CAPACITY TO PURSUE ECONOMIC AND SOCIAL GOALS

In November 2014 the European Commission has launched the Investment Plan for Europe, an ambitious initiative having its roots in the need for greater confidence in the overall economic environment, for increased predictability and transparency in policy-making and the regulatory framework, for more effective use of scarce public resources, as well as enhanced trust in the economic potential of investment projects under development and reliable risk-bearing capacity to stimulate project promoters in unlocking invest-ment (EC, 2014, p.4). The fundamental goal of this Plan, which at the same time represents also a challenge, consists in pooling financial liquidity from EU budget, member states, NPBs and other public and private contributors and channeling them to smarter, long-term investments in order to support Europe's, competitiveness, the achievement of sustainable jobs and growth.

Two reinforcing pillars of the Investment Plan, which are directly connected with promotional banks' activity, are represented by the mobilization of at least EUR 315 billion until 2017 (through the creation of a European Fund for Strategic Investments in partnership between the European Commission and the European Investment Bank), with the stated purpose of boosting strategic investments and improve the access to investment finance for Small and Medium-Sized Enterprises (SMEs) and mid-cap companies, and secondly by the development of a framework meant to facilitate the meeting between EU financing and targeted real economy sectors. Both pillars request a strong cooperation between promotional banks, as important stakeholders, and the European Investment Bank. On the one hand, NPBs can contribute directly to the capital of the European Fund for Strategic Investments or can co-finance individual projects. Secondly, NPBs expertise will add a valuable contribution during the EC's screening exercise for identifying potentially viable projects with European significance to further channel the European financing.

The final recipients of long-term European strategic investments sup-ported by the European Fund for Strategic Investments are those projects in the fields of infrastructure, education, research and innovation, renewable energy and energy efficiency, although there will be adopted also a flexible approach towards identifying the specific needs of a country or region and selecting projects with no pre-established thematic or geographic rationale, but simply by assessing their value added and impact.

European Parliament (2015, article 23) agrees that the EFSI should sup-port a wide range of financial products (equity, debt and guarantees) due to its twofold reason of being, namely to best accommodate market's needs and to stimulate private investment in projects. It is strongly highlighted that

the EFSI should not be a substitute for private market finance or products provided by national promotional banks or institutions but should instead act as a catalyst for private finance by addressing market failures so as to ensure the most effective and strategic use of public money and should act as a means of further enhancing cohesion across the Union.

An interesting remark belongs to a group of researchers (Rubio, Rinaldi and Pellerin-Carlin 2016, p. 50) which warn that the increased involvement promotional banks will play in the functioning of EFSI might distort the objectivity of the process of screening for economically viable projects, the result being that EFSI financial products will be directed mostly to those countries having powerful national promotional banks.

Wruuck (2016) acknowledges the broad geographical coverage achieved by EFSI, but concludes that until now it is more known about EFSI's activity than its economic impact because the expected benefits cover multi-year time periods and depend on the implementation of projects.

In July 2015 the European Commission (2015) has launched a communication with an in-depth focus on the increased role promotional banks have to play for implementing the Investment Plan and enhancing its impact on investment, growth and employment. It encourages the setting up of national promotional banks, as well as effective ways of further involvement for existing ones, "due to their particular expertise and their knowledge of the local context, business and investor communities as well as national policies and strategies" (EC, 2015, p.2).

The European Committee of the Regions (2016, p.3) ascertains that although promotional banks currently operate with different business models, their important role in countering the effects of the economic and financial crisis cannot be neglected or underestimated, particularly on the background of low public investment at local, regional or national level.

The European Association of Public Banks - EAPB (2015a, p.10) welcomes the EC's Investment Plan and appreciates that the Plan fully recognizes the important role public, promotional banks have exerted since the beginning of the 2008 financial crisis, by providing dedicated financial instruments to jump-start investments of SMEs as well as of large-scale projects. EAPB outlines NPBs potential for further contribution to re-launching the European economy, in line with their public mandates, by relying on the cooperation mechanisms to be established at European level.

A World Bank policy report (de Luna-Martinez and Vicente, 2012) attributes to promotional banks the role of instrument in the service of the government, meant to promote economic growth by addressing the financing needs of households, SMEs or large companies. Draghi (2013, p.2), president of European Central Bank, is more concerned on the higher challenges SMEs, relative to larger companies, have to face when gaining access to financing, the more so as the euro area financial system is heavily bank-based. He advocates for the design of adequate financial instruments to combine the lending capacity of the European Investment Bank as well as resources from national promotional banks to support SMEs financing.

It can be noticed from those above mentioned that regulatory authorities widely agree that NPBs' involvement in real economy has to target particularly the SMEs sector, as it is more prone to experience liquidity shortages and failures in obtaining financing through bank credit, especially in times of financial turmoil or economic downturns. During these periods, banks' risk aversion increases, translating into a precautionary financial behavior. The direct consequence relates to a strengthening of creditworthiness assessment for each potential borrower, the more so as the informational asymmetry is higher. SMEs are the first to confront with barriers in accessing bank credit, rather than larger companies.

Dalberg (2010, p. 4) defines this drawback as the missing middle, namely "those businesses with perhaps the greatest potential to grow and create jobs being the very ones that have the least access to the investment they need to finance that development".

Therefore, promotional banks have to play an increasing role in complementing the financing that SMEs obtain from banks, from capital market (SME Asset-Backed Securities sector), or from innovative financial instruments such as crowdfunding (European Central Bank, 2014). Their comparative advantages rely on a deeper knowledge of national markets, which can be materialized both in terms of direct funding and provision of guarantees for SME lending.

Bassanini et al. (2015, p.2) are proponents of NPBs' ability to bridge, at least partially, the long-term financing gap. Their credibility might be explained through several reasons: long track record of activities, reliability of their business model characterized by public mission and non-volatile financial behavior, political institutional weight, in-depth knowledge of local communities, strong financial position due to stable funding structure, habit to support long-term investment.

In completing the already mentioned views, Berlin Economics (2014, p.6) agrees with the effectiveness and focused nature of NPBs in achieving economic, ecological and social policy goals and enumerates several of their main contributions, as follows:

1. Increase of government support programs and of subsidies' transparency and efficiency;
2. Help the enlargement and deepening of commercial banks` activities;
3. Development of the government bond market as they typically refinance themselves through local bonds;
4. Stimulate through their financing the development of SMEs, research and innovation, exports, energy efficiency projects, investments in housing or infrastructure.

The European Association of Public Banks (2015b, p.1) adds the contribution NPBs might play in the field of municipality financing, due to municipalities' participation in financing infrastructure projects and SMEs.

A new investment area NPBs might focus on is related to climate change mitigation projects. Smallridge et al. (2013) recognize the unique role NPBs compared to other players, such as bilateral international agencies or multilateral development banks, can exert in scaling up private sector investments for supporting low-carbon, climate-resilient development activities or projects. This is due to their intrinsic features, namely good, privileged knowledge on the national private sector's barriers to investment, enhanced potential for taking on risks related to the provision of long-term financing and their basic rationale of complementing and catalyzing private sector players.

The European Commission (2013) has identified another market failure to be addressed by NPBs and other interested financial intermediaries, namely the restricted, low access to finance faced by SMEs active in the cultural and creative sector. Therefore, it has been designed and launched the Creative Europe Program, with the fundamental aim of preserving and enhancing countries' cultural diversity and intrinsic cultural value, as well as mitigating people perception of culture as a non-economic activity[1]. Under this framework, financial intermediaries will provide loans to SMEs acting in the culture sector, which are guaranteed through the Cultural and Creative Sectors Loan Guarantee Facility. The selection of financial intermediaries is meant to be as comprehensive as possible, by covering different geographical markets and various cultural and creative sectors, such as architecture, libraries, artistic crafts, audiovisual (including film, television, video games and multimedia), cultural heritage, design, festivals, music, performing arts, publishing, radio and visual arts.

When summing up the recent range of countercyclical activities performed by promotional banks across Europe, three main trends emerge, namely: an expansion of activities in terms of scope, respectively in terms of scale and increased Europeanisation (Deutsche Bank, 2015, p.15). Regarding the latter trend, it can be described by two complementing features. The first one relates to the direct provision of loans to other NPBs (as is the case of KfW in Germany which provided global loans to promotional banks in Italy and Spain) or consulting and advice services to other NPBs or to governments planning to set up new financial institutions with promotional mission. The second feature is related to the contribution that NPBs made, from their financial resources, to the capital of the newly launched European Fund for Strategic Investments, as well as to their increased cooperation with the European Commission and the European Investment Bank in implementing their new financial instruments.

The launch of the Investment Plan for Europe has marked the beginning of a shift of focus in terms of EU funding programs, from the traditional approach based on European Commission's direct financial contributions in the form of grants (through the European Structural and Investment Funds - ESIF) towards a newer one, consisting of several innovative financial instruments. The common denominator of all EC's funding programs resides in NPBs active role to be fulfilled in the implementation of EU financial instruments managed both under shared management and directly by the European Commission and the European Investment Bank.

Whittle, Malan and Bianchini (2016, p.13), in a study requested by the European Parliament's Committee on Budgets, enumerate the particular involvement and role NPBs' play in implementing the EU financial instruments tailored for SMEs needs, as follows:

- Shared management of those EU financial instruments which are implemented on a decentralized basis at national / regional level;
- Act as financial intermediaries in implementing financial instruments managed directly by the European Investment Bank and the European Investment Fund ;
- NPBs co-investment in EU financial instruments schemes, in order to strengthen multiplier and leverage effects of EC's financing;
- Awareness-raising among other financial players in the banking system and among the SME target group on the specificities of EU financial instruments designed for SMEs;
- Information and advisory role to assist SMEs in accessing those EU financial instruments appropriate for their financial needs.

Table 1. Typology of EU financial instruments for the 2014-2020 programming period

---

A) EU Financial instruments under shared management

The **European Structural and Investment Funds (ESIFs)** represent the European Union's main investment policy tool, with a planned budget of €454 billion for 2014-2020 period. Financial resources will be channeled for investments in key EU priority areas, such as updating/developing skills and adaptability of Europe's workforce, job creation, SMEs competitiveness, infrastructure investment in areas such as broadband, IT and telecoms, and water supplies, sustainable growth of European economy. It comprises six funds, each one with its thematic objectives and budget, namely:

✓ The *European Regional Development Fund* covers all Member states and has a strong focus on 4 key priority areas: Research and Innovation, the Digital Economy, SME competitiveness and the Low Carbon Economy. Its total 2014-2020 budget is of €196 billion.

✓ The *European Social Fund*, with a total budget of €86 billion, is the main instrument for addressing people's needs (education, employment, develop start-ups and businesses, supports disadvantaged groups, efficient public services).

✓ The *Cohesion Fund* channels financing to 15 EU Member States, namely Bulgaria, Croatia, Cyprus, the Czech Republic, Estonia, Greece, Hungary, Latvia, Lithuania, Malta, Poland, Portugal, Romania, Slovakia and Slovenia. Its total budget is of €63 billion and will be allocated to the development of trans-European transport networks and to projects addressing EU environmental priorities.

✓ The *European Agricultural Fund for Rural Development* allocates funds to projects meant to alleviate the challenges EU rural areas face in terms of economic, environmental and social development. Its total budget for 2014-2020 is of €98 billion.

✓ The *European Maritime and Fisheries Fund* benefits from a total budget of €5 billion and focuses on a balanced territorial development of sustainable and competitive fisheries and aquaculture areas.

✓ The *Youth Employment Initiative* has been assigned a total budget of €3 billion to be used for tailored measures to decrease the level of youth unemployment, such as integrating young people on the labor market, education or training.

B) EU Financial instruments managed directly by EC and European Investment Bank

✓ *COSME* is the EU program designed for the Competitiveness of Enterprises and Small and Medium-sized Enterprises, benefiting from a planned budget of €2.3 billion. It aims at increasing and smoothing SMEs' access to guarantees, loans and equity capital in all phases of their lifecycle: creation, expansion, or business transfer. It relies on two pillars:

• The *Loan Guarantee Facility* (LGF). Its dedicated budget will fund guarantees and counter-guarantees for financial intermediaries to stimulate them in providing more loans and lease finance to SMEs, as it is widely known that SMEs usually do not hold enough collateral and are perceived as riskier.

• The *Equity Facility for Growth* (EFG) will target investments in risk-capital funds that provide venture capital and mezzanine finance to expansion and growth-stage SMEs, in particular those operating across borders.

✓ *InnovFin – EU Finance for Innovators* represents a new generation of financial instruments and advisory services developed and launched by the European Commission and the European Investment Bank. Its goal is to ease access to finance for innovative small, medium and large companies in Europe. The total budget of €2.7 billion will be allocated to several thematic products addressing specific financing needs of research and innovation sectors, namely: *InnovFin Large Projects, InnovFin MidCap Growth Finance, InnovFin MidCap Guarantee, InnovFin SME Guarantee* and *InnovFin Advisory* services.

✓ *Creative Europe* program has been designed by EC in order to support cultural, creative and audiovisual sectors. Its budget of €1.46 billion will be allocated through a Loan Guarantee Facility.

✓ *LIFE program* for the environment and climate change resides on two new financial instruments:

• The Private Finance for Energy Efficiency (PF4EE) benefits of a budget of €80 million for 2014 – 2017 which will be used to provide loans for financing investments in energy efficiency enhancing projects.

• The Natural Capital Financing Facility (NCFF) will employ its €100-125 million budget for providing loans to projects which promote the preservation of natural capital, adaptation to climate change, ecosystem services, green infrastructure, biodiversity and innovative pro-biodiversity.

Source: author, based on information collected from http://ec.europa.eu/growth/access-to-finance/

Table 2 synthesizes European national promotional banks that have applied for funding from EU newly launched financial instruments and have been authorized to act as financial intermediaries on behalf of the European

Table 2. NPBs carrying out lending or guarantees from EU financial resources

Country	Financial intermediary name	Type of financing provided	Investment focus	Budget of the program	Start date of the program	Sources of finance for the program
Bulgaria	Bulgarian Development Bank	Micro-loans to be implemented through commercial banks	Micro-enterprises and individuals	EUR 6,250,000	December 2015	European Investment Fund and the European Progress Microfinance Facility
Croatia	HBOR	Loans	Micro-entrepreneurs for promoting self-employment, modernization and expansion of existing business	Not available	February 2015	European Investment Fund and the European Union
		Loans	General Hospital construction project, to contribute to the upgrading of health care services and standards	EUR 40 million	June 2015	European Investment Bank
		Guarantees	SMEs including micro-enterprises and individuals	Not available	August 2014	Competitiveness and Innovation Framework Programme (CIP) - EU Guarantees managed by the European Investment Fund
		Loans	small and medium-sized companies and medium-capitalized companies in the industry, services, tourism and other sectors, as well as public and private companies investing in knowledge-based, infrastructure and environmental projects	EUR 800 million	March 2014	European Investment Bank
		Loans	modernization and upgrading of two existing hotels and associated tourism facilities in Mlini, and the construction of a new hotel in Srebreno, Croatia	EUR 25 Million	January 2014	European Investment Bank

continued on following page

Table 2. Continued

Country	Financial intermediary name	Type of financing provided	Investment focus	Budget of the program	Start date of the program	Sources of finance for the program
Czech Republic	Českomoravská záruční a rozvojová banka (CMZRB)	Guarantees	SMEs	Guaranteed amount up to 70% of the loan principal Guaranteed loan amount up to CZK 10,000,000 Guaranty period up to 6 years	January 2015	COSME Loan Guarantee Facility (EU program)
		Guarantees	SMEs	Envisaged portfolio volume - EUR 114 million	April 2016	European Fund for Strategic Investments resources to enhance the deployment of existing COSME Loan Guarantee Facility (EU program)
Estonia	KredEx	Guarantees	SMEs	EUR 120 million	April 2016	European Fund for Strategic Investments resources to enhance the deployment of existing COSME Loan Guarantee Facility (EU program)
France	Bpifrance	Guarantees	Research-based and innovative SMEs and Small Mid-caps	EUR 420 million	April 2016	European Fund for Strategic Investments resources to enhance the deployment of existing InnovFin Guarantee Facility
		Guarantees	innovative SMEs and Small Mid-caps	EUR 200 million	April 2016	InnovFin SME Guarantee
Germany	KfW	Guarantees	SMEs	EUR 1000 million	April 2016	European Fund for Strategic Investments resources to enhance the deployment of existing COSME Loan Guarantee Facility (EU program)
		Guarantees	Research-based and innovative SMEs and Small Mid-caps	EUR 500 million	April 2016	European Fund for Strategic Investments resources to enhance the deployment of existing InnovFin Guarantee Facility

continued on following page

Table 2. Continued

Country	Financial intermediary name	Type of financing provided	Investment focus	Budget of the program	Start date of the program	Sources of finance for the program
Italy	Cassa Depositi i Prestiti	Guarantees	SMEs	EUR 200 million	April 2016	European Fund for Strategic Investments resources to enhance the deployment of existing COSME Loan Guarantee Facility (EU program)
		Loans	urban/architectural reconstruction of private residential buildings and houses located in the Italian regions of Emilia Romagna, Lombardia and Veneto affected by two strong seismic events in 2012	EUR 1000 million	December 2015	European Investment Bank
Poland	Bank Gospodarstwa Krajowego	Guarantees	SMEs	EUR 193 million	April 2016	European Fund for Strategic Investments resources to enhance the deployment of existing COSME Loan Guarantee Facility (EU program)
Slovakia	Slovenská záručná a rozvojová banka (SZRB)	Loans	SMEs and mid-caps for the support of youth employment	EUR 15 million	January 2015	European Investment Bank
Spain	Instituto de Crédito Oficial (ICO)	Loans	Infrastructure projects in priority sectors: transport, energy, environmental and social facilities	EUR 50 million	May 2016	European Investment Bank, through European Fund for Strategic Investments
Sweden	Almi	Guarantees	innovative SMEs	EUR 63 million	April 2016	InnovFin SME Guarantee

Source: information and data collected and synthesized by the author, from www.eif.org and www.eib.org

institutions (European Investment Fund, European Investment Bank) and carry out lending activities or providing guarantees to end-customers in their country of residence, either directly or indirectly, by resorting on commercial banks' territorial network.

As from the table above, Croatia holds the most active NPB, in terms of the number of finance contracts recently signed with EU institutions and also the most diversified range of projects financed. The overwhelming majority of the EU financial resources are channeled by NPBs to SMEs. Another finding is that only eleven NPBs from 11 EU countries have applied for obtaining funding through the newly launched EC's financial instruments. In some countries not the promotional bank, but rather private commercial banks have applied for benefiting of financing from European budget.

Definitely, there is still large room for promotional banks across Europe to become major players in the implementation of the Investment Plan for Europe. The European Investment Bank (2016, pp.2-3) is fully aware of NPBs potential, derived from their particular expertise and knowledge of the local context and intends to explore and design new modes of enhanced cooperation as well as products which capitalize on comparative strengths of the NPBs. In addition, the EIB acknowledges the diversity of NPBs' business model and the heterogeneity of the regulatory and economic environment in which they operate. As a matter of consequence, the EIB envisages the design of tailor made approaches, comprising various financial products, in addition to co-financing at project level, such as: risk-sharing products, securitization structures, venture capital funds, co-investing in/with Investment Platforms, etc.

In addition to the Europeanisation main characteristics, it can be observed the emergence and consolidation of another distinctive feature, apart from those previously indicated by Deutsche Bank (2015). For enhancing their role in addressing market failures and amplifying their long-lasting beneficial impact on society, economy and environment, several European NPBs have decided to join together by creating various associations and networks. The German Development Institute (2015, p.1) argues that the emergence of these new associations contributes in a valuable way to NPBs fundamental aim of financing sustainable development.

EMPIRICAL EVIDENCES FROM EXISTING LITERATURE ON THE IMPACT EXERTED BY NPBS ON FINANCIAL AND ECONOMIC FUNDAMENTALS

Increasingly more voices (De Luna-Martinez and Vicente, 2012; Griffith-Jones, 2015) outline that despite their size and importance, the promotional banks' activity and outcomes are placed in an undeserved obscurity. Little is known about NPBs' fundamental role and mission, about the peculiarities of their business model, financial services and risk profile, and about how they distinguish from other state-owned financial institutions or private financial intermediaries.

Table 3. Promotional financial institutions' forms of association at European level

The *Network of European Financial Institutions for Small and Medium Sized Enterprises (NEFI)* was founded in 1999 and consists currently of 17 promotional financial institutions from 17 EU member states. Its objective is to monitor and collect information on financial, political and legal policies and measures adopted by the European Institutions in the fields of European economic and financial policies, which prove relevance for promotional financial institutions that focus mainly on smoothing SMEs' access to finance. NEFI serves also as a contact for the European Institutions, as it provides know-how and information on all promotional banking issues. NEFI members act complementary but in tight cooperation with the national banking system through co-financing, risk-sharing and advisory services in order to address SMEs financing needs, as well as providing financing in the fields of environment and infrastructure.

The *European Association of Public Banks (EAPB)* was founded in May 2000 and comprises as members public owned banks, development banks and funding agencies at the European level. At present it represents the specific interests of over 90 financial institutions, which hold a European market share of around 15% and a total balance sheet of about € 3.500 billion. It serves as a contact point for the European Parliament and the European Commission for issues related to providing know-how and information in all banking issues and represents its members in front of professional organizations, media and the general public. In addition, it commits to regularly and promptly inform its members regarding relevant and topical financial, political and legal developments, policies and measures adopted by the European institutions in the fields of banking law, and of economic and financial policies and encourages networking, exchange of best practices and cooperation among public sector banks in Europe.

The *Long-term Investors Club (LTIC)* was founded in 2009 on the joint initiative of three national promotional banks (Caisse des Dépots from France, Cassa Depositi e Prestiti from Italy and KfW from Germany) and the European Investment Bank. At present it comprises 18 major financial institutions with the mission of financing economic development and institutional investors (sovereign wealth funds, pension funds, public retirement funds, insurance funds) from all over the world, representing a total balance sheet of USD 5.4 trillion. LTIC members have agreed on several key principles, such as playing a positive role in the global economy by supporting sustainable economic growth, active support of social and environmental improvement. The reasons underlying the creation of LTIC reside in the prospects for long-term investment growth both in advanced countries (infrastructure, innovation, environmental programs, ageing population) and emerging countries (transportation, energy, urbanization) which require financial institutions to enhance their long-term investment identity and strengthen cooperation. It worth's mentioning two main common achievements of LTIC members, represented by the launch in 2010 of two major equity investment funds: the Marguerite fund and the InfraMed Infrastructure Fund.

The *European Long-Term Investors Association (ELTI)* was launched in July 2013 and currently gathers 27 European long-term financial institutions, representing a total balance sheet of 2.3 trillion Euros. Its full members are national financial institutions dedicated to the promotion of public policies at national and EU level, but also associate members represented notably by multilateral financial institutions, regional financial institutions, and non-banking institutions such as pension funds. ELTI's purpose is to promote quality long-term investment in real economy, in close alignment with the objectives and initiatives developed at the European Union level, in order to foster sustainable, smart and inclusive economic growth and employment.

Source: data collected and synthesized by the author from associations' websites, as follows: http://www.eapb.eu/, http://www.nefi.eu/, http://www.ltic.org/, http://www.eltia.eu/.

Schmit et al. (2011, p.31) observe that most authors focus their research on comparing and contrasting public and private-owned banks, instead of defining precise criteria for establishing a clear definition of the diverse public banks' typology (national and regional development banks, municipal credit institutions, export credit agencies, public savings banks). In a similar fashion, Rudolph (2010, p.2) claims that most existing studies in the literature do not perform any distinction between state-owned development / promotional banks and state-owned commercial banks, but through their findings blame all the state-owned financial institutions for their adverse impact on economic growth.

Therefore, there is an imperative need for decision makers, professionals in the financial system and researchers to perform targeted qualitative and quantitative analyses devoted exclusively to promotional banks' institutional and financial features, as well as to their effectiveness in achieving their mission, to their particular challenges and prospects for development. The more so as the current public debates and consultations within European Commission envisage a key role to be played by NPBs in obtaining funding from EU financial instruments and channeling it further towards pre-established destinations and recipients.

Rudolph (2009) summarized several drawbacks identified by economic literature (lack of good governance, of appropriate management skills, of transparency and misguided incentives for credit allocation) which discredited the activity performed by state-owned financial institutions in supporting the regional or nation-wide economic development. By putting in balance these shortcomings with the active role several state-owned banks played since the 2008 financial crisis, he raises the question of whether the presence of some government ownership in the banking system would be beneficial. By relying on a case study approach of four full state-owned development banks, he found that they are not dependent on state financial support for performing their current activities, but rather they raise financing from financial markets. This indicates that although NPBs depict a prevalent state ownership, they can be financially independent regarding the collection and allocation of funds.

The policy research working paper published by De Luna-Martinez and Vicente (2012, pp.17-18) examined the key findings of a questionnaire survey launched by the World Bank and the World Federation of Development Financial Institutions, in order to illustrate the features and challenges faced by promotional banks in low and middle-income countries. The study covered 90 NPBs in 61 countries, for data until end-2009. According to the size criterion, half of the surveyed NPBs have been grouped as small, 33% as medium, 11% were identified as large entities and 5% as megabanks. The countercyclical role played during the 2008 financial crisis is depicted by an increase of their loan portfolio between 20% and over 100%, although 16% of NPBs in the sample experienced negative loan portfolio growth. In terms of the quality of loan portfolio, more than half of NPBs reported non-performing loan ratios of less than 5%, while 15% of NPBs recorded ratios of over 30%. Another issue of interest has been NPBs profitability, which, on average, proved to position below the average return recorded by the banking system. In respect of return on assets, at end-2009 over half of surveyed NPBs exceeded the average recorded by their national banking systems, meanwhile in terms of return on equity only 20% of NPBs over-performed the national average.

A strand of economic literature investigated the relationship between bank ownership and the pattern of lending across economic cycles, although most studies don't explicitly discriminate between state-owned commercial banks and development or promotional banks (Deutsche Bank, 2015).

Sapienza (2004) studied the lending behavior of Italian state-owned banks and found that although they favor borrowers located in poor, depressed areas, their lending decision-making is affected by the electoral cycles. Micco and Panizza (2006) examined the lending behavior of a global sample of over 6000 state-owned banks. Empirical results show that public banks operating in developing countries seem to depict a less pro-cyclical lending than public banks located in industrial countries. Consequently, public bank lending depicts a very different response to the business cycle, depending on the degree of development of the country of residence, but overall their lending is less sensitive to macroeconomic shocks than private owned banks' lending.

Andrianova, Demetriades, and Shortland (2009) argue that countries witnessing high degrees of banks' government ownership are more prone to record long-term economic growth than countries with less state-owned banks. The authors explain this finding by relying on the developmental role played by state-owned banks in developing and industrialized countries, which help containing moral hazard behaviors and contribute to long-term economic growth.

Iannotta, Nocera, and Sironi (2011) performed an empirical analysis on a sample of 210 large Western European banks during a time span from 2000 to 2009, by investigating three research hypotheses. Their findings indicated that government-owned banks are characterized by a lower default risk, mainly due to the explicit or implicit government guarantees, but depict higher insolvency risk than private banks. In respect of their lending behavior across the economic cycle, there is no significant difference between government owned banks and private banks. However, the surveyed European government owned banks are exposed to political influence and tend to increase their lending more than private commercial banks during election years.

Bertray, Demirgüc-Kunt, and Huizinga (2012) surveyed a global sample of 1633 banks from 111 countries over the 1999-2010 periods to investigate state-owned banks' financial behavior in times of business cycle fluctuations. Their findings indicate that state-owned banks in countries with good governance depict less procyclical lending patterns than private commercial banks, while in high-income countries the public banks' countercyclical feature is more pronounced. In addition, their non-performing loans ratio is more evenly distributed across a business cycle and the non-deposit liabilities increases at a stable pace in times of economic booms. The authors concluded that state banks indeed exhibit a useful role in stabilizing credit both over the business cycle and during periods of financial instability.

Cull and Martínez Pería (2012) investigated whether bank ownership might exert an impact on credit growth in developing countries from Eastern Europe (Bulgaria, Croatia, Czech Republic, Hungary, Poland, Romania, Slovakia, and Slovenia) and Latin America before and during the 2008 crisis. Their findings are mixed, even contradictory across regions. Although ownership matters in discriminating between the financial behaviors of banks, state-owned banks in Latin America acted countercyclical, meanwhile those in Eastern Europe countries proved more pro-cyclical.

A singular research attempt belongs to Francisco, Mascaró, Mendoza, and Yaron (2008) who developed a methodology meant to assess the performance of development or promotional banks from the viewpoint of their effectiveness in meeting the social objectives. The evaluation takes into account two components, namely the subsidy dependence index, which refers to the subsidies they received from state in order to achieve these objectives and the output index, which indicates the level to which the NPBs contribute to achieving the social objectives of the state. The authors suggest the use of this methodology as a quantitative tool within the broader policymakers' framework for evaluating the performance of NPBs, as it may help in the decision making process for the optimal allocation of scarce public funds for NPBs that pursue social goals.

In 2010 a study by Dalberg Global Development Advisors, an international consulting firm, examined the methods and effectiveness of the national development banks in Europe. The findings have indicated NPBs' ability to trigger both positive long-lasting development impact and good financial returns for most of their projects, as well as a very cost-efficient use of public funds for their governments (Dalberg Global Development Advisors, 2010, p.5).

Griffith-Jones (2015, pp.3, 10) investigated two alternative scenarios to find out which of them is susceptible to generate private investment increases at euro-zone level, for the period 2014-2020. The first scenario assumed that governments across EU countries will maintain the austerity policies by cutting government expenditures to compress the debt-to-GDP ratios. The second scenario assumed that both public and private investments will record a progressive increase until 2020, as a strategy for enhancing economic growth and employment. By employing a Cambridge-Alphametric Model, the author obtained significant results for the investment-led scenario, consisting in up to an additional 5 million jobs in the EU by 2020, higher levels of GDP growth and decreases in debt-to-GDP ratios. These findings outline that a national or regional investment-led strategy in which lending from NPBs as well as financial resources from EU budget hold a central role, tends to be not only economically viable but also creates prospects for strengthening entrepreneurship and innovation, leading to higher levels of growth and employment.

RECENT INVOLVEMENT OF NPBS IN DETERMINING SOCIAL AND ECONOMIC FUNDAMENTALS

This last section of the chapter aims at investigating the recent patterns depicted by the relationship between promotional banks' size, expressed in terms of total assets, and several macroeconomic fundamentals. The sources of data as of 2014 year-end have been manifold: the amount of total assets has been extracted from the annual reports of each NPB in the sample, total assets of the national banking systems have been collected from European Central Bank's Statistical Data Warehouse while the Eurostat database has been the source for macroeconomic indicators.

To obtain information on promotional banks' importance for the national economy, it has been computed several indicators. The share of individual NPB's total assets in national banking system's total assets (see Figure 1) illustrates that Cassa Depositi e Prestiti concentrates almost 13% from Italian banking system, the highest share among all the NPBs in the sample. Five NPBs record a market share above 5%, eight NPBs oscillate in the range of 1 – 3.4% of market share, while NPBs in Slovakia, Estonia, Luxembourg and Austria hold less than 1%.

Another indicator of NPBs' significance is related to their contribution to a country's financial depth, computed as the ratio of NPBs total loans to GDP (see Figure 2). Keeping in mind one of the specificities of NPBs business model, regarding the provision of financing through first-tier or second-tier lending models, or through a combination of the two models, the total loans term in the computation formula adds customer loans and bank loans (if applicable). Not surprisingly, the promotional bank from Italy exerts the highest contribution to financial depth (over 18%), closely followed by Netherlands' NPB and KfW in Germany. Although Czech Republic's NPB holds a market share of 2.5% in terms of total assets, its lending activity as percent of GDP is of only 0.27%. The reverse situation can be observed for the NPB in Luxembourg, which holds negligible market share in the national banking system but contributes to financial depth with 1.76%. The structure of its

Figure 1. The share of NPBs' total assets in national banking system's total assets (2014 year-end data)
Source: author

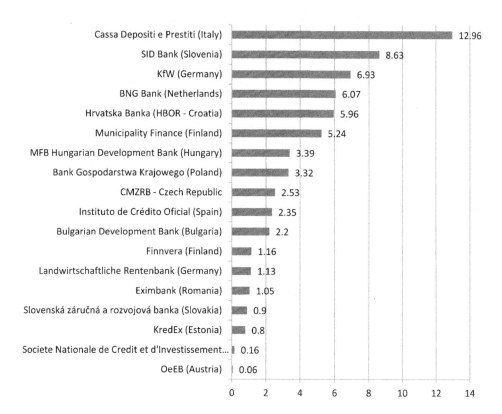

financial statements provides the explanation: loans to banks (second tier model) are the predominant asset item. Most banks in the sample position below the sample's average contribution to financial depth (of 4.66%).

The following series of graphs aims at exhibiting the strength of the relationship between the size of promotional banks, measured in terms of total assets amount, and various macroeconomic indicators. The below mentioned graphs are exhibiting the status of all the 18 NPBs included in the analysis. However, as most banks concentrate in the same part of the graph, being difficult to nominate each of them (due to overlapping of their names), it has been chosen to add the names of only those NPBs which appear to be outliers, depicting specific features from the remaining NPBs.

By plotting GDP expressed in current prices with NPBs total assets, it can be observed (Figure 3) that most promotional banks concentrate in the quadrant depicting low GDP level and low amount of assets. The outliers

Figure 2. NPBs individual contribution to financial depth (2014 year-end data)
Source: author

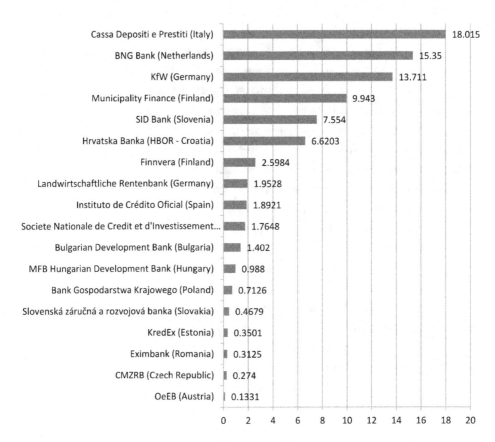

are KfW in Germany and the Italian NPB which position in the high GDP – high total assets quadrant. The R^2 level indicates that, by estimating a linear relationship between GDP and NPBs total assets, the latter explains 60% of GDP's variability.

Although empirical literature argues that the level of debt-to-GDP ratio is expected to decrease due to the long-lasting catalyzing effect to be exerted by NPBs on private investment activity, by taking a snapshot of the relationship between debt-to-GDP and NPBs' total assets (see Figure 4) the evidence is inconclusive. Most European NPBs hold total assets far less than €50,000 million, therefore their beneficial influence on government's deficit/surplus as percentage of GDP is still marginal. Estonia, Germany and Luxembourg are the only countries recording government surplus.

Figure 3. Relationship between GDP and NPBs' total assets (2014 year-end data)
Source: author

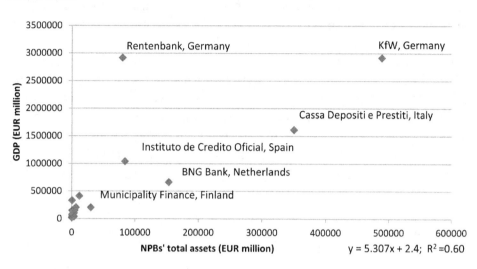

Figure 4. Relationship between Debt-to-GDP ratio and NPBs' total assets (2014 year-end data)
Source: author

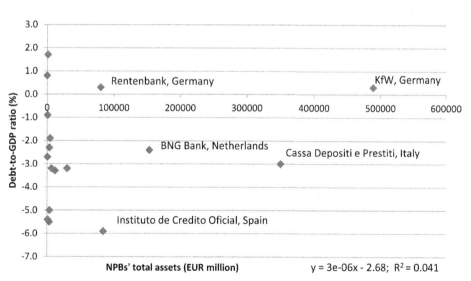

Another issue of interest is whether the size of promotional activity positively determines the level of wellbeing. As a measure of social wellbeing it has been considered the level of GDP per capita (see Figure 5), a metric widely used in the literature. Luxembourg exhibits the highest standard of living (over €60,000 per inhabitant) despite its NPB hold total assets of less than €2,000 million. Six NPBs (Rentenbank and KfW from Germany, Municipal Finance and Finnvera from Finland, BNG Bank in Netherlands, OeEB from Austria) operate in countries with GDP per capita of around €30,000. Nine NPBs holding the lowest total assets levels concentrate within the €4,000 - €15,000 per inhabitant range. It seems that there are many other factors that influence the degree of social wellbeing, apart from NPBs size, as the NPBs total assets explain only 5% of the GDP per capita variability.

By analyzing the fundamental objectives of their promotional activity, it can be observed that most NPBs in the sample depict the mission of providing financing for housing building or reconstruction. Figure 6 illustrates that those which are very active in focusing on housing issues operate in countries with a higher level of production in construction index. However, the linear relationship between NPBs size and the index level is weak, suggesting that

Figure 5. Relationship between GDP per capita and NPBs' total assets (2014 year-end data)
Source: author

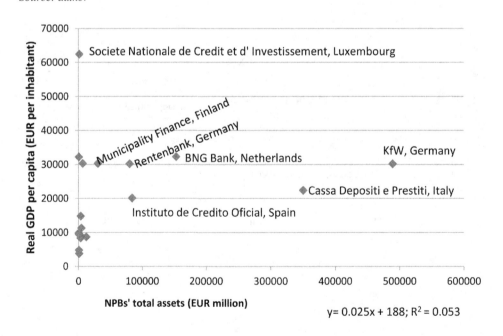

Figure 6. Relationship between production in construction index and NPBs' total assets (2014 year-end data)
Source: author

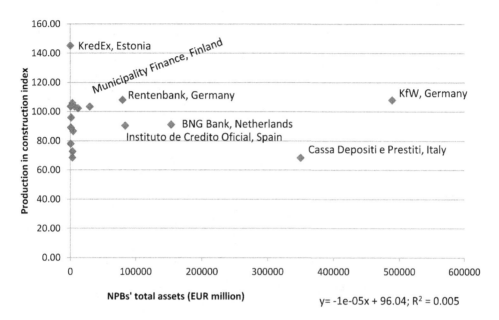

NPBs are not the sole, nor the most important determinant of housing market developments.

In terms of the relationship between employment and promotional banks' total assets, the wide majority of NPBs are located in countries whose employment rate ranges between 65-75%. NPBs in Germany and Netherlands depict both higher employment rates, of almost 80% of active population, and larger amounts of total assets (Figure 7). NPBs activity exerts an indirect influence on labor force market, as they primarily assess, select and finance investment projects and SMEs or companies that proved their ability in creating economic and social value added. The productive use of financial resources obtained from NPBs is susceptible to create also more full-time jobs, to increase skills of existing workers and enhance self-employment (in the case of entrepreneurs or start-ups).

To assess whether the presence of a NPB might stimulate the export activity of a country, it has been comparatively plotted the exports/GDP ratio against NPBs total assets. The Figure 8 illustrates that Societe Nationale de Credit et d'Investissement located in Luxembourg makes discordant note with the other 17 NPBs in the sample, as the country exhibits the highest share of exports in national GDP (of 203.3%). One reason is the targeted,

Figure 7. Relationship between employment and NPBs' total assets (2014 year-end data)
Source: author

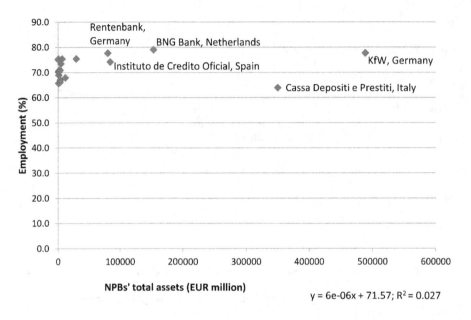

Figure 8. Relationship between Exports/GDP and NPBs' total assets (2014 year-end data)
Source: author

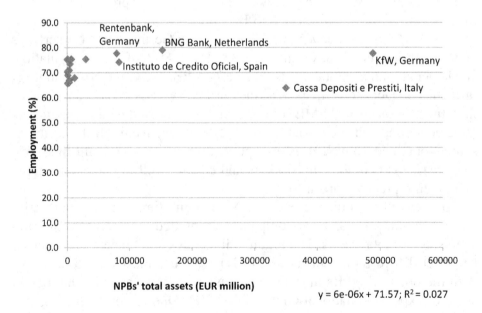

specialized mission of the promotional bank in Luxembourg, which provides mostly medium and long-term financing for innovations and exports, as well as for financing Luxembourg companies' investments abroad. The remaining NPBs in the sample do not put stronger emphasis on promoting exports, but they target specific fields of economic and social activity which cannot make the object of exports.

For examining NPBs contribution to boosting innovation it has been employed as proxy the research and development (R&D) expenditure as percent of GDP (Figure 9). It can be noticed that countries as Austria, Finland and Germany depict the highest levels of the R&D expenses, around 3% of national GDP. Thus, NPBs located in these countries have the potential to exert a greater influence towards the further improvement of the ratio. Although the scatter plot is quite heterogeneous, most banks operate in countries with a level of R&D expenses/GDP lower than 1.5%. Economic literature widely acknowledges that research and development (R&D) are key drivers of economic growth hence NPBs have to address this gap through the funding they provide. As the linear relationship estimated in the graph shows, NPBs size explains only 5% of the variability of research and development expenditure as share in GDP.

Some NPBs provide financing for the development of alternative sources of energy. To explore this statistical relationship it has been plotted Figure 10, which illustrates the link between energy efficiency and NPBs total assets. Austria positions itself on the top of the hierarchy, with the largest share

Figure 9. Relationship between Research and development expenditure as share in GDP and NPBs' total assets (2014 year-end data)
Source: author

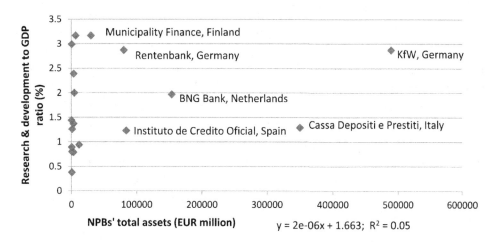

Figure 10. Relationship between electricity generated from renewable sources and NPBs' total assets (2014 year-end data)
Source: author

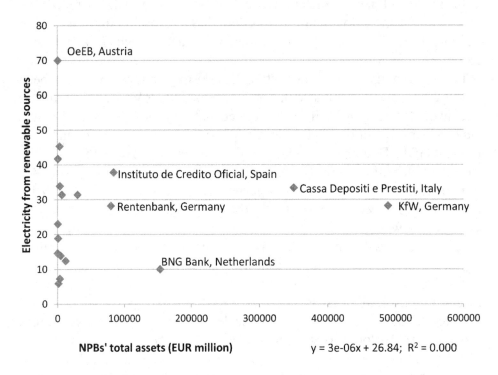

of electricity generated from renewable sources as percent of gross national electricity consumption. OeEB, Austria's promotional bank, contributes significantly to mitigating climate change by investing at end-2015 almost €400 million in renewable energy sources (hydro plants, wind, solar, geo-thermal and electricity from biomass/wastes) and energy efficiency projects.

By summing up the findings drawn from the visual representations above it can be extracted several conclusions. First, although several promotional banks appear always distinctly, due to their total asset larger amount compared to their peers (it is the case of Rentenbank and KfW from Germany, Cassa Depositi e Prestiti from Italy, BNG Bank from Netherlands, Instituto de Credito Oficial from Spain), their country of residence does not perform in all cases significantly better, in terms of various economic and social indica-tors considered, than those in the sample. The positioning of a country in respect of given macro-economic and social fundamentals is due to a complex mix of intrinsic factors and causes, promotional banks being just a detail of the larger picture.

As United Nations (2012, p.4) explain, domestic economic trends and vulnerabilities change continually but NPBs maintain their essential role in development. It is outlined that

the role, institutional structure, funding and potential success of NPBs depend on the financial systems and economic structures in which they are inserted. Two things are certain, though: no country has managed to achieve developmental goals rapidly without the systematic and coherent mobilization and deployment of social resources for public ends, and no country has been able to rely entirely upon competing commercial banks to achieve these goals.

Second, no matter what proxy indicator we employ for measuring NPBs size (total assets, total loan portfolio), it is subject of limitations regarding the economic and financial significance of a promotional bank within the domestic economy. This is mainly due to the fact that their economic impact cannot always be assessed directly and over a short to medium time horizon. Their impact, closely resulting from their mission, has to be evaluated by relying on specific, niche market segments. Despite their small size, they might play a fundamental role by defreezing financing towards some sectors of activity, market participants (start-ups, SMEs) or investment projects that mainstream banking ignores or rejects from financing due to uncertainty related to future prospects and cash-flows.

Deutsche Bank Research (2015, p.10) agrees that performing size comparisons across promotional banks and assessing their economic role has to be treated with caution as "some activities they engage in may have a limited impact on their balance sheet size, e.g. seed and start-up funding or advisory services, but are still of relevance to the economy".

Policy-makers are well aware of the economic and social value added by promotional banks, the more so as the European Commission has chartered the pivotal role to be further played by NPBs in implementing its new financial instruments. At present, we are witnessing a process of designing, developing and launching new promotional banks in several European countries. These national incentives are encouraged by the European Commission (2015), which provides guidance to those EU member states willing to set up a new promotional bank.

The European Committee of the Regions (2016, pp.4-5) highlights that the criteria to be envisaged by a national authority intending to develop an effective promotional banking business model should comprise the mitigation of market failures, increase of employment, awareness on local communities' interests and needs and pursuit of public economic development objectives.

There are also advanced two main proposals: first, local and regional authorities should have a more prevailing role in the strategic focus and governance of national promotional banks due to enhanced knowledge of regional vulnerabilities. Second, for establishing a reliable promotional bank model, the EC and the European Investment Bank have to analyze the existing NPBs' business models as well as the specific individual characteristics of each country, in order to define best practices framework.

The German Development Institute (2015, p.2) appreciates that the current trend of creating new promotional banks reflects a shift from private financial system towards greater emphasis on public, state-owned banks. NPBs can overcome the limitations of the private banks in funding the real economy, especially of particular sectors such as infrastructure, renewable energy, or other areas where important environmental externalities exist. Rudolph (2009, p.4) claims that before establishing a new promotional bank, the government has to clearly identify which market failures the NPB is going to solve or alleviate: lack of financial support to the agricultural sector, infrastructure sector or SMEs.

The unique position hold by NPBs within their domestic financial market, their strong knowledge of country's development needs and local opportunities, and their broad experience in long-term financing are perceived by Smallridge et al. (2013, p.16) as natural NPBs' strengths and capacities in order to place in leadership positions in particular economic segments.

An interesting opinion belongs to Bassanini et al. (2015, p.16) which explain that national and international organizations, as well as decision-makers shouldn't aim at returning to the economic and financial pre-crisis path because it proved to be unsustainable from an economic, social and environmental standpoint. They draw attention that in charting NPBs' future activities and prospects for development, policymakers should have in mind the identification of new sources for real economy growth and competitiveness, based on knowledge intensive activities, high productivity and environmental sustainability.

A singular attempt to date belongs to Whittle, Malan and Bianchini (2016, p.16) which conducted a mapping exercise in order to identify the current coverage across the EU-28 of NPBs, irrespective of their status: already well-established, recently established ones, and not yet set up. Their findings indicated that almost all EU countries have in place NPBs, some of them with long-established, significant experience in implementing EC's financial instruments designed for SMEs (such as KfW from Germany, Cassa Depositi e Prestiti from Italy and BGK from Poland). The only countries where there are currently not set up any NPBs are Belgium, Greece and Malta.

In the following, to gain a comprehensive perspective on the most recent incentives for creating a national promotional bank, it has been summarized the country of residence and the particular mission to be performed by each NPB (Table 4).

These recent past developments as well as the prospects for future emergence of new national promotional banks reflect the actuality of the topic and the important place it holds on decision-makers' agenda. In adopting the decision to design and launch a national promotional bank, the screening of the existing best practices in this field is of crucial importance.

Table 4. Recently launched European NPBs

Country	Year of establishment	Name of the NPB	Mission
France	2012	Bpifrance	promotes competitiveness by providing loan guarantee instruments and equity for start-ups and SMEs
France	2013	Agence France Locale	provides French local authorities with optimized, alternative financing solutions by raising cost-efficient resources in capital markets
Latvia	2013	Latvian Development Financial Institution Altum	financing SMEs and start-ups, supporting other areas of business activity with the purpose of enhancing the development of the Latvian economy, employment and societal welfare
UK	2014	British Business Bank	supply of finance for small businesses in the UK at all stages of their development: starting up, scaling up and staying ahead
Ireland	2014	Strategic Banking Corporation of Ireland	focuses on facilitating the provision of flexible financing products to small and medium Irish businesses
Portugal	2014	Development Financial Institution (Instituição Financeira de Desenvolvimento)	manages the European Structural and Investment Funds allocated to Portugal for the 2014-2020 financing period, with the main purpose of addressing market failures regarding SMEs' access to debt, equity and quasi-equity funding
UK	2015	Green Investment Bank	specialized in financing UK's green economy, by channeling financing towards UK based green infrastructure projects, with particular focus on energy efficiency, waste and bio-energy, offshore wind, and onshore renewable
Greece	Not yet launched	Institution for Growth	promote competitiveness, growth, innovation and employment through the provision of short and long-term debt and equity capital to SMEs
Malta	Not yet launched	Malta Development Bank	finances both traditional and emerging economic sectors that show potential for further growth, with focus on infrastructure investments

Source: author, based on information from NPBs websites and EC's press releases

REFERENCES

Andrianova, S., Demetriades, P., & Shortland, A. (2009). *Is Government Ownership of Banks Really Harmful to Growth?* University of Leicester Discussion Paper in Economic 09/11.

Bassanini, F., Pennisi, G., & Reviglio, E. (2015). *The Development/Promotional Banks: From the Financial and Economic Crisis to Sustainable and Inclusive Development.* Retrieved from http://www.bassanini.it/wp-content/uploads/2015/02/Bassanini_Pennisi_Reviglio_CDP-developmentbanks-FINALE-n.-207-numero-142014.pdf

Berlin Economics GmbH (2014). *Establishment of a Promotional Bank in Ukraine, Analysis and Recommendations.* Final report financed by the Federal Ministry of Finance of Germany.

Bertray, A. C., Demirgüc-Kunt, A., & Huizinga, H. (2012). *Bank Ownership and Credit over the Business Cycle: Is Lending by State Banks Less Procyclical?* European Banking Center Discussion Paper No. 2012-013.

Club. (n.d.). Retrieved from: http://www.ltic.org/

COSME Financial Instruments. (2016) *COSME Financial Instrucments.* GROWTH. Retrieved from: http://ec.europa.eu/growth/access-to-finance/cosme-financial-instruments/index_en.htm

Creative Europe. (n.d.) *About.* Creative Europe. Retrieved from: https://ec.europa.eu/programmes/creative-europe/about_en

Cull, R., & Martínez Pería, M. S. (2012). *Bank Ownership and Lending Patterns during the 2008-9 Financial Crisis: Evidence from Latin America and Eastern Europe.* World Bank Policy Research Working Paper No. 6195.

Dalberg Global Development Advisors. (2010). The Growing Role of Development Finance Institutions in International Development Policy. Author.

De Luna-Martínez, J., & Vicente, C. L. (2012). *Global Survey of Development Banks.* World Bank Policy Research Working Paper No.5969.

Deutsche Bank Research (2015). *Promoting investment and growth: the role of development banks in Europe.* EU Monitor Global Financial Markets.

Draghi M. (2013). *Introductory statement.* Hearing at the Committee on Economic and Monetary Affairs of the European Parliament, Brussels, Belgium.

EAPB. (n.d.). Retrieved from: http://www.eapb.eu/

European Association of Public Banks. (2015a). *EAPB Annual Report 2014-2015*. Author.

European Association of Public Banks (2015b). *EAPB Position Paper on EU Commission public consultation on long term finance and on possible impact of the CRR and CRD IV on bank financing of the economy.* Author.

European Central Bank. (2014). *SME access to finance in the euro area: Barriers and potential policy remedies.* Author.

European Commission. (2013). *CREATIVE EUROPE Programme the Cultural and Creative Sectors Loan Guarantee Facility.* Directorate-General for Education and Culture, Culture and media, Media Programme and media literacy. Retrieved from http://www.creativeeuropeireland.eu/content/resources/18.%20faq-financial-instrument.pdf

European Commission. (2014). An Investment Plan for Europe. Communication From The Commission To The European Parliament, The Council, The European Central Bank, The European Economic And Social Committee, The Committee Of The Regions And The European Investment Bank.

European Commission. (2015). Working together for jobs and growth: The role of National Promotional Banks (NPBs) in supporting the Investment Plan for Europe. Communication from the Commission to the European Parliament and the Council.

European Committee of the Regions. (2016). *Opinion - Working together for jobs and growth: The role of National and Regional Promotional Banks (NPBs) in supporting the Investment Plan for Europe.* Communication from the Commission to the European Parliament and the Council, COM (2015) 361 final, 117th plenary session.

European Investment Bank. (2016). *Rules applicable to operations with Investment Platforms and National Promotional Banks or Institutions.* SB/10/16 18. Author.

European Investment Fund. (2016). *What we do.* European Investment Fund. Retrieved from: http://www.eif.org/what_we_do/

European Long-Term Investors. (n.d.). Retrieved from: http://www.eltia.eu/

European Parliament (2015). *Regulation (EU) 2015/1017 of the European Parliament and of the Council on the European Fund for Strategic Investments, the European Investment Advisory Hub and the European Investment Project Portal and amending Regulations (EU) No 1291/2013 and (EU) No 1316/2013*. The European Fund for Strategic Investments.

European Structural and Investment Funds. (n.d.). *Exploring the Data by Fund*. European Structural and Investment Funds. Retrieved from: https://cohesiondata.ec.europa.eu/funds

Francisco, M., Mascaró, Y., Mendoza, J. C., & Yaron, J. (2008). *Measuring the Performance and Achievement of Social Objectives of Development Finance Institutions*. World Bank Policy Research paper no. 4506.

German Development Institute. (2015). *Financing Global Development: The BRICS New Development Bank*. Briefing paper, no.13/2015. Author.

Griffith-Jones, S. (2015). *The case and role for development banks: The European example*. Retrieved from http://policydialogue.org/files/events/Stephany_Paper.pdf

GROWTH. (n.d.) *Access to finance for SMEs*. GROWTH. Retrieved from: http://ec.europa.eu/growth/access-to-finance/

Iannotta, G., Nocera, G., & Sironi, A. (2011). *The Impact of Government Ownership on Bank Risk and Lending Behaviour*. Available at SSRN: http://ssrn.com/abstract=1774887

InnovFin – EU Finance for Innovators. (2014). *EU and EIB Group join forces to support up to 48 billion in R&I Investment*. European Commission. Retrieved from: http://europa.eu/rapid/press-release_IP-14-670_en.htm

LIFE Program. (n.d.). *Financial Instruments*. Climate Action. Retrieved from: http://ec.europa.eu/clima/policies/budget/life/instruments/index_en.htm

Micco, A., & Panizza, U. (2006). Bank Ownership and Lending Behaviour. *Economics Letters*, *93*(2), 248–254. doi:10.1016/j.econlet.2006.05.009

NEFI. (n.d.). Retrieved from: http://www.nefi.eu/

Progressive Economy Workshop. (2016). *EFSI, development banks and job creation*. Retrieved from: http://www.progressiveeconomy.eu/sites/default/files/events/EFSI-workshop-summary2704.pdf

Rubio, E., Rinaldi D., & Pellerin-Carlin T. (2016). *Investment in Europe: making the best of the Juncker plan with case studies on digital infrastructure and energy efficiency*. Jacques Delors Institute, Studies and Reports.

Rudolph, H. P. (2009). *State Financial Institutions: Mandates, Governance, and Beyond*. World Bank Policy Research Working Paper No. 5141.

Rudolph, H. P. (2010). *State Financial Institutions: Can They Be Relied on to Kick-Start Lending?*. World Bank Crisis Response, Note no. 12.

Sapienza, P. (2004). The Effect of Government Ownership on Bank Lending. *Journal of Financial Economics, 72*(2), 357–384. doi:10.1016/j.jfineco.2002.10.002

Schmit M., Gheeraert L., Denuit T., & Warny C. (2011). *Public Financial Institutions in Europe*. European Association of Public Banks.

Smallridge, D., Buchner, B., Trabacchi, C., Netto, M., Gomes Lorenzo, J. J., & Serra, L. (2013). *The Role of National Development Banks in Catalyzing International Climate Finance*. Inter-American Development Bank.

United Nations. (2012). *The Continuing Relevance of Development Banks*. UN Conference on Trade And Development, Policy Brief no. 04/April 2012.

Whittle M., Malan J. & Bianchini D. (2016). *New Financial Instruments and the Role of National Promotional Banks*. Directorate-General for Internal Policies, Policy Department D: Budgetary Affairs.

Wruuck, P. (2016). *Promoting investment in Europe: where do we stand with the Junker Plan?* Deutsche Bank Research June 17, 2016. Internet resources: European Investment Bank, EIB and ICO: first EFSI operation with national promotional bank signed 12 May, 2016, from: http://www.eib.org/infocentre/press/releases/all/2016/2016-115-bei-e-ico-primera-operacion-del-plan-de-inversiones-para-europa-que-se-firma-con-un-banco-de-promocion-nacional.htm

ENDNOTE

[1]   It should be mentioned that several banks already provide culture loans from own funds and no EC' guarantee. It is the case of KfW, a promotional bank from Germany which provides since 2011 loans for financing the German film industry.

Chapter 3

Exploratory Assessment of National Promotional Banks' Business Models' Resemblance

INTRODUCTION

The purpose of the research performed in this chapter is to take a closer look at the business model implemented by the national promotional banks in EU, with a focus on the period following the financial crisis. It has been investigated whether NPBs have aligned their business practices and balance sheets structure, by operating homogeneously irrespective of the country of origin, or there is evidence of heterogeneity across financial positions and financial indicators.

Cluster analysis is the best suited statistical method for the purpose of this research as it provides, through a series of algorithms, a classification of banks included in the sample into distinct groups or clusters, by relying on a pre-established set of continuous variables. The chapter has been organized as follows: the first sub-chapter describes the peculiarities of the methodology employed, the two research hypotheses and the underlying data. The second sub-chapter presents the empirical results obtained, for each research hypothesis, and discusses the findings.

DOI: 10.4018/978-1-5225-1845-7.ch003

Copyright ©2017, IGI Global. Copying or distributing in print or electronic forms without written permission of IGI Global is prohibited.

Cluster Analysis Methodology and Variables' Selection

Cluster analysis is a statistical technique concerned with classifying data, its fundamental goal being to uncover several groups of observations from initially unclassified data (Landau & Everitt, 2004, p.311). It is also known as numerical taxonomy or automatic data classification (Kaufman and Rousseeuw, 2005). Klotz and Lindermeir (2015, p.148) argue that, at present, cluster analysis is perceived as one of the three most important multivariate analysis methods, due to its ability to unveil hidden patterns and features within a data set and to identify groups or clusters based on data similarities. According to Everitt, Landau, Leese & Stahl (2011, p.7) cluster analysis is essentially about discovering groups existing in a larger data set, and it should not be confused with discriminant analysis and other assignment or supervised learning methods. In this latter case, the groups are known a priori therefore the purpose of the empirical analysis is not to discover new information but to create and validate rules for including new cases into one or other of the already known groups.

Thiprungsri (2011, p.8) explains that cluster analysis is performed when researchers intend to "ask the question whether a given group can be partitioned into subgroups which have different characteristics". These subgroups can be further defined by relying on the common characteristics depicted by the banks included in the subgroup. The rationale is that the banks assigned to a group are the most similar, while the remaining are not. Timm (2002) enumerates some cases which may distort or heavily influence the results obtained through cluster analysis, namely the amount of random noise existing in the data set, the presence of outliers, the variables included in the analysis, the proximity measures used and the linkage methods employed.

The study in this chapter employs a widely used cluster analysis method, called agglomerative hierarchical clustering. The particularity of this method resides in the creation and chaining of clusters. It starts with a number of clusters equal with the number of individual banks in the sample, each bank being assumed to represent a single-member cluster. First, individual banks sharing the highest degree of similarity (from the standpoint of several predefined variables) are merged in the same group. During next stages, the more resembling clusters are linked together, the result being the creation of progressively larger groups. Finally, all the groups formed earlier are joined in the same big, unique group. As Landau and Everitt (2004, p.312) point out, in the agglomerative technique small clusters are merged together to form larger clusters of increasingly dissimilar elements. In the process of clusters' formation the computational algorithms ensure that banks in the same cluster are the most resembling while those in other clusters are dissimilar. Klotz and Lindermeir (2015, p.149) explain that the process of grouping individual banks into clusters "is driven by a high degree of homogeneity within the clusters and dissimilarity between objects of different groups".

The two major computational steps in cluster analysis are:

1. Measuring the proximity (in terms of similarity or dissimilarity) between individual banks,
2. Measuring the proximity between groups of individual banks, for larger cluster formation purpose (Kachigan, 1991).

The general term of proximity isn't interpreted as closeness in terms of physical distance, but stands for dissimilarity or similarity regarding the characteristics of banks.

To measure the proximity between individual banks and establish whether they should merge in the same group it has to be computed a distance or resemblance measure. In this study it has been used the squared Euclidean distance, a metric widely employed in the literature due to its ability to identify with greater accuracy the dissimilarities between banks. Consequently, two banks are deemed to be close or similar when the level of the squared Euclidean distance is small. The higher its value, the more dissimilar the two banks considered. The proximity between two individual banks can be computed with the formula:

$$\text{Squared Euclidean distance} = \sum_{i=1}^{n} \left(pi - qi \right)^2$$, where p_i and q_i $(i = 1, \dots n)$ are two points in the Euclidean n-space

For measuring the inter-group proximities and decide whether two groups should merge it has to be defined another algorithm, called linkage rule. Economic literature exhibits a variety of methods, the most widely used being single linkage (nearest-neighbor distance), complete linkage (furthest-neighbor distance) and Ward's method. As Everitt et al. (2011) outline, the main discrepancies between the results obtained by employing these various methods arise due to the different definition of distance or similarity between groups.

For instance, Ward's method relies on a computational algorithm that joins two clusters based on the size of an error sum-of-squares criterion. More specifically, it minimizes the within-group sum-of-squared-errors, while maximizing between-group variance.

The sum of squares by combining clusters A and B = $\dfrac{nA \times nB}{nA + nB}\left(cA - cB\right)^2$

where

nA and *nB* represent the number of banks in clusters *A* and *B,* respectively
cA and *cB* are the centers of the two clusters

The single linkage clustering technique takes into account the similarity between the closest banks located in two clusters, while the complete linkage method computes the distance between two clusters as the largest distance between two banks in two clusters. Hubert (1974) acknowledges that single and complete link for hierarchical clustering are data analysis routines, but claims that the clustering obtained can be primarily used as a descriptive device due to the lack of standardized statistical tools for assessing the adequacy of the sub-groups created.

To sum up, the clustering technique may be viewed as a succession of different computational algorithms for merging individual banks and respectively pairs of clusters, the final purpose being to classify an initial broad data set into more meaningful, homogenous groups.

Hierarchical classifications generated by means of agglomerative cluster analysis provide also an output in a graphical, two-dimensional tree-like diagram form, called dendrogram, which exhibits all the clustering stages, from individual clusters to the big, single cluster. As Klotz and Lindermeir (2015) argue, this tree of successive clusterings add value for the interpretation of results, allowing the researcher to choose its own stopping rule for obtaining the appropriate number of clusters, according to the research hypotheses envisaged. Landau and Everitt (2004) emphasize, too the subjectivity of determining the number of clusters by choosing a given distance at which clusters merge. They explain that a researcher will choose a distance metric that will allow him to obtain the clustering solution best describing the intrinsic structure of the initial data set. In a similar fashion, Norušis (2008, p. 364) points out that in the process of identifying a good clustering solution, the researcher has to observe the characteristics depicted by the clusters formed at successive steps and decide when it is achieved a reliable solution, which comprises a reasonable number of fairly homogeneous clusters.

At this point of the methodological presentation it has to be outlined that the clustering solution is not unique, but it heavily depends on a series of factors and algorithms. The clustering might change as the researcher expands the set of variables or attributes describing banks' financial behavior or business model. Also, the assignment of a bank to a specific cluster is strongly influenced by the computational algorithms chosen, such as the proximity metric and the linkage rule. Another observation relates to including in the analysis a representative sample of banks, as the final clustering results cannot be extrapolated to the entire population.

To account for the stability of NPBs clustering in each year under study, in the context of potential outliers, it has been employed three linkage rules for merging groups of banks, namely Ward's distance, single linkage and complete linkage. Consequently, the cluster analysis has been performed distinctly for each linkage algorithm and the results indicated in the dendrograms have been synthesized in a comparative manner.

This three-fold approach, which is common in economic literature applying the clustering technique, acts as a validation tool as it allows the comparative assessment of NPBs clustering and checks for the robustness and stability of the results across both time periods and linkage methods. All the clustering procedures implied by cluster analysis were conducted using SPSS software.

The focus of the research in this chapter is to perform an in-depth case analysis and comparisons in terms of NPBs business model's particularity to identify groups that share similar characteristics. The sample under study comprises the 18 national promotional banks established in the EU, the data covering the years 2011 to 2014. The newly established NPBs have not been included in the study due to low data availability. The financial data has been obtained from NPBs' annual reports and financial statements. Table 1 below illustrates the list of NPBs included in the analysis, the country of residence and the year of launch.

The cluster analysis aims at performing a screening and classification of NPBs' business models, in terms of two main research hypotheses. The first hypothesis is related to identifying resembling NPBs in respect of the overall activity performed. For conducting the analysis it has been included in the study three variables, namely: total assets to reflect bank size, NBPs profitability expressed by means of return on equity (ROE) and a measure of capital adequacy to risks called tier 1.

The second hypothesis aims at identifying similar NPBs by taking an in-depth look at their balance sheet structure. Thus, it has been computed several indicators as proxy for the financial position, namely: the share of loans (includes both direct lending to customers and second-tier lending) in total assets, the share of financial assets to total assets and total liabilities. The highest the share of total loans in NPBs total assets, the more dedicated is a NPB to fulfilling its societal and development mission. The indicator also measures the scale of lending activity, acting as a proxy for the credit

Table 1. Description of NPBs under analysis

National Promotional Bank	Country	Year of Establishment
OeEB	Austria	2008
Bulgarian Development Bank	Bulgaria	1999
Hrvatska Banka (HBOR)	Croatia	1992
Českomoravská záruční a rozvojová banka (CMZRB)	Czech Republic	1992
KredEx	Estonia	2001
Municipality Finance	Finland	1990
Finnvera	Finland	1999
Landwirtschaftliche Rentenbank	Germany	1949
KfW	Germany	1948
MFB Hungarian Development Bank	Hungary	2006
Cassa Depositi e Prestiti	Italy	1850
Societe Nationale de Credit et d'Investissement	Luxembourg	1978
BNG Bank	Netherlands	2005
Bank Gospodarstwa Krajowego	Poland	1924
Eximbank	Romania	1992
SID Bank	Slovenia	1994
Slovenská záručná a rozvojová banka	Slovakia	1991
Instituto de Crédito Oficial	Spain	1971

Source: author

risk exposure, coming both from customers and bank interconnectedness. NPBs depicting a high ratio of financial assets to total assets are susceptible of following a riskier, investment-type financial behavior, moving away from their basic financial intermediation function subordinated to local, regional or national development. These NPBs are more exposed to market and liquidity risks.

Before proceeding with the cluster analysis it is useful to examine the main descriptive statistics of the two datasets of variables, because the properties of these time series will directly impact the assignment of a given bank to a specific cluster. Tables 2 and 3 below summarize the set of initial variables included in each clustering model, as well as the computed level of their primary statistics.

The mean of a time series represent a measure of its central tendency. It can be noticed that the variable total assets recorded quite the same mean value in 2011 and 2013, with the highest mean value recorded at 2014 year-

Table 2. Descriptive statistics of the variables included in the first cluster analysis model

	Statistic	Total Assets (€ Thousand)	Tier 1 (%)	ROE (%)
Year 2011	Mean	63417041	26.32	6.46
	Maximum	494818000	75	27.08
	Minimum	196615	11.72	0
	Standard deviation	1.29E+08	20.84	7.49
Year 2012	Mean	67877007	27.22	7.48
	Maximum	509424000	80.6	38.04
	Minimum	191684	10.64	0
	Standard deviation	1.35E+08	19.83	9.90
Year 2013	Mean	63952805	29.21	6.31
	Maximum	464755000	78	30.58
	Minimum	201333	9.3	0.26
	Standard deviation	1.27E+08	19.24	7.26
Year 2014	Mean	68057464	28.33	5.06
	Maximum	489100123	65	21.66
	Minimum	176529	10.8	0
	Standard deviation	1.36E+08	16.72	5.36

Source: author, based on data computed with Eviews software

end. Tier 1 indicator of capital adequacy exhibited increasing mean values during 2011-2013, followed by a small contraction in 2014. In respect of ROE, it depicted similar mean values in 2011 and 2013, with a peak in 2012 and a minimum in 2014. Thus, NPBs seemed concerned to strengthen their capital base during the four years under study, have increased their business size in terms of total assets held meanwhile the mean profitability oscillated one year from another.

The maximum and minimum values recorded during the time span analyzed are a pair of summary statistics that help computing the range between raw data. The broader the range between a variable's values, the sharper the fluctuations recorded by the variable. The maximum level of total assets has always been recorded by KfW from Germany, while the minimum level belongs to KredEx from Estonia in each and every year. In respect of tier 1 indicator, the maximum value is always recorded by Eximbank from Romania, while the minimum value always belongs to Cassa Depositi e Prestiti (Italy). This might indicate that the Romanian promotional bank has adopted a very

Table 3. Descriptive statistics of the variables included in the second cluster analysis model

	Statistic	Share of Loans in Total Assets	Share of Financial Assets in Total Assets	Total Liabilities
Year 2011	Mean	60.15	20.32	60714734
	Maximum	93.06	55.67	477101000
	Minimum	8.71	1.31	60165
	Standard deviation	25.76	15.65	1.24E+08
Year 2012	Mean	57.63	18.71	64923303
	Maximum	90.02	60.85	491203000
	Minimum	7.03	4.99	60165
	Standard deviation	26.29	13.87	1.30E+08
Year 2013	Mean	59.93	20.42	60854723
	Maximum	86.62	55.62	444200100
	Minimum	14.64	5.91	62200
	Standard deviation	25.27	14.87	1.22E+08
Year 2014	Mean	58.71	20.53	65339648
	Maximum	84.58	52.16	468121000
	Minimum	9.24	8.08	35785
	Standard deviation	23.37	11.57	1.32E+08

Source: author, based on data computed with Eviews software

precautionary, conservative financial behaviour by holding large amounts of capital and low risky assets, while the Italian promotional bank operates close to the minimum requirements. As regards ROE, Municipality Finance (Finland) always exhibited the highest profitability level in all the four years considered, while the minimum levels of ROE have been recorded successively by KredEx, Slovenská záručná a rozvojová banka (Slovakia) in 2012 and 2013 and by MFB Hungarian Development Bank (Hungary) in 2014.

Standard deviation adds complementary information on the dispersion of the observations in the sample around their mean. High values are a sign of greater spread of a time series' values around its mean, indicating the presence of extreme values or data variability. By far, the highest standard deviation has been recorded for the total assets variable and the lowest for ROE.

Consequently, according to the descriptive statistics discussed above, it seems that the source of dissimilarity between individual NPBs mainly comes from their size, followed by capitalization indicators, and last but not least from their profitability level. Further, the purpose of the cluster analysis is to identify and cluster those NPBs of similar size, which depict also similarities in terms of capitalization and profitability.

The ratio of loans to total assets recorded a slightly decreasing trend of its mean value, ranging between 57.63 and 60.15%. The ratio of financial assets in total assets exhibits a quite constant level, around 20%. Total liabilities recorded quite the same mean value in 2011 and 2013, with the highest mean value recorded at 2014 year-end.

In terms of the maximum and minimum levels of the ratio of loans to total assets, no bank depicts a steady evolution. The maximum level is hold by Hrvatska Banka (HBOR - Croatia) in 2011, by SID Bank (Slovenia) in 2012, by Finnvera (Finland) in 2013 and again by HBOR in 2014. The minimum level also shows fluctuations across banks, being recorded by KredEx (Estonia) in 2011, by Slovenská záručná a rozvojová banka (Slovakia) in 2012, and by CMZRB (Czech Republic) in 2013 and 2014. As regards the share of financial assets in total assets, during 2011-2013 the maximum level is continuously hold by Eximbank (Romania), while in 2014 it is hold by Bank Gospodarstwa Krajowego (Poland). The minimum level of the indicator is recorded by the NPB from Bulgaria in 2011, the one from Croatia in 2012 and 2013, and KfW (Germany) in 2014. It can be noticed that, in terms of assets' structure, there isn't a stable pattern exhibited by a given bank over the four-year time frame. The maximum level of total liabilities has always been recorded by KfW from Germany, while the minimum level belongs to Societe Nationale de Credit et d'Investissement (Luxembourg) in each and every year. All the three variables depict large values of standard deviation, indicating the presence of wide data fluctuations. However, the largest variation across NPBs is due to total liability amount, followed by the share of loans in total assets and the share of financial assets in total assets.

The synthesis of the descriptive statistics attributed to the variables in the second cluster model indicates that the source of dissimilarity between individual NPBs mainly originates from their liability size and subsequently from their lending and financial assets' trading activity.

Identification and Interpretation of NPBs Clustering

The methodological steps mentioned in the previous sub-chapter have been implemented distinctly, for each cluster analysis research hypothesis, and lead to a series of findings which have been summarized in Tables 4 and 5. Both tables describe the order individual NPBs joined a cluster and the order of clusters' appearance. To ensure that the clusters obtained preserve their homogeneity, it has been chosen as stopping rule a linkage distance of five. Consequently, it has been analyzed and interpreted the clusters formed in the lowest distance interval, namely (0 - 5). Another common observation applicable to both tables relates to the order a NPB joins a cluster: the later it merges a cluster, the more dissimilar with the ones already assigned to the cluster.

Table 4 provides synthesized information on the first clustering model, by listing the NPBs according to the cluster within which they have been assigned (see Appendix 1 for a detailed presentation of dendrograms obtained for each linkage rule and each of the four years). We recall that the specifica-

Table 4. NPBs clustering during 2011-2014 (model 1)

Year	Number of Clusters	Ward Method	Single Linkage	Complete Linkage
2011	1	MFB (Hungary), SID Bank (Slovenia), KredEx (Estonia), Rentenbank (Germany), ICO (Spain), Bank Gospodarstwa (Poland), Finnvera (Finland), SNCI (Luxembourg), OeEB (Austria), KfW (Germany), CassaDepositi e Prestiti (Italy), CMRZB (Czech Republic), BNG Bank (Netherlands), Municipality Finance (Finland)	MFB (Hungary), SID Bank (Slovenia), KredEx (Estonia), Rentenbank (Germany), ICO (Spain), Bank Gospodarstwa (Poland), Finnvera (Finland), SNCI (Luxembourg), OeEB (Austria), KfW (Germany), Cassa Depositi e Prestiti (Italy), CMRZB (Czech Republic), BNG Bank (Netherlands), Municipality Finance (Finland)	MFB (Hungary), SID Bank (Slovenia), KredEx (Estonia), Rentenbank (Germany), ICO (Spain), Bank Gospodarstwa (Poland), Finnvera (Finland), SNCI (Luxembourg), OeEB (Austria)
	2	Bulgarian Development Bank (Bulgaria), HBOR (Croatia), SZRB (Slovakia), Eximbank (Romania)	Bulgarian Development Bank (Bulgaria), HBOR (Croatia), SZRB (Slovakia), Eximbank (Romania)	KfW (Germany), CassaDepositi e Prestiti (Italy), CMRZB (Czech Republic), BNG Bank (Netherlands), Municipality Finance (Finland)
	3			Bulgarian Development Bank (Bulgaria), HBOR (Croatia), SZRB (Slovakia), Eximbank (Romania)
2012	1	Bank Gospodarstwa (Poland), Finnvera (Finland), MFB (Hungary), SID Bank (Slovenia), OeEB (Austria), KredEx (Estonia), SNCI (Luxembourg), Rentenbank (Germany), ICO (Spain), KfW (Germany), BNG Bank (Netherlands), CMRZB (Czech Republic), CassaDepositi e Prestiti (Italy), Municipality Finance (Finland)	Bank Gospodarstwa (Poland), Finnvera (Finland), OeEB (Austria), KredEx (Estonia), MFB (Hungary), SID Bank (Slovenia), SNCI (Luxembourg), Rentenbank (Germany), ICO (Spain), KfW (Germany), BNG Bank (Netherlands), CMRZB (Czech Republic), CassaDepositi e Prestiti (Italy)	Bank Gospodarstwa (Poland), Finnvera (Finland), MFB (Hungary), SID Bank (Slovenia), OeEB (Austria), KredEx (Estonia), SNCI (Luxembourg), Rentenbank (Germany), ICO (Spain), KfW (Germany), BNG Bank (Netherlands), CMRZB (Czech Republic), CassaDepositi e Prestiti (Italy)
	2	HBOR (Croatia), SZRB (Slovakia), Bulgarian Development Bank (Bulgaria), Eximbank (Romania)	Municipality Finance (Finland)	Municipality Finance (Finland)
	3		HBOR (Croatia), SZRB (Slovakia), Bulgarian Development Bank (Bulgaria)	HBOR (Croatia), SZRB (Slovakia), Bulgarian Development Bank (Bulgaria), Eximbank (Romania)
	4		Eximbank (Romania)	

continued on following page

Table 4. Continued

Year	Number of Clusters	Ward Method	Single Linkage	Complete Linkage
2013	1	CMRZB (Czech Republic), Finnvera (Finland), CassaDepositi e Prestiti (Italy), OeEB (Austria), KredEx (Estonia), MFB (Hungary), SID Bank (Slovenia), SNCI (Luxembourg), Rentenbank (Germany), ICO (Spain), KfW (Germany), BNG Bank (Netherlands), Municipality Finance (Finland)	CMRZB (Czech Republic), Finnvera (Finland), OeEB (Austria), KredEx (Estonia), MFB (Hungary), SID Bank (Slovenia), SNCI (Luxembourg), Rentenbank (Germany), KfW (Germany), BNG Bank (Netherlands), ICO (Spain), CassaDepositi e Prestiti (Italy)	CMRZB (Czech Republic), Finnvera (Finland), OeEB (Austria), KredEx (Estonia), MFB (Hungary), SID Bank (Slovenia), SNCI (Luxembourg), Rentenbank (Germany), ICO (Spain), KfW (Germany), BNG Bank (Netherlands), CassaDepositi e Prestiti (Italy)
	2	Bulgarian Development Bank (Bulgaria), HBOR (Croatia), SZRB (Slovakia), Bank Gospodarstwa (Poland), Eximbank (Romania)	Municipality Finance (Finland)	Municipality Finance (Finland)
2013	3		Bulgarian Development Bank (Bulgaria), HBOR (Croatia), SZRB (Slovakia), Bank Gospodarstwa (Poland)	Bulgarian Development Bank (Bulgaria), HBOR (Croatia), SZRB (Slovakia), Bank Gospodarstwa (Poland), Eximbank (Romania)
	4		Eximbank (Romania)	
2014	1	Bulgarian Development Bank (Bulgaria), HBOR (Croatia), SZRB (Slovakia), Eximbank (Romania)	Bulgarian Development Bank (Bulgaria), HBOR (Croatia), SZRB (Slovakia)	Bulgarian Development Bank (Bulgaria), HBOR (Croatia), SZRB (Slovakia), Bank Gospodarstwa (Poland)
	2	Bank Gospodarstwa (Poland), Municipality Finance (Finland), CMRZB (Czech Republic), Finnvera (Finland),Rentenbank (Germany), KfW (Germany),CassaDepositi e Prestiti (Italy),ICO (Spain), BNG Bank (Netherlands),SID Bank (Slovenia),OeEB (Austria), KredEx (Estonia), SNCI (Luxembourg), MFB (Hungary)	Eximbank (Romania)	Eximbank (Romania)
	3		Bank Gospodarstwa (Poland)	CMRZB (Czech Republic), Finnvera (Finland),Rentenbank (Germany), KfW (Germany),CassaDepositi e Prestiti (Italy),ICO (Spain), BNG Bank (Netherlands),SID Bank (Slovenia),OeEB (Austria), KredEx (Estonia), SNCI (Luxembourg), MFB (Hungary)
	4		ICO (Spain), BNG Bank (Netherlands),SID Bank (Slovenia),OeEB (Austria), KredEx (Estonia), SNCI (Luxembourg), CMRZB (Czech Republic), MFB (Hungary), Finnvera (Finland),Rentenbank (Germany), KfW (Germany),CassaDepositi e Prestiti (Italy)	Municipality Finance (Finland)
	5		Municipality Finance (Finland)	

Source: author, based on data computed with SPSS software

tion of this model comprises the variables: total assets (in logarithm), ROE and Tier 1. As it can be noticed from the table, although most banks have been included in the same cluster for the entire sample period and the composition of the cluster changed very slightly over time, some NPBs have changed their cluster through the sampled period of 2011-2014. Therefore, these particular NPBs have modified their financial parameters one year from another, by exhibiting increased dissimilarity with their initial peers.

It can be noticed that the highest fragmentation between NPBs in terms of size, profitability and capital adequacy indicators has been recorded in 2014 (under the single linkage rule for computing clusters' proximity), when it has been obtained the most clusters.

Table 5. NPBs clustering during 2011-2014 (model 2)

Year	Number of Clusters	Ward Method	Single Linkage	Complete Linkage
2011	1	HBOR (Croatia), SID Bank (Slovenia), Cassa Depositi e Prestiti (Italy), KfW (Germany), Finnvera (Finland), Bulgarian Development Bank (Bulgaria)	HBOR (Croatia), SID Bank (Slovenia), Cassa Depositi e Prestiti (Italy), KfW (Germany), Finnvera (Finland), Bulgarian Development Bank (Bulgaria)	HBOR (Croatia), SID Bank (Slovenia), Cassa Depositi e Prestiti (Italy), KfW (Germany), Finnvera (Finland), Bulgarian Development Bank (Bulgaria)
	2	Eximbank (Romania), KredEx (Estonia)	Rentenbank (Germany), Municipality Finance (Finland), OeEB (Austria), MFB (Hungary), SZRB (Slovakia), BNG Bank (Netherlands)	Rentenbank (Germany), Municipality Finance (Finland), OeEB (Austria), MFB (Hungary), SZRB (Slovakia), BNG Bank (Netherlands)
	3	SZRB (Slovakia), BNG Bank (Netherlands), Rentenbank (Germany), Municipality Finance (Finland), OeEB (Austria), MFB (Hungary)	ICO (Spain)	Eximbank (Romania), KredEx (Estonia)
	4	CMRZB (Czech Republic), Bank Gospodarstwa (Poland), ICO (Spain), SNCI (Luxembourg)	SNCI (Luxembourg)	CMRZB (Czech Republic), Bank Gospodarstwa (Poland), ICO (Spain), SNCI (Luxembourg)
	5		CMRZB (Czech Republic), Bank Gospodarstwa (Poland)	
	6		Eximbank (Romania), KredEx (Estonia)	

continued on following page

Table 5. Continued

Year	Number of Clusters	Ward Method	Single Linkage	Complete Linkage
2012	1	Rentenbank (Germany), Municipality Finance (Finland), OeEB (Austria), MFB (Hungary), BNG Bank (Netherlands), Bulgarian Development Bank (Bulgaria), HBOR (Croatia),SID Bank (Slovenia),CassaDepositi e Prestiti (Italy), KfW (Germany),Finnvera (Finland)	Rentenbank (Germany), Municipality Finance (Finland), OeEB (Austria), MFB (Hungary), BNG Bank (Netherlands)	Rentenbank (Germany), Municipality Finance (Finland), OeEB (Austria), MFB (Hungary), BNG Bank (Netherlands), Bulgarian Development Bank (Bulgaria), SID Bank (Slovenia),KfW (Germany),CassaDepositi e Prestiti (Italy), Finnvera (Finland), HBOR (Croatia)
	2	SNCI (Luxembourg), KredEx (Estonia), ICO (Spain), CMRZB (Czech Republic), SZRB (Slovakia), Eximbank (Romania), Bank Gospodarstwa (Poland)	KfW (Germany), CassaDepositi e Prestiti (Italy), Bulgarian Development Bank (Bulgaria), HBOR (Croatia),SID Bank (Slovenia), Finnvera (Finland)	Eximbank (Romania), Bank Gospodarstwa (Poland)
	3		SNCI (Luxembourg), KredEx (Estonia)	CMRZB (Czech Republic), SZRB (Slovakia)
	4		ICO (Spain)	SNCI (Luxembourg), KredEx (Estonia), ICO (Spain)
	5		CMRZB (Czech Republic), SZRB (Slovakia)	
	6		Bank Gospodarstwa (Poland)	
	7		Eximbank (Romania)	
2013	1	SID Bank (Slovenia),Finnvera (Finland),HBOR (Croatia),CassaDepositi e Prestiti (Italy), KfW (Germany),Bulgarian Development Bank (Bulgaria),OeEB (Austria), SZRB (Slovakia),Rentenbank (Germany), Municipality Finance (Finland), BNG Bank (Netherlands)	SID Bank (Slovenia),Finnvera (Finland), HBOR (Croatia), CassaDepositi e Prestiti (Italy), KfW (Germany), Bulgarian Development Bank (Bulgaria), OeEB (Austria), SZRB (Slovakia), Rentenbank (Germany), Municipality Finance (Finland), BNG Bank (Netherlands)	SID Bank (Slovenia),Finnvera (Finland), HBOR (Croatia), CassaDepositi e Prestiti (Italy), KfW (Germany), Bulgarian Development Bank (Bulgaria), OeEB (Austria), SZRB (Slovakia), Rentenbank (Germany), Municipality Finance (Finland), BNG Bank (Netherlands)

continued on following page

Table 5. Continued

Year	Number of Clusters	Ward Method	Single Linkage	Complete Linkage
2013	2	Eximbank (Romania),Bank Gospodarstwa (Poland), SNCI (Luxembourg), KredEx (Estonia), CMRZB (Czech Republic),ICO (Spain), MFB (Hungary)	Eximbank (Romania), Bank Gospodarstwa (Poland)	Eximbank (Romania), Bank Gospodarstwa (Poland)
	3		SNCI (Luxembourg), KredEx (Estonia)	SNCI (Luxembourg), KredEx (Estonia), CMRZB (Czech Republic), ICO (Spain), MFB (Hungary)
	4		CMRZB (Czech Republic), ICO (Spain)	
	5		MFB (Hungary)	
2014	1	KfW (Germany), CassaDepositi e Prestiti (Italy), HBOR (Croatia), SID Bank (Slovenia),Finnvera (Finland), Bulgarian Development Bank (Bulgaria), SZRB (Slovakia), SNCI (Luxembourg), Rentenbank (Germany), Municipality Finance (Finland), OeEB (Austria), BNG Bank (Netherlands), Eximbank (Romania)	KfW (Germany), CassaDepositi e Prestiti (Italy), HBOR (Croatia), SID Bank (Slovenia),Finnvera (Finland),Rentenbank (Germany), Municipality Finance (Finland), OeEB (Austria), Bulgarian Development Bank (Bulgaria), SZRB (Slovakia), SNCI (Luxembourg), BNG Bank (Netherlands)	KfW (Germany), CassaDepositi e Prestiti (Italy), HBOR (Croatia), SID Bank (Slovenia),Finnvera (Finland), Bulgarian Development Bank (Bulgaria), SZRB (Slovakia), SNCI (Luxembourg)
	2	ICO (Spain), MFB (Hungary), KredEx (Estonia), CMRZB (Czech Republic), Bank Gospodarstwa (Poland)	Eximbank (Romania)	Rentenbank (Germany), Municipality Finance (Finland), OeEB (Austria), BNG Bank (Netherlands), Eximbank (Romania)
	3		ICO (Spain), MFB (Hungary)	ICO (Spain), MFB (Hungary), KredEx (Estonia), CMRZB (Czech Republic)
	4		CMRZB (Czech Republic)	Bank Gospodarstwa (Poland)
	5		KredEx (Estonia)	
	6		Bank Gospodarstwa (Poland)	

Source: author, based on data computed with SPSS software

By comparatively assessing the clustering solutions obtained in each of the four years and for each linkage rule, it can be drawn several observations:

- When applying Ward's method for computing the distance between clusters and joining them, the initial sample of 18 NPBs has been divided in two main, stable clusters for each and every year considered. Moreover, the composition of the two clusters remains the same during each year. There is a smaller cluster comprising the promotional banks from Bulgaria, Croatia, Romania and Slovakia and a larger one reconciling all the remaining banks.

- The single linkage rule has generated most clusters. In 2011 it identified the same clusters' composition as Ward method. Starting with 2012, it generated 4 stable clusters, namely: a big one, another cluster comprising the NPBs from Bulgaria, Croatia and Slovakia, and two single-membership clusters represented by Eximbank from Romania and respectively by Municipality Finance from Finland. There can be also noticed that a single bank (Bank Gospodarstwa from Poland) changed its patterns and hence the cluster it joined in each year. This might suggest that this bank has recorded ample fluctuations of its financial indicators one year from another, so that each year it has been assigned to a different cluster, with completely different membership. By examining the values recorded by its financial indicators it can be noticed that this bank continuously improved its capitalization ratio (from 13.4% in 2011 to 55.4%), while profitability levels fluctuated sharply one year from another.

- The complete linkage applies a rule for computing the distance between clusters that is completely opposite to the single linkage one. However, the results generated are not strikingly different. In three out of four years the promotional banks from Bulgaria, Croatia, Romania and Slovakia have been always positioned in the same cluster, excepting 2014 when the bank from Romania becomes an outlier and creates its own cluster. Municipality Finance from Finland holds its own cluster during 2012 – 2014.

- Another interesting observation is that, irrespective the linkage rule employed, during 2011 - 2013 the banks: Bulgarian Development Bank (Bulgaria), HBOR (Croatia), SZRB (Slovakia) and Eximbank (Romania) were always the last banks joining the cluster. It means that their financial indicators are broadly different from all the remaining NPBs and this peculiarity persisted across three out of four years analyzed.

To gain a closer insight into the particularities of each cluster identified during each year, one has to rely on raw financial indicators values. For the interpretation of the results it has been relied on the classification performed by means of single linkage method, as it is more sensitive to outliers and generated a more fragmented clustering. The clustering identified for the year 2011 records the following characteristics:

- The promotional banks included in the first cluster record tier 1 capital levels between 12 – 20%, below the sample's average. In terms of assets size and profitability they range close to the sample's average.
- The second cluster comprises four NPBs that hold the highest tier 1 ratios (between 52 and 75%) in the entire sample, well above the sample's average of 26.32%. This high capitalization has been explained by the economic literature through a natural conservatism which is due to their governance and limited access to 3rd party capital (McCarroll and Habberfield, 2012). They exhibit also the lowest profitability in the sample, between 0.66 and 2% (the sample's average being of 6.46%) and an asset size which is below, but close to the sample's average.

The year 2012 witnessed the following classification of NPBs:

- A big cluster comprising 13 promotional banks, with quite resembling features: tier 1 capital ratio fluctuates in the range 10 – 21%, below the sample's average of 27.22%, meanwhile ROE and asset size oscillate around the sample's average levels.
- A second cluster represented by only one bank, namely Municipality Finance (Finland). It obtained the highest level of ROE, of 38%, well above the sample's average of 7.49%. The asset size exceeds the sample's average while the capitalization is close to the sample's average (26.22%, the average being of 27.22%).
- A third cluster composed by NPBs from Bulgaria, Croatia and Slovakia. These banks depict the lowest profitability in the entire sample of banks, between 0 and 1.65%, and one of the highest tier 1 ratios, ranging between 50 and 60%. Their asset size ranges close, but below the sample's average value.
- The last cluster consists of only one bank, Eximbank from Romania. It holds the highest capital adequacy ratio, of 80%, although the profitability is low, of only 1.12% and the bank's size is below, but close to the sample's average.

During 2013 and 2014 the classification of banks into clusters remained unchanged, as they succeeded to preserve their positioning relative to sample's average. The two outlier banks maintained their top positions in terms of ROE (it is the case of Municipality Finance) and tier 1 ratio (Eximbank).

The second research hypothesis has performed a cluster analysis with a different model specification, which focuses on NPBs' balance sheet structure. It is useful to recall that the variables used for identifying promotional banks' classification are the share of loans in total assets, the share of financial assets in total assets and total liabilities (expressed in natural logarithm for standardization purposes). The results obtained in the form of several dendrograms have been synthesized in Table 5 below (see Appendix 2 for a detailed presentation of dendrograms obtained for each linkage rule and each of the four years).

A main observation, compared with the previous research direction, relies on the increased fragmentation ranging between 2 and 7 clusters, as well as the appearance of more outlier banks, that hold their unique cluster. This increased heterogeneity between NPBs in terms of balance sheet structure, reflected by the number of clusters obtained, is a proof that their business model is complex and has to be analyzed from distinct perspectives. If from the standpoint of capital resilience and profitability NPBs classified themselves in 4 main typologies, the findings are more nuanced when assessed from the standpoint of financial structure.

Turning to the results summarized in table 3.5, the highest fragmentation between NPBs' indicators has been recorded under the single linkage rule for computing clusters' proximity, ranging between 5 and 7 clusters.

Taking a comparative look at the clustering solutions generated for each of the four years and for each linkage rule, it can be extracted several features, as follows:

- Ward's method divided the initial sample of 18 NPBs in four clusters for the 2011 year-end data and in two main clusters during 2012 – 2014. Generally, the composition of these clusters remained relatively unchanged for the last three years considered. Promotional banks from Czech Republic, Estonia, Poland and Spain always shared the same second cluster, while banks from Hungary, Luxembourg, Romania and Slovakia migrated from one cluster to another.
- The single linkage rule has identified the most clusters. In 2011 it identified the same clusters' composition as Ward's method for 3 out of 6 clusters. The remaining 3 clusters have been obtained by splitting a big cluster created according to Ward's method. The year 2012 wit-

nessed the broadest fragmentation between NPBs, while years 2013 and 2014 exhibit the presence of a big and stable cluster, and of several small clusters with changing composition due to shifts in their resembling patters. The NPBs from Czech Republic, Estonia, Hungary, Luxembourg, Poland, Romania and Spain are susceptible to depict particular features from the remaining ones, as they used to hold their unique cluster or to group in pairs.

- The complete linkage has identified in 2011 exactly the same clusters' number and composition as Ward's method. For the next three years it generates a big cluster whose composition is similar with the one identified by the other two linkage rules, and a series of small clusters with changing composition, comprising banks from Czech Republic, Estonia, Hungary, Luxembourg, Poland, Romania and Spain.
- Irrespective the linkage rules employed, during 2011 - 2014 the promotional banks from Czech Republic, Estonia, Hungary, Luxembourg, Poland, Romania and Spain were always the last banks joining the cluster, meaning that their financial structure is apart from all the NPBs in the sample and persists across the four years considered.

To examine the particularities of each cluster identified during each year it has been taken into account the values of the balance sheet indicators, under the single linkage method. The classification identified for the year 2011 depicts the following characteristics:

- NPBs included in the first cluster depict the highest levels of loans to total assets ratio, ranging between 75.8 – 93%, and the lowest levels of financial assets to total assets ratio, ranging between 1.31 – 10.22%. In respect of total liability, its level fluctuates around the sample's average. One can conclude that these banks are the more committed to fulfilling their mission of channeling funding towards real economy, as most of their activity gravitates around lending.
- The common features of NPBs included in the second cluster relate to above the average values for loans to total assets ratio (ranging between 60 – 72.92%), and closely around the sample's average levels for the other two indicators.
- the third cluster is represented solely by the promotional bank from Spain. It holds a Low share of loans in total assets, of only 34% compared with the sample's average of 60%, a low share of financial assets in total assets (8.97% the sample's average being of 20.32%) and one of the highest levels for its liability side.

- The fourth cluster is also represented by a single bank, operating in Luxembourg. It exhibits the lowest level of total liabilities of all NPBs in the sample, a low share of financial assets in total assets of 8.57% and a low share of loans in total assets, of 46.34% compared with the sample's average of 60%.
- The fifth cluster includes two NPBs, CMRZB (Czech Republic) and Bank Gospodarstwa (Poland) which record almost equal values for all of the three indicators. They hold a low ratio of loans to total assets, between 34-38%, a high share of financial assets in total assets (34.23 – 35.44%, the sample's average being 20.32%) and a total liability level almost equal to the entire sample's average.
- The sixth cluster comprises two NPBs, namely Eximbank (Romania) and KredEx (Estonia) which share similar features, such as: the lowest ratio of loans to total assets in the sample, the highest ratio of financial assets in total assets (twice more than the sample's average of 20.32%) and one of the lowest levels of total liabilities. Thus, these banks do not follow the genuine promotional business model focused on lending activity but instead prove a more investment-oriented financial behavior.

According to the clustering identified for 2012 year-end, there are seven main groups:

- The NPBs that joined the first cluster are exactly the same that were included in the second cluster identified for the year 2011 and exhibit the same particular features as in the preceding year. They show above the average values for loans to total assets ratio (ranging between 62 – 73.52%), one of the highest levels for the financial assets to total assets ratio (ranging between 18 – 26.8% while the sample's average is of 18.7%) and closely around the sample's average levels for the total liabilities.
- The second cluster has exactly the same component NPBs as the first cluster identified for the year 2011. The main characteristics of these banks maintained: the highest levels of loans to total assets ratio, ranging between 80 – 90%, and the lowest levels of financial assets to total assets ratio, ranging between 5 – 12%.
- The third cluster is represented by SNCI (Luxembourg) and KredEx (Estonia), its common features relying on below average levels for loans/total assets, one of the lowest levels of financial assets/total assets and the smallest level of total liabilities.

- The NPB from Spain records below average levels for loans/total assets and financial assets/total assets and an above average level for its total liabilities.
- The fifth cluster joins CMRZB (Czech Republic) and SZRB (Slovakia). Both banks depict the smallest level of loans to total assets, ranging between 7 – 15.26%, a value slightly exceeding the sample's average for the ratio of financial assets to total assets and close to the average levels of total liabilities. Taking a look at the financial statement for year-end 2012 it can be noticed that the main part of their financial activity is summarized in the item cash and balances with central banks, which comprises mainly the amounts due under reverse repo transactions. It means that these banks prefer to lend on short-term maturities to the central bank, instead to lend to customers either directly or through second-tier lending.
- Bank Gospodarstwa (Poland) records a low level of loans/total assets of only 28.10%, a slightly above the average level for total liabilities and one of the highest share of financial assets in total assets, of 36.84% compared with the sample's average of 18.71%. It has a diversified holding of debt securities issued by banks, central and local government, and shares in financial institutions and other undertakings.
- Eximbank from Romania is the last NPB joining the clustering tree. It exhibits a low level of loans/total assets of only 27.07%, a below average level for total liabilities and the feature that makes it the most apart: the highest share of financial assets in total assets of all NPBs in the sample, of 60.85%. According to the balance sheet for 2012 year-end they are represented by financial securities held until maturity issued by the Central Bank of Romania or by the Ministry of Finance.

The classification performed for 2013 year-end data revealed a repositioning of NPBs compared with the preceding two years: the first two clusters merged into a single big cluster gathering 11 out of 18 banks.

- The first big cluster joins NPBs sharing several common features, such as: the highest levels of loans to total assets ratio, ranging between 70.7 – 86.62%, and values fluctuating around the sample's average for the other two indicators.
- The second cluster comprises Eximbank (Romania) and Bank Gospodarstwa (Poland), which exhibit low levels of loans to total assets of around 25-36% compared with the sample's average of 60%, close to the average levels for total liabilities and the highest levels

of financial assets to total assets of all NPBs considered (54.5-55.6%, exceeding the average of 20.42%). If in the preceding year these two banks held the first two positions in the ranking in terms of the level of financial assets to total assets, one year later the catch-up effect joined both banks in the same cluster.

- The third cluster gathers SNCI (Luxembourg) and KredEx (Estonia) depict below average values for the share of loans in total assets, one of the lowest levels of the share of financial assets in total assets and the smallest level of total liabilities of all NPBs.

- CMRZB (Czech Republic) and ICO (Spain) record the smallest level of loans to total assets, ranging between 14.6 –27%, a value slightly exceeding the sample's average for the ratio of financial assets to total assets and close to the average levels of total liabilities.

- The last cluster identified is composed by a single bank, namely MFB from Hungary. It holds one of the highest levels of the ratio of financial assets to total assets of 35.5%, a small level of loans/total assets ratio and a close to average level of total liabilities.

The last year considered witnessed a similar classification of NPBs with the 2013 one, namely a big cluster and several small clusters comprising satellite banks whose resemblance patterns are fluctuating one year from another.

- The first, big cluster maintained the features in the preceding years, namely the highest levels of loans to total assets ratio, ranging between 61.8 – 84.58%, and values fluctuating around the sample's average for the other two indicators.

- Eximbank from Romania has its own cluster, recording the second highest share of loans in total assets of 54.49%, the second highest share of financial assets in total assets of 40.5%, and a below but close to sample's average level for total liabilities.

- The third cluster joins NPBs from Spain and Hungary, with relatively small levels of loans to total assets ratio and close to average levels of the remaining two indicators.

- The fourth cluster is represented by the NPB from Czech Republic which records the lowest level of loans to total assets ratio of all banks (9.24% while the sample's average is of 58.71%), a slightly below average level of financial assets to total assets and equal to average level for total liabilities.

- The fifth cluster is also described by only one bank from Estonia which exhibits low levels, below the sample's average for all the three indicators of financial position.
- The last cluster comprises the promotional bank from Poland whose main feature resides in holding the highest level of financial assets to total assets ratio of all banks in the sample (52.16% while the sample's average is of 20.53%). In terms of total liabilities it positions above the average, meanwhile the share of loans to total assets is small, of only 24.42%.

Interestingly, with the passing of time, the NPBs that exhibited the highest levels of loans to total assets ratio record a decreasing trend, from a maximum of 93% in 2011 (held by HBOR from Croatia) until a value of 84.5% at 2014 year-end, recorded by the same bank. The maximum level recorded by the share of financial assets to total assets always exhibited a stable pattern, ranging between 55-60%, with a small decrease in 2014, until 52%.

This second research direction proved the persistence of dissimilarities between NPBs, as well as the changing patterns across years for some of them. The presence of heterogeneity might indicate that these banks do not act according to the genuine promotional business model, as they prefer to invest in acquiring debt securities and shares or to engage in transactions with pre-established maturity (usually reverse repo agreements) with the central bank. This reluctance in lending to customers, in managing large amounts of loans and hence in exposing themselves to credit risk, liquidity risk or market risk might be explained by the fact that they are financed with public, not private money. Another explanation might reside in the fact that their ownership structures, mostly public, didn't understand the mission and specificities of promotional banks' functioning. As a matter of consequence, the tone at the top is adopted by medium-level management and transposed in practice, sometimes by losing sight of promotional basic mission.

REFERENCES

Everitt, B. S., Landau, S., Leese, M., & Stahl, D. (2011). *Cluster Analysis* (5th ed.). West Sussex, UK: Wiley, John & Sons Ltd. doi:10.1002/9780470977811

Hubert, L. (1974). Approximate evaluation techniques for the single-link and complete link hierarcihal clustering procedures. *Journal of the American Statistical Association*, 69(347), 698–704. doi:10.1080/01621459.1974.10480191

Kachigan, S. K. (1991). *Multivariate Statistical Analysis: A Conceptual Introduction.* New York, NY: Radius Press.

Kaufman, L., & Rousseeuw, P. J. (2005). *Finding groups in data: an introduction to cluster analysis.* New York: John Wiley and Sons.

Klotz, S., & Lindermeir, A. (2009). Multivariate credit portfolio management using cluster analysis. *The Journal of Risk Finance, 16*(2), 145-163.

Landau, S., & Everitt, B. S. (2004). *A handbook of statistical analyses using SPSS.* Chapman & Hall/CRC Press LLC.

Norušis, M. J. (2008). SPSS 17.0 Statistical Procedures Companion. In Cluster Analysis. Prentice Hall.

Thiprungsri, S. (2011). *Cluster analysis for anomaly detection in accounting* (PhD Dissertation). Rutgers, The State University of New Jersey.

Timm, N. H. (2002). Applied Multivariate Analysis. Springer-Verlag.

Chapter 4
Nonparametric Estimation of National Promotional Banks' Efficiency and Productivity

INTRODUCTION

Existing research on national promotional banks is still scarce, a main impediment being the lack of long time series or a predefined database comprising detailed balance sheet indicators. The only data available is that on NPBs websites, which has to be extracted from financial statements and annual reports.

As de Luna Martinez and Vicente (2012, p.2) document, the World Bank has increasingly received, during the last years, several requests concerning the availability of data as well as the elaboration of new studies about NPBs. Decision makers and financial institutions in various countries have motivated their requests by the need to strengthen the role, independence and corporate governance of their own NPBs in order to become more profitable and financially self-sustainable organizations and avoid any undue political interference in their regular business conduct.

Some papers have introduced delineation between state-owned and private-owned banks when attempting to empirically assess various features of a given banking system, but evidences are mixed in terms of efficiency and profitability across countries.

DOI: 10.4018/978-1-5225-1845-7.ch004

Copyright ©2017, IGI Global. Copying or distributing in print or electronic forms without written permission of IGI Global is prohibited.

Schmit et al. (2011, p. 31) observe that public banks in developed countries are less efficient from the standpoint of profit and costs management than their privately-owned peers. The same finding is supported by Micco, Panizza, & Yanez (2007), which explain that the financial performance differential is driven by political factors and depicts a widening trend particularly during election years. By analyzing a global sample of promotional banks during the 2007-2009 years, de Luna Martinez and Vicente (2012) concluded that they maintained their financial stability and profitability although profit maximization is not a main objective.

Despite the inconclusive empirical findings in terms of state-owned banks' efficiency and financial performance, several authors advocate for the economic and social beneficial effects and value added through the activity of NPBs which may explain their underperformance compared to private ones.

Sobreira and Zendron (2011, p.6) state that NPBs focus should always be on alleviating productive sectors' or country's financing needs, without being driven by profitability issues. Iannotta et al. (2011) argue that NPBs lower profitability might be due either to the pursuance of political goals or to their mere social object of activity, namely the provision of financing to investment projects that private-owned banks are reluctant to fund or in time periods of financial market stress, in order to defreeze the credit supply. Irrespective their intrinsic motivation, promotional banks' mission is closely mirrored by their lending behavior and risk profile.

Schmit et al. (2011, p. 34) agree with the explanation of public banks' poor performance by means of their social and development mission, which emphasizes the mitigation of financial market inefficiencies and the financing of less profitable economic sectors but with increased social utility for the local communities.

The lower profitability recorded by NPBs can also be interpreted through a different perspective, related to the degree of risk forbearance. According to Rudolph (2010, p.3), promotional banks with a public policy mandate usually depict riskier loan portfolios and higher operational costs as a result of financing riskier, unpredictable investment projects than commercial banks do. For the going concern of their business, NPBs target the achievement of reasonable returns instead of profit maximization; therefore, the quite natural lower returns shouldn't be perceived as lack of efficiency in conducting their activity, but as a consequence of operating in difficult market segments.

An important observation belongs to Gutierrez et al. (2011). Although they recognize the poor past financial performance recorded by promotional banks, it is outlined the necessity that NPBs remain financially viable, to consolidate their presence in the financial market as they hold best knowledge on local communities' needs. In addition, the authors point out that in times of financial distress NPBs have to fulfill and reconcile two challenging tasks, namely the long-term development role and the short-term countercyclical role dealing with providing liquidity to systemically important markets and containing the credit crunch.

This chapter aims at investigating two complementing research directions, to shed light on NPBs financial activity's efficiency and productivity. To my knowledge, it is the first empirical attempt devoted exclusively to assessing the efficiency and productivity of promotional banks, in a comparative fashion.

The two methods employed within this chapter depict a non-parametric nature, being the most appropriate for the purpose of the analysis and the specificities of the dataset used. Existing literature also advocates for the use of new approaches in assessing banks' financial performance, apart from the traditional analysis of financial ratios. International Monetary Fund (2007, p.10) explains that commonly-used financial indicators (ROA, cost-to-income ratios etc.) "convey useful information on financial performance, but offer little guidance to identify best practices and are clearly insufficient to assess operating efficiency. The later is further complicated by the fact that productive processes usually entail the combination of many inputs to produce several outputs". Banerjee (2012, p.5) criticizes the use of financial ratios approach because they are single factor measures of performance, cannot embed issues related to product mix or input prices and may be misleading indicators of efficiency.

The first sub-chapter applies the Data Envelopment Analysis technique. Its outcome is represented by the computation of relative efficiency scores for each promotional bank, allowing the researcher to perform discrimination between efficient and inefficient banks and make a ranking. Thus, one gains an understanding on how each NPB performs relative to others in the sample, which are its closest peers and how it can improve its performance to become efficient.

The second sub-chapter employs a DEA-type Malmquist index of total factor productivity to measure the productivity changes over time for each NPB in the sample. In addition, a main advantage of this technique resides in the decomposition of total productivity into changes in technical efficiency, due to a catch-up effect and changes in technology, due to frontier movement.

Measuring NPBs Relative Efficiency: A Data Envelopment Analysis Approach

Data envelopment analysis (DEA) is a method widely used by researchers, as well as international organizations in an attempt to quantify the performance depicted by financial institutions, in terms of the degree of relative efficiency. It consists in applying a linear programming technique for computing the relative efficiency of a bank, by mathematically aggregating multiple inputs and outputs.

Barr and Siems (1996) highlight the main distinction between DEA and statistical methods: the former is an extreme-point method that compares each bank in the sample only with the best practice ones meanwhile the latter evaluates each bank according to a central tendency by using econometric techniques.

This peculiarity of DEA helps explaining the term *relative efficiency* in that a bank previously identified as being fully efficient for a given dataset, time period or peer group, can become inefficient if one changes the input or output variables included in the initial dataset or the group composition. Another consequence is that the findings obtained by using DEA cannot be extrapolated to the entire population, but are valid only for the sample considered. In addition, the efficiency scores obtained are not the unique, generally valid solution, but a satisfactory one which resulted from the solving of an optimization problem.

Repkova (2014, p. 590) outlines that this specific feature of DEA might constitute a useful decision-making tool, as "knowing which efficient banks are most comparable to the inefficient bank enables the analyst to develop an understanding of the nature of inefficiencies and reallocate scarce resources to improve productivity". A different, but complementary view belongs to Ferreira (2011, p.7) which argues that all the features underlying DEA method are closely related to the microeconomic concept of efficiency and the microeconomic view of production functions.

Delineation between non-parametric techniques (represented by DEA) and parametric ones resides also in terms of the methodologies employed. Banerjee (2012, p. 7) points out DEA's focus on technological optimization, whereas parametric techniques imply the economic optimization. Therefore, the purpose of DEA is to measure technical efficiency, namely whether banks are using too many inputs for producing a given level of outputs (banks' ability to minimize the use of input variables) or they are producing too few outputs given the level of inputs (or alternatively banks' ability to maximize the amount of outputs obtained).

The final aim of this methodology is to build an efficient frontier represented by a combination of the most efficient banks in the initial sample. A research performed by the International Monetary Fund (2007, p.11) explains that DEA methodology "exploits information on the input-output mix of individual entities to construct an efficient frontier enveloping the data, and then uses the frontier as a benchmark to assess various efficiency indicators for individual entities".

Technically speaking, if a bank reaches an efficiency score of 1, it is positioned on the frontier and is called fully efficient, being a benchmark for the inefficient ones. All other banks are deemed inefficient, the level of inefficiency being computed as the difference between 1 and their computed efficiency score. The highest the inefficiency, the more far away from the frontier is a bank.

The efficiency scores are computed individually for each bank in the sample, by solving a linear optimization problem for each bank. The simplified formula computes technical efficiency as the ratio of the weighted sum of outputs to the weighted sum of inputs:

$$\sum_{j=1}^{n} x_n \times output_{nj} \Big/ \sum_{j=1}^{m} y_m \times input_{mj}$$

where

n = the number of output variables generated for bank j
m = the number of input variables used by bank j
x_n = the weight attributed to each output variable
y_m = the weight attributed to each input variable

The vector of weights is also the solution of the optimization problem, being computed distinctly for each bank in the sample. According to Guzowska, Kisielewska, Nellis, & Zarzecki (2004), this flexibility in establishing individual weights contributes to the enhancement of bank's degree of efficiency, allowing the bank to appear in the best possible light.

Further it can be performed a classification of DEA models, based on two main criterions:

1. Returns to Scale

According to a study performed by IMF (2007, p.12), returns to scale are measuring the changes incurred in the production process of an entity, due to a proportional increase in all inputs. In other words, the concept of returns to scale allows the comparison between the actual, observed size of a bank and its efficient scale.

One can distinguish between a model with constant returns to scale (CRS) and another one employing variable returns to scale (VRS). The basic DEA model has been developed by Charnes, Cooper and Rhodes (1978) under the assumption of constant returns to scale. Their rationale was that in the constant returns to scale hypothesis there is no significant relationship between the scale of operations and the level of computed efficiency and all entities considered are operating at an optimal scale.

In 1984 Banker, Charnes and Cooper have modified the initial DEA model in order to allow the computation of efficiency scores in the assumption of variable returns to scale, by arguing that in practice most entities are confronted either with economies or diseconomies to scale. Titko and Jureviciene (2014, p. 1127) explain that the CRS assumption has to be interpreted as an equiproportionate increase in inputs which generates an equiproportionate increase in output. On the other hand, the VRS assumption means that equiproportionate increases in inputs are followed by a greater (or less) than equiproportionate increase in output. More specifically, an entity exhibits increasing returns to scale if by increasing all inputs with an arbitrary value x it will be obtained an increase of all outputs with a value bigger than x. The alternative is represented by an entity recording descending returns to scale, when the increase of inputs will yield outputs increases smaller than x.

Nenovsky, Chobanov, Mihaylova, and Koleva (2008, p. 19) suggest that VRS-model is more indicated when estimating "the large banks and the total banking system's average efficiency, because the increasing competition, technology improvement and regulatory changes affect the banks' behavior and impede some of them from operating at their optimal level". Andries (2011) adds a series of other factors which can impede some banks to operate at an optimum scale and hence advocate for the use of VRS, namely imperfect competition, asymmetric information, financing constraints, the prudential requirements especially those related to capital adequacy.

2. DEA Model's Orientation (Input or Output Oriented)

A feature of DEA as an extreme point method resides in its duality, meaning that the same problem can generate optimal solutions in two equivalent and interchangeable ways, in terms of two alternative distance orientations. An input orientation envisages an as much as possible reduction of input amounts while keeping relatively unchanged the present levels of outputs and is the equivalent of solving a minimization problem. The output orientation is specific to the solving of a maximization problem and aims at increasing as much as possible output levels by relying on a pre-established mix of input amounts.

An important observation has been stressed by Coelli (1996, p. 23), arguing that both input and output oriented models are able to estimate the same efficient frontier and identify the same set of efficient banks. The difference lies in the computed efficiency scores associated to those banks that are not positioned on the best-practices frontier, which differ between the two models.

The next step before performing the DEA analysis relies on ensuring that the data fulfils some goodness-of-fit criteria. A rule of thumb for assessing sample's adequacy and the robustness of computations relies on monitoring the degrees of freedom. As in any other non-parametric or statistical analysis, the degrees of freedom record an increase when new banks are included in the sample and a decrease when new variables are added. Varias and Sofianopoulou (2012, p. 257) mention in this regard the following rule to comply with:

$$n \geq \max \{ m \times s, 3(m + s) \}$$

where

n = the number of entities in the sample
m = the number of input variables
s = the number of output variables

A second requirement is to apply the principle of homogeneity in selecting those entities to be included in the analysis. According to Haas and Murphy (2003, p.530), the running of DEA method implicitly assumes the presence of homogeneity "among the considered entities in terms of the nature of the operations they perform, the measures of their efficiency and the conditions under which they operate". For that reason, if banks are not homogeneous in terms of the size of their activity, the efficiency measures may reflect the underlying differences in risk profile, credit culture, corporate governance, rather than inefficiency.

To sum up the previous methodological frame, the main arguments that advocate for the use of DEA method as a reliable tool for assessing an entity's performance are:

- Allows the simultaneous testing of multi-input multi-output models;
- Unlike statistical methods, there is no need to investigate the existence of a functional relationship between input and output variables;

- It doesn't require an a priori hypothesis validation regarding the analytical form of the production function. It simply generates efficiency estimates by solving a minimization or maximization problem (IMF 2007, Nenovsky et al. 2008, Scippacercola and Sepe 2014).
- The multicollinearity problem between input and output variables has no impact on efficiency estimates;
- It accounts for technical efficiency only as any differentials in terms of input costs or product differentiation between the entities are not taken into account (Toci, 2009);
- Unlike the statistic approaches, the computation of efficiency scores doesn't need long time series (Nenovsky et al. 2008, Toci 2009);
- The relative efficiency is computed for each bank in the sample and ranked against the efficiency scores of other banks in the analyzed sample, not against a theoretical maximum;
- Each inefficient bank is attributed a set of benchmark or peer banks, represented only by the efficient ones, which depict a similar structure of input-output variables with the inefficient bank;
- DEA findings are easy to understand and interpret;
- The mathematical algorithms it relies on for solving the minimum or maximum optimization problem are more easy to follow and verify than the stochastic, statistical methods; the more sophisticated and complex are the latter, the most are they compared with black boxes.

As indicated by Nenovsky et al. (2008, p.14), DEA methodology depicts also some disadvantages, such as: sensitiveness to extreme values, failure in decomposing banks' deviation from the efficient production frontier into inefficiency and random error components. Banerjee (2012, p. 7) too observes that the efficiency scores are very sensitive to outliers and shocks as all deviations from the estimated frontier are treated as inefficiency. A possible explanation is provided by Andries (2011) which argues that DEA's deterministic nature has as implicit hypothesis that all deviations from efficiency are caused by the entity under analysis, despite the influence of external factors that might affect its performance.

To compute the efficiency scores of the 18 European NPBs it has been employed the software DEAP (Data Envelopment Analysis Program) Version 2.1, developed by Tim Coelli. It is important to mention that the case study involves all promotional banks with long track records (those established since 2012 have not been considered due to the low availability of historical data), hence providing reliable, stable estimations of efficiency scores. Regarding the principle of homogeneity, the DEAP software automatically scales all quantitative data on input and output variables, by dividing it with sample's mean therefore there is no need to apply a standardization technique in order to smooth the time series.

It has been tested an output-oriented DEA model, with variable returns to scale and a single-input single-output specification. Keeping in mind that promotional banks' mission is subordinated to channeling financing to societal and development investment projects, it has been chosen the output orientation in order to emphasize NPBs' ability to increase or optimize the amount of outputs they produce by using a given level of inputs they hold in a particular year.

The reason for testing a single-input single-output specification resides in a specificity of NPBs business model, namely the broad heterogeneity of the operations through which they attract funding. By observing the composition of NPBs total liabilities, it can be noticed that some banks use mainly one or two types of liabilities, while not resorting at all to other sources for attracting financing, such as deposits from customers and banks or borrowings from international institutions. This lack of standardization in terms of liabilities' composition justifies the choice for the development of a parsimonious model specification, with only one input and one output. Another consequence resides in avoiding the decrease of degrees of freedom, due to the use of unnecessary or less important variables.

As regards the process of defining the input and output variables, it has been followed the intermediation approach which assumes that a bank gathers liabilities (deposits, borrowed funds, debt issuance) from financial institutions and non-bank customers and transforms them, by using own labor force and capital into outputs such as loans and other types of financial investments. For the purpose of this study the input variable is represented by total liabilities in order to account for all liability items, irrespective of their type, in the balance sheet of each NPB. The output variable consists of the volume of loans granted to banks and customers, through the first and second-tier lending models. It cannot be assessed distinctly the efficiency of lending through first-tier and respectively second-tier as some NPBs resort exclusively to only one of the two approaches and the sample of observations would have been imbalanced.

The research premises outlined above are in line with IMF (2007, p. 12) conclusions stating that "the technologies used by the banks have to be comparable (i.e. the institutions have to be dedicated to similar activities)" and that the configuration of inputs and outputs must adequately reflect the specific nature of banking activity.

The study employs bank-level data collected from NPBs financial statements, the DEA analysis being run distinctly for each year in the time span 2011 – 2014. The results generated by performing DEA analysis are two-fold, consisting in the computation of technical efficiency for each NPB in each of the 4 years considered and the identification of the most appropriate peers for each inefficient NPB.

Table 1 summarizes the peer promotional banks attributed to each inefficient NPB, in each year under study, as well as the necessary strategy (expressed in terms of peer weights) to be adopted in order to improve their efficiency level.

The NPBs that position themselves on the efficient frontier (HBOR from Croatia, KfW from Germany, Societe Nationale de Credit et d'Investissement from Luxembourg and Cassa Depositi e Prestiti from Italy) have no peer, but they become benchmarks or peers for the remaining inefficient ones.

In 2011 and 2012, HBOR from Croatia has been designated as peer for 14 times, followed by Cassa Depositi e Prestiti (Italy) for 9 times and Societe Nationale de Credit et d'Investissement (Luxembourg) for 5 times. In 2013 and 2014, HBOR maintained its influence, been identified as peer for 15 times, KfW (Germany) for 10 times and Societe Nationale de Credit et d'Investissement (Luxembourg) for 5 times. These results suggest that, in order to improve their efficiency score, most promotional banks have to implement a business strategy closely related to HBOR one. As the qualitative analysis developed in the previous chapters shows up, the main peculiarities of HBOR operations in the liability side of the balance sheet are a high reliance on the issuance of debt securities and on borrowings from international financial institutions. It is also the most active European promotional bank in terms of applying for EC's funding under various financial instruments. On the asset side, it employs most of the financing collected for providing loans, preponderantly through a second-tier lending model.

Another finding indicates that 5 out of the 18 NPBs exhibit each year the same peer promotional banks. It is the case of Bulgarian Development Bank (Bulgaria), Eximbank (Romania), OeEB (Austria), Slovenská záručná a rozvojová banka (Slovakia) and KredEx (Estonia) whose related peers, represented by those NPBs they have to follow in order to become more efficient, are always HBOR (Croatia) and Societe Nationale de Credit et d'Investissement (Luxembourg). The highest weight is attributed to the promotional bank located in Luxembourg, meaning that these 5 NPBs have to target in a greatest proportion its business model.

The main results of DEA technique, represented by the computation of efficiency scores, are synthesized in Table 2.

Table 1. NPBs and their peers

Promotional banks in the sample	2011		2012		2013		2014	
	Peer promotional banks	Peer weights	Peer promotional banks	Peer weights	Peer promotional banks	Peer weights	Peer promotional banks	Peer weights
Bulgarian Development Bank (Bulgaria)	Hrvatska Banka (HBOR - Croatia)	0.298	Hrvatska Banka (HBOR - Croatia)	0.203	Hrvatska Banka (HBOR - Croatia)	0.233	Hrvatska Banka (HBOR - Croatia)	0.278
	Societe Nationale de Credit et d'Investissement (Luxembourg)	0.702	Societe Nationale de Credit et d'Investissement (Luxembourg)	0.797	Societe Nationale de Credit et d'Investissement (Luxembourg)	0.767	Societe Nationale de Credit et d'Investissement (Luxembourg)	0.722
Eximbank (Romania)	Hrvatska Banka (HBOR - Croatia)	0.262	Hrvatska Banka (HBOR - Croatia)	0.255	Hrvatska Banka (HBOR - Croatia)	0.273	Hrvatska Banka (HBOR - Croatia)	0.278
	Societe Nationale de Credit et d'Investissement (Luxembourg)	0.738	Societe Nationale de Credit et d'Investissement (Luxembourg)	0.745	Societe Nationale de Credit et d'Investissement (Luxembourg)	0.727	Societe Nationale de Credit et d'Investissement (Luxembourg)	0.722
Českomoravská záruční a rozvojová banka (CMZRB - Czech Republic)	Cassa Depositi e Prestiti (Italy)	0	Cassa Depositi e Prestiti (Italy)	0.007	KfW (Germany)	0.003	KfW (Germany)	0.005
	Societe Nationale de Credit et d'Investissement (Luxembourg)	1	Societe Nationale de Credit et d'Investissement (Luxembourg)	0.993	Hrvatska Banka (HBOR - Croatia)	0.997	Hrvatska Banka (HBOR - Croatia)	0.995
Landwirtschaftliche Rentenbank (Germany)	Cassa Depositi e Prestiti (Italy)	0.319	Cassa Depositi e Prestiti (Italy)	0.282	KfW (Germany)	0.169	KfW (Germany)	0.163
	Societe Nationale de Credit et d'Investissement (Luxembourg)	0.681	Societe Nationale de Credit et d'Investissement (Luxembourg)	0.718	Hrvatska Banka (HBOR - Croatia)	0.831	Hrvatska Banka (HBOR - Croatia)	0.837
KfW (Germany)	-	1	-	1	-	1	-	1

continued on following page

Table 1. Continued

Promotional banks in the sample	2011 Peer promotional banks	Peer weights	2012 Peer promotional banks	Peer weights	2013 Peer promotional banks	Peer weights	2014 Peer promotional banks	Peer weights
Instituto de Crédito Oficial (Spain)	Cassa Depositi e Prestiti (Italy)	0.346	Cassa Depositi e Prestiti (Italy)	0.379	Hrvatska Banka (HBOR - Croatia)	0.784	Hrvatska Banka (HBOR - Croatia)	0.835
	Societe Nationale de Credit et d'Investissement (Luxembourg)	0.654	Societe Nationale de Credit et d'Investissement (Luxembourg)	0.621	KfW (Germany)	0.216	KfW (Germany)	0.165
Hrvatska Banka (HBOR - Croatia)	-	1	-	1	-	1	-	1
Cassa Depositi e Prestiti (Italy)	-	1	-	1	KfW (Germany)	0.665	KfW (Germany)	0.728
					Hrvatska Banka (HBOR - Croatia)	0.335	Hrvatska Banka (HBOR - Croatia)	0.272
Societe Nationale de Credit et d'Investissement (Luxembourg)	-	1	-	1	-	1	-	1
MFB Hungarian Development Bank (Hungary)	Cassa Depositi e Prestiti (Italy)	0.007	Cassa Depositi e Prestiti (Italy)	0.003	KfW (Germany)	0.002	KfW (Germany)	0.001
	Societe Nationale de Credit et d'Investissement (Luxembourg)	0.993	Societe Nationale de Credit et d'Investissement (Luxembourg)	0.997	Hrvatska Banka (HBOR - Croatia)	0.998	Hrvatska Banka (HBOR - Croatia)	0.999
OeEB (Austria)	Hrvatska Banka (HBOR - Croatia)	0.084	Hrvatska Banka (HBOR - Croatia)	0.123	Hrvatska Banka (HBOR - Croatia)	0.167	Hrvatska Banka (HBOR - Croatia)	0.265
	Societe Nationale de Credit et d'Investissement (Luxembourg)	0.916	Societe Nationale de Credit et d'Investissement (Luxembourg)	0.877	Societe Nationale de Credit et d'Investissement (Luxembourg)	0.833	Societe Nationale de Credit et d'Investissement (Luxembourg)	0.735

continued on following page

Table 1. Continued

Promotional banks in the sample	2011		2012		2013		2014	
	Peer promotional banks	Peer weights	Peer promotional banks	Peer weights	Peer promotional banks	Peer weights	Peer promotional banks	Peer weights
Bank Gospodarstwa Krajowego (Poland)	Cassa Depositi e Prestiti (Italy)	0.021	Cassa Depositi e Prestiti (Italy)	0.028	KfW (Germany)	0.014	KfW (Germany)	0.016
	Societe Nationale de Credit et d'Investissement (Luxembourg)	0.979	Societe Nationale de Credit et d'Investissement (Luxembourg)	0.972	Hrvatska Banka (HBOR - Croatia)	0.986	Hrvatska Banka (HBOR - Croatia)	0.984
SID Bank (Slovenia)	Cassa Depositi e Prestiti (Italy)	0.007	Cassa Depositi e Prestiti (Italy)	0.005	KfW (Germany)	0.003	KfW (Germany)	0.002
	Societe Nationale de Credit et d'Investissement (Luxembourg)	0.993	Societe Nationale de Credit et d'Investissement (Luxembourg)	0.995	Hrvatska Banka (HBOR - Croatia)	0.997	Hrvatska Banka (HBOR - Croatia)	0.998
Slovenská záručná a rozvojová banka (Slovakia)	Hrvatska Banka (HBOR - Croatia)	0.079	Hrvatska Banka (HBOR - Croatia)	0.055	Hrvatska Banka (HBOR - Croatia)	0.057	Hrvatska Banka (HBOR - Croatia)	0.112
	Societe Nationale de Credit et d'Investissement (Luxembourg)	0.921	Societe Nationale de Credit et d'Investissement (Luxembourg)	0.945	Societe Nationale de Credit et d'Investissement (Luxembourg)	0.943	Societe Nationale de Credit et d'Investissement (Luxembourg)	0.888
Municipality Finance (Finland)	Cassa Depositi e Prestiti (Italy)	0.084	Cassa Depositi e Prestiti (Italy)	0.08	KfW (Germany)	0.053	KfW (Germany)	0.059
	Societe Nationale de Credit et d'Investissement (Luxembourg)	0.916	Societe Nationale de Credit et d'Investissement (Luxembourg)	0.92	Hrvatska Banka (HBOR - Croatia)	0.947	Hrvatska Banka (HBOR - Croatia)	0.941
Finnvera (Finland)	Cassa Depositi e Prestiti (Italy)	0.001	Cassa Depositi e Prestiti (Italy)	0.002	KfW (Germany)	0.003	KfW (Germany)	0.008
	Societe Nationale de Credit et d'Investissement (Luxembourg)	0.999	Societe Nationale de Credit et d'Investissement (Luxembourg)	0.998	Hrvatska Banka (HBOR - Croatia)	0.997	Hrvatska Banka (HBOR - Croatia)	0.992

continued on following page

Table 1. Continued

Promotional banks in the sample	2011		2012		2013		2014	
	Peer promotional banks	Peer weights	Peer promotional banks	Peer weights	Peer promotional banks	Peer weights	Peer promotional banks	Peer weights
KredEx (Estonia)	Hrvatska Banka (HBOR - Croatia)	0.041	Hrvatska Banka (HBOR - Croatia)	0.027	Hrvatska Banka (HBOR - Croatia)	0.031	Hrvatska Banka (HBOR - Croatia)	0.032
	Societe Nationale de Credit et d'Investissement (Luxembourg)	0.959	Societe Nationale de Credit et d'Investissement (Luxembourg)	0.973	Societe Nationale de Credit et d'Investissement (Luxembourg)	0.969	Societe Nationale de Credit et d'Investissement (Luxembourg)	0.968
BNG Bank (Netherland)	Cassa Depositi e Prestiti (Italy)	0.515	Cassa Depositi e Prestiti (Italy)	0.478	KfW (Germany)	0.284	KfW (Germany)	0.317
	Societe Nationale de Credit et d'Investissement (Luxembourg)	0.485	Societe Nationale de Credit et d'Investissement (Luxembourg)	0.522	Hrvatska Banka (HBOR - Croatia)	0.716	Hrvatska Banka (HBOR - Croatia)	0.683

Source: author, based on the results obtained by running DEA with DEAP software

Table 2. NPBs' efficiency measures

Promotional bank	2011		2012		2013		2014	
	Technical efficiency	Scale efficiency	Technical efficiency	Scale efficiency	Technical efficiency	Scale efficiency	Technical efficiency	Scale efficiency
Bulgarian Development Bank (Bulgaria)	0.603	0.205	0.782	0.231	0.658	0.229	0.424	0.095
Eximbank (Romania)	0.103	0.215	0.223	0.213	0.279	0.216	0.332	0.095
Českomoravská záruční a rozvojová banka (CMZRB - Czech Republic)	0.279	0.144	0.151	0.134	0.133	0.142	0.088	0.045
Landwirtschaftliche Rentenbank (Germany)	0.692	0.098	0.764	0.111	0.795	0.111	0.843	0.036
KfW (Germany)	1	0.09	1	0.105	1	0.11	1	0.035
Instituto de Crédito Oficial (Spain)	0.381	0.098	0.483	0.111	0.314	0.111	0.288	0.036
Hrvatska Banka (HBOR - Croatia)	1	0.147	1	0.154	1	0.158	1	0.055
Cassa Depositi e Prestiti (Italy)	1	0.097	1	0.11	0.97	0.11	0.996	0.035
Societe Nationale de Credit et d'Investissement (Luxembourg)	1	1	1	1	1	1	1	1
MFB Hungarian Development Bank (Hungary)	0.617	0.123	0.681	0.143	0.29	0.146	0.303	0.051
OeEB (Austria)	0.191	0.362	0.333	0.285	0.35	0.26	0.316	0.097
Bank Gospodarstwa Krajowego (Poland)	0.442	0.11	0.343	0.12	0.308	0.122	0.314	0.04
SID Bank (Slovenia)	0.854	0.123	0.906	0.137	0.812	0.142	0.747	0.049
Slovenská záručná a rozvojová banka (Slovakia)	0.482	0.373	0.055	0.412	0.559	0.421	0.326	0.166
Municipality Finance (Finland)	0.627	0.101	0.701	0.114	0.777	0.114	0.782	0.037
Finnvera (Finland)	0.836	0.142	0.907	0.144	0.94	0.139	0.91	0.043
KredEx (Estonia)	0.026	0.502	0.162	0.564	0.154	0.55	0.075	0.371
BNG Bank (Netherlands)	0.795	0.098	0.83	0.11	0.877	0.11	0.791	0.036
Average efficiency	0.607	0.224	0.629	0.233	0.623	0.233	0.585	0.129
Standard deviation	0.320	0.226	0.337	0.227	0.322	0.226	0.338	0.232

Source: author, based on the results obtained by running DEA with DEAP software

Scale efficiency has been computed as the ratio of technical efficiency scores estimated through a CRS DEA model and technical efficiency scores estimated through a VRS DEA model. It provides information on whether a promotional bank operates in an area of increasing or decreasing returns to scale. The results indicate that all NPBs in the sample depict decreasing returns to scale, meaning that any increase of inputs with a given amount will trigger a smaller increase of outputs. The average scale efficiency ranges between 0.129 and 0.233, the minimum level being recorded in 2014. According to Repkova (2014, p. 594) low levels of scale efficiency are caused by banks' inappropriate size of business or range of activities. The highest scale efficient bank appears to be KredEx (Estonia), while at the opposite are NPBs in Finland, Germany, Italy, Poland and Spain with the highest degree of scale inefficiency.

We recall that the technical efficiency scores have been computed for a VRS DEA model with an output orientation, in order to find out by how much output levels can be expanded without changing the amounts of input used. By analyzing the value recorded by the average efficiency score of all NPBs in the sample in each of the four years considered, it can be noticed that it doesn't record ample fluctuations one year from another. The lowest average efficiency has been recorded at end 2014, of 0.585 meaning that on average NPBs use efficiently only 58.5% of their total liabilities to produce the amount of outputs. Thus, the level of promotional banks' average inefficiency in attaining their optimal level of outputs is in the range 37.1 - 41.5%.

In respect of individual NPBs efficiency measurement, the fully efficient ones that describe the best-practices frontier are HBOR from Croatia, KfW from Germany and Societe Nationale de Credit et d'Investissement from Luxembourg in all the four years considered, while Cassa Depositi e Prestiti from Italy proved to operate efficiently only in 2011 and 2012, although in the subsequent two years its level of inefficiency is negligible (between 0.4% and 3%). Consequently, in 2013 and 2014 the efficient frontier is described by three promotional banks. As it has been performed a cross-country study based on a pooled database, the common frontier depicts a particularity in terms of being made up of the best performing promotional banks from the countries included in the sample. As for the remaining banks, their level of efficiency varies greatly in the period 2011-2014. To gain a more informative view on their positioning relative the frontier it has been performed a ranking from fully efficient to less efficient NPBs in Table 3 and the distribution of their efficiency scores in Figure 1.

Table 3. NPBs ranking according to the technical efficiency score

Ranking	2011	2012	2013	2014
1	HBOR (Croatia), KfW (Germany), Societe Nationale de Credit et d'Investissement (Luxembourg), Cassa Depositi e Prestiti (Italy)	HBOR (Croatia), KfW (Germany), Societe Nationale de Credit et d'Investissement (Luxembourg), Cassa Depositi e Prestiti (Italy)	HBOR (Croatia), KfW (Germany), Societe Nationale de Credit et d'Investissement (Luxembourg)	HBOR (Croatia), KfW (Germany), Societe Nationale de Credit et d'Investissement (Luxembourg)
2	SID Bank (Slovenia)	Finnvera (Finland)	Cassa Depositi e Prestiti (Italy)	Cassa Depositi e Prestiti (Italy)
3	Finnvera (Finland)	SID Bank (Slovenia)	Finnvera (Finland)	Finnvera (Finland)
4	BNG Bank (Netherlands)	BNG Bank (Netherlands)	BNG Bank (Netherlands)	Landwirtschaftliche Rentenbank (Germany)
5	Landwirtschaftliche Rentenbank (Germany)	Bulgarian Development Bank (Bulgaria)	SID Bank (Slovenia)	BNG Bank (Netherlands)
6	Municipality Finance (Finland)	Landwirtschaftliche Rentenbank (Germany)	Landwirtschaftliche Rentenbank (Germany)	Municipality Finance (Finland)
7	MFB Hungarian Development Bank (Hungary)	Municipality Finance (Finland)	Municipality Finance (Finland)	SID Bank (Slovenia)
8	Bulgarian Development Bank (Bulgaria)	MFB Hungarian Development Bank (Hungary)	Bulgarian Development Bank (Bulgaria)	Bulgarian Development Bank (Bulgaria)
9	Slovenská záručná a rozvojová banka (Slovakia)	Instituto de Crédito Oficial (Spain)	Slovenská záručná a rozvojová banka (Slovakia)	Eximbank (Romania)
10	Bank Gospodarstwa Krajowego (Poland)	Bank Gospodarstwa Krajowego (Poland)	OeEB (Austria)	Slovenská záručná a rozvojová banka (Slovakia)
11	Instituto de Crédito Oficial (Spain)	OeEB (Austria)	Instituto de Crédito Oficial (Spain)	OeEB (Austria)
12	Českomoravská záruční a rozvojová banka (CMZRB - Czech Republic)	Eximbank (Romania)	Bank Gospodarstwa Krajowego (Poland)	Bank Gospodarstwa Krajowego (Poland)
13	OeEB (Austria)	KredEx (Estonia)	MFB Hungarian Development Bank (Hungary)	MFB Hungarian Development Bank (Hungary)
14	Eximbank (Romania)	Českomoravská záruční a rozvojová banka (CMZRB - Czech Republic)	Eximbank (Romania)	Instituto de Crédito Oficial (Spain)
15	KredEx (Estonia)	Slovenská záručná a rozvojová banka (Slovakia)	KredEx (Estonia)	Českomoravská záruční a rozvojová banka (CMZRB - Czech Republic)
16	-	-	Českomoravská záruční a rozvojová banka (CMZRB - Czech Republic)	KredEx (Estonia)

Source: author, based on DEAP estimation of efficiency scores

Figure 1. NPBs distribution by year and range of efficiency scores
Source: author, based on DEAP estimation of efficiency scores

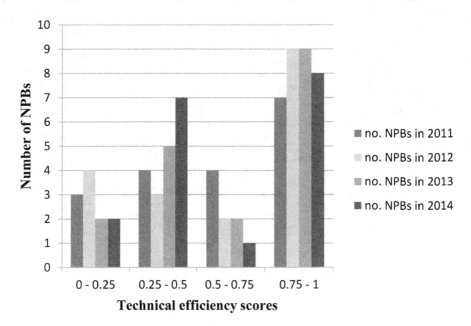

In each year of the period 2011-2014, the top-5 hierarchy derived from technical efficiency scores comprises some common NPBs, namely Finnvera (Finland), BNG Bank (Netherlands) and Landwirtschaftliche Rentenbank (Germany). These banks are the closest of the best-practices frontier regarding their ability to maximize the lending activity.

It can also be noticed that several promotional banks maintain, most of the time (in 3 out of the 4 years considered), the place hold in this ranking. It is the case of Finnvera (Finland) placed on 3rd place, BNG Bank (Netherlands) on 4th place and Bulgarian Development Bank (Bulgaria) on 8th position. On the other hand, Českomoravská záruční a rozvojová banka (CMZRB - Czech Republic) and KredEx (Estonia) are always positioned within the top-5 of less efficient banks, at the bottom of the hierarchy.

However, there is no sustained, predictable pattern in the evolution of efficiency scores one year from another, as some NPBs record sudden upward jumps of 1 to 3 positions, while others show downward movements.

At this point of the analysis an important remark has to be highlighted: although the comparative assessment of efficiency focuses strictly on the NPBs included in the sample, these state-owned banks operate in distinct banking systems and economic environments, with different intrinsic characteristics, determinant factors and dynamics. Consequently, the relative efficiency scores recorded in each year by each NPB indirectly incorporate some of the influence exerted by foreign-owned banks operating in the domestic banking system. These foreign banks bring a different internal governance, business strategies and risk profiles, are in line with the newest e-banking technologies for better reaching customers and fulfilling their financial needs, depict good management of administrative costs. By stimulating competition in the banking system, they put pressure also on state-owned banks to adapt their activities and enter in a catch-up process, without losing sight of their public mission. In this respect Nenovsky et al. (2008) argue that the co-existence of domestic and foreign-owned banks creates a stimulus for the former to permanently improve their efficiency level.

Figure 1 illustrates how the distribution of the number of NPBs fluctuated during 2011-2014, by considering a cut-off of 0.25. Most efficiency scores lie in the range 0.75-1, in all the four years, with a maximum of 9 NPBs out of 18 recorded in 2012 and 2013. The next range which is best represented in terms of the number of banks is 0.25-0.5. It also experienced the widest change in terms of the number of banks whose scores positioned in this range, from 3 NPBs in 2012 up to 7 in 2014. The remaining two ranges do not exhibit dramatic changes in the number of efficient banks and the drop is less pronounced (1 up to 2 NPBs).

Assessing NPBs Total Factor Productivity: A Malmquist Index Approach

The assessment of banking systems' productivity is a matter of interest for both financial institutions and public authorities due to the tight interdependence between the levels of banks productivity and the public perception of overall banking performance and contribution to the real economy development. Some authors (Andries, 2011) indicate that increased productivity is compatible with better cost management, better allocation of financial resources and improvements in the quality of banking services. Casu et al. (2004) analyze banking productivity through a macro-prudential perspective, claiming that productivity increases positively contribute to banking systems' financial soundness and stability on condition that the profits generated through regular banking activity are channeled towards the increase of bank's capitalization or level of equity and of buffers in the form of provisions meant to cover expected losses.

The most common and basic approach for measuring banking productivity is represented by the computation of several financial ratios. The main drawback resides in the fact that we have no information on the intrinsic leading factors that trigger a change in the productivity level. Economic literature developed a productivity index called Malmquist Total Factor Productivity Change Index which is able not only to reveal the change in productivity recorded by a bank or banking system over a given time span, but also the source of these changes by decomposing total factor productivity in two components: technical efficiency change (catch up effect) and technological progress, for each bank included in the sample. In other words, Malmquist indices allow the assessment of the productivity evolution over a time period by taking into account both the time and the cross-section dimensions of the data.

Sten Malmquist, a Swedish economist and statistician was the first who derived, in 1953, a quantity index to be used in consumption analyses. A few decades later, Caves et al. (1982) adapted Malmquist's idea in order to expand its use for production analyses and named the resulting productivity changes index after Sten Malmquist. From now on, the application of Malmquist total factor productivity index by relying on the results obtained by performing first a Data Envelopment Analysis has become widely spread in the literature.

Toci (2009) states that the Malmquist Total Factor Productivity Change Index is a natural extension of applying DEA. He explains that over time the efficiency frontier records shifts due to changes in production technology. Some banks succeed in taking advantage of the new technology and act as best-practice benchmarks being positioned on the frontier, while others fail to catch-up the frontier. These banks are inefficient relative to frontier banks, but not inefficient in absolute terms. The author concludes that although DEA estimations indicate no significant improvements in the level of average efficiency for a given sample of banks, this hasn't necessarily be interpreted as a productivity decline.

In computing Malmquist indices one has to estimate first the distance functions, by employing DEA, under different time period technologies and a chosen orientation (output-oriented or input-oriented). As Kirikal, Sõrg & Vensel (2004) explain, an output-oriented productivity index aims at measuring how much output has been produced, using a given level of inputs and the current state of technology, relative to what could have been produced. Similarly, an input-orientation approach measures changes in productivity by comparing the input amounts used for producing a given level of outputs under a reference technology with the optimum reduction in input amounts.

The formula proposed by Caves et al. (1982) to compute output-based Malmquist productivity index can be defined as:

$$M_{t,\,t+1}\left(y^t, y^{t+1}, x^t, x^{t+1}\right) = \left[\frac{D^t\left(y^{t+1}, x^{t+1}\right)}{D^t\left(y^t, x^t\right)} \times \frac{D^{t+1}\left(y^{t+1}, x^{t+1}\right)}{D^{t+1}\left(y^t, x^t\right)}\right]^{1/2}$$

where:

$M_{t,\,t+1}$ = Malmquist productivity index measuring changes between t and $(t+1)$ time periods

y^t, y^{t+1} = output vectors at t, respectively $(t+1)$ period

x^t, x^{t+1} = input vectors at t, respectively $(t+1)$ period

D^t, D^{t+1} = distance function based on period t, respectively $(t+1)$ technology

The first ratio in Caves et al. (1982) formula denotes the Malmquist index computed for period t. It measures the productivity change recorded from period t to period $(t+1)$ on the assumption of using period t technology as a reference point. The second ratio represents the Malmquist index computed for period $(t + 1)$ and measures productivity change from period t to period $(t + 1)$ this time by using period $(t + 1)$ technology as a benchmark. A value of Malmquist index greater than unity denotes productivity growth or improvements in banking performance, while a value less than 1 indicates productivity decline. A Malmquist index equal to 1 indicates stagnation.

Fare et al. (1994) had rewritten the basic Caves et al. (1982) formula in order to better outline the two components of Malmquist productivity change, by decomposing it as follows:

$$M_{t,\,t+1}\left(y^t, y^{t+1}, x^t, x^{t+1}\right) = \frac{D^{t+1}\left(y^{t+1}, x^{t+1}\right)}{D^t\left(y^t, x^t\right)} \times \left[\frac{D^t\left(y^{t+1}, x^{t+1}\right)}{D^{t+1}\left(y^{t+1}, x^{t+1}\right)} \times \frac{D^t\left(y^t, x^t\right)}{D^{t+1}\left(y^t, x^t\right)}\right]^{1/2}$$

where:

$$\frac{D^{t+1}\left(y^{t+1}, x^{t+1}\right)}{D^t\left(y^t, x^t\right)}$$

represents the technical efficiency change or the catching-up to the frontier effect. It measures the change in relative efficiency scores between the t and $(t+1)$ periods. In other words, it reflects the convergence towards, or divergence from the best practice frontier depicted for each bank in the sample (Angelidis et al. 2005). Kirikal, Sõrg & Vensel (2004, p.28) explains that technical efficiency level "is greater than, equal to, or less than 1 if the producer is moving closer to, unchanging, or diverging from the production frontier".

$$\left[\frac{D^t\left(y^{t+1}, x^{t+1}\right)}{D^{t+1}\left(y^{t+1}, x^{t+1}\right)} \times \frac{D^t\left(y^t, x^t\right)}{D^{t+1}\left(y^t, x^t\right)} \right]^{1/2}$$

represents the technological change and reflects the shift or evolution recorded by the production frontier, as a consequence of technology developments (frontier shift effect). According to Angelidis et al. (2005), technological change indicates the improvement or the deterioration in the performance achieved by the best practice (fully efficient) banks in the sample. The level recorded by technological change "is greater than, equal to, or less than 1 when the technological best practice is improving, unchanged, or deteriorating, respectively" (Kirikal, Sõrg & Vensel 2004, p.28).

Technological change, which triggers efficient frontier shifts, has its roots in several developments of banking activity driven by new information technology or, generally speaking, technological progress. Examples of such beneficial developments consist of the diversification of financial products and services provided to retail and corporate customers (electronic payments, internet banking, self banking, e-banking, mobile banking, contactless cards), the strengthening of back-office activity, by relying on economic and statistical models to evaluate the credit, liquidity, market and operational risks or scoring techniques and discriminant analyses to decide whether to finance or not the credit demands (Boitan, 2015, p.22). Toci (2009, p.6) adds that shifts in the frontier might be due to the simplification of banking regular processes as a result of technological progress, to innovations, shocks to the economy, episodes of financial distress or crises, change in regulations, etc.

Several authors agree that information technology play an important role in improving bank performance. Berger (2003) argues that the economic effects of employing new software technologies exert an impact on banking systems' productivity by improving the quality of banking products and services, expanding their range, increasing the processing speed of banking regular operations, and enhancing the degree of satisfaction felt by customers. Ho and Mallick (2006) claim that information technology contributes to decreasing operational costs incurred by banking activity. Frame and White (2009) surveyed banking developments over several decades and concluded that financial innovations driven by technological change (e.g. subprime mortgage loans, online banking, asset securitization, credit scoring, bank risk management through value-at-risk and stress-testing tools) recorded a significant evolution and rapid pace growth. Saeed and Bampton (2013) suggest that information and communication technology play an important role especially in developed countries, its influence being related to lower operating costs, good quality banking services and enhancement of profits.

The study developed in this sub-chapter focuses on computing the output-oriented Malmquist index, and decomposing it in order to measure the contributions exerted by the progress in technology (technological change) and improvement in efficiency (technical efficiency change) on the growth of national promotional banks' productivity. The Malmquist indexes are constructed by relying on Data Envelopment Analysis' distance functions and a panel data sample that reconciles the 18 European NPBs and all the 4 years considered. As in the preceding sub-chapter, it has been maintained the financial intermediation approach and the configuration of input and output variables. Both methods have been applied by using the program developed by Coelli (1996), called DEAP version 2.1.

Table 4 reports the Malmquist index total productivity changes over the four years considered as well as its 4-year average, computed for each NPB in the sample.

A first observation is that 10 out of 18 NPBs recorded a TFP change below 1 during 2011-2012, 9 recorded a sub unitary change in 2012-2013 while during 2013-2014 their number jumped to 12 NPBs. Therefore, negative productivity growth (productivity decline) dominates the sample, for all the time periods considered. Overall, the mean growth rate of the industry is around 8.9% for the year 2012-2013, while the remaining time periods exhibit productivity declines of 0.2 - 5.6 percent.

By analyzing individual NPBs productivity change in each time period it can be noticed that the highest positive growth in productivity during 2011-2012 has been achieved by KredEx (Estonia), followed by Eximbank (Romania) and Bulgarian Development Bank (Bulgaria). During 2012-2013 the largest productivity growth has been attributed to Slovenská záručná a rozvojová banka (Slovakia), followed by Eximbank (Romania), while in 2013-2014 Societe Nationale de Credit et d'Investissement (Luxembourg) and again Eximbank (Romania) witnessed productivity increases. The largest individual productivity decline has been recorded by Slovenská záručná a rozvojová banka (Slovakia) in 2011-2012, by MFB Hungarian Development Bank (Hungary) in 2012-2013 and by Českomoravská záruční a rozvojová banka (CMZRB - Czech Republic) in 2013-2014.

Table 4. Malmquist index dynamics, expressed as total factor productivity change

Promotional bank	2011-2012	2012-2013	2013-2014	Bank's average
Bulgarian Development Bank (Bulgaria)	1.219	0.855	0.791	0.955
Eximbank (Romania)	1.784	1.305	1.547	1.545
Českomoravská záruční a rozvojová banka (CMZRB - Czech Republic)	0.417	0.961	0.625	0.668
Landwirtschaftliche Rentenbank (Germany)	1.038	1.072	1.016	1.042
KfW (Germany)	0.967	1.076	0.956	1.000
Instituto de Crédito Oficial (Spain)	1.19	0.67	0.882	0.914
Hrvatska Banka (HBOR - Croatia)	0.87	1.06	1.035	0.988
Cassa Depositi e Prestiti (Italy)	0.94	0.998	0.981	0.973
Societe Nationale de Credit et d'Investissement (Luxembourg)	0.83	1.029	2.966	1.608
MFB Hungarian Development Bank (Hungary)	1.063	0.447	1.077	0.862
OeEB (Austria)	1.142	0.986	1.001	1.043
Bank Gospodarstwa Krajowego (Poland)	0.702	0.946	0.979	0.876
SID Bank (Slovenia)	0.982	0.952	0.936	0.957
Slovenská záručná a rozvojová banka (Slovakia)	0.105	10.683	0.681	3.823
Municipality Finance (Finland)	1.046	1.142	0.965	1.051
Finnvera (Finland)	0.914	1.032	0.885	0.944
KredEx (Estonia)	5.817	0.954	0.983	2.585
BNG Bank (Netherlands)	0.981	1.088	0.862	0.977
Period's average	**0.944**	**1.089**	**0.998**	**1.010**

Source: author, based on DEAP software computations

Some NPBs succeeded to maintain a positive productivity growth path during each time period considered, namely: Eximbank (Romania) and Landwirtschaftliche Rentenbank (Germany), with a productivity growth average of 54.5 percent and 4.2 percent, respectively. Other four NPBs always positioned on a productivity decline path, more or less pronounced: Českomoravská záruční a rozvojová banka (CMZRB - Czech Republic), Cassa Depositi e Prestiti (Italy), Bank Gospodarstwa Krajowego (Poland) and SID Bank (Slovenia). The remaining banks show mixed evidence of productivity developments one year from another.

The total factor productivity change has been further decomposed into technical efficiency change and technological change (see Table 5), in order to discriminate which component contributed most to Malmquist indexes path over time and across NPBs.

During 2011-2012, the main source of total productivity growth has been the catch-up effect for 15 out of 18 promotional banks. In 2013 relative to 2012 the catch-up effect has exerted a significant influence for only 9 NPBs which recorded a value exceeding 1, while the period 2013-2014 market a sharp drop as the productivity of only one bank in the sample is still determined by the catch-up effect. The decreasing path of the average technical efficiency change computed for each time period suggests that with the passing of time the catch-up effect diminishes its influence in triggering NPBs' productivity. Another finding relates to a shift in the main source for productivity changes during the four years considered, namely the compression path of average catch-up effect which overlaps on a sustained increasing trend in average technological change. On average, the catch-up effect has been most prominent in 2012 relative to 2011 (1.136), meanwhile the frontier shift effect has been the most significant in 2014 relative to 2013 (2.966).

Taking a look at individual NPBs' technical efficiency change, most of them depict a converging path towards the best practice efficiency frontier in 2012 relative to 2011. Českomoravská záruční a rozvojová banka (CMZRB - Czech Republic), Bank Gospodarstwa Krajowego (Poland) and Slovenská záručná a rozvojová banka (Slovakia) are the only promotional banks falling behind the efficient frontier in 2012 as compared to 2011 frontier. The picture is worsening in 2013 relative to 2012 and 2014 compared to 2013 as increasingly more NPBs are getting further from the 2013 frontier compared to their position relative the 2012 frontier. In 2013-2014 only Societe Nationale de Credit et d'Investissement (Luxembourg) maintained its position on the 2014 efficient frontier, compared to its position relative to the 2013 frontier.

In terms of technological change, 2012 compared to 2011 witnessed a technological regress for all banks in the sample, as the technology best practice is worsening. The subsequent two time periods show technological progress, an improvement of the performance achieved by the best practice (fully efficient) banks in the sample. Put in other words, the values greater than 1 indicate productivity gain recorded by a NPB, meaning that for a given amount of inputs it obtains higher output amounts in 2013 than in the preceding year. The same conclusion is valid also for 2014 compared to 2013.

Another finding can be obtained by correlating the results obtained in the previous sub-chapter with the dynamics recorded by technological change. More specifically, economic theory states that if the efficient frontier shifts

Table 5. Malmquist index decomposition into technological change and technical efficiency change

Promotional bank	Technical efficiency change			Technological change		
	2011-2012	2012-2013	2013-2014	2011-2012	2012-2013	2013-2014
Bulgarian Development Bank (Bulgaria)	1.468	0.831	0.267	0.83	1.029	2.966
Eximbank (Romania)	2.149	1.268	0.522	0.83	1.029	2.966
Českomoravská záruční a rozvojová banka (CMZRB - Czech Republic)	0.502	0.934	0.211	0.83	1.029	2.966
Landwirtschaftliche Rentenbank (Germany)	1.25	1.042	0.343	0.83	1.029	2.966
KfW (Germany)	1.164	1.046	0.322	0.83	1.029	2.966
Instituto de Crédito Oficial (Spain)	1.432	0.651	0.297	0.83	1.029	2.966
Hrvatska Banka (HBOR - Croatia)	1.048	1.03	0.649	0.83	1.029	2.966
Cassa Depositi e Prestiti (Italy)	1.132	0.97	0.331	0.83	1.029	2.966
Societe Nationale de Credit et d'Investissement (Luxembourg)	1	1	1	0.83	1.029	2.966
MFB Hungarian Development Bank (Hungary)	1.279	0.434	0.363	0.83	1.029	2.966
OeEB (Austria)	1.376	0.958	0.337	0.83	1.029	2.966
Bank Gospodarstwa Krajowego (Poland)	0.846	0.919	0.33	0.83	1.029	2.966
SID Bank (Slovenia)	1.182	0.925	0.316	0.83	1.029	2.966
Slovenská záručná a rozvojová banka (Slovakia)	0.126	10.381	0.23	0.83	1.029	2.966
Municipality Finance (Finland)	1.26	1.11	0.325	0.83	1.029	2.966
Finnvera (Finland)	1.101	1.003	0.299	0.83	1.029	2.966
KredEx (Estonia)	7.004	0.927	0.331	0.83	1.029	2.966
BNG Bank (Netherlands)	1.181	1.058	0.291	0.83	1.029	2.966
Period's average	**1.136**	**1.059**	**0.336**	**0.83**	**1.029**	**2.966**

Source: author, based on DEAP software computations

outwards in the *(t+1)* period and is described by the same efficient banks as in the *t* period, those banks exhibit technological progress but no efficiency change. DEA findings in the previous sub-chapter suggested that the fully efficient NPBs that build the best-practices frontier are HBOR from Croatia, KfW from Germany and Societe Nationale de Credit et d'Investissement from Luxembourg in all the four years considered. Consequently, for these 3 banks the frontier shift is due to technological progress, while their degree of efficiency is steady.

Table 6. Malmquist index 4-year average (2011-2014)

Promotional bank	Technical efficiency change	Technological change	Total factor productivity change
Bulgarian Development Bank (Bulgaria)	0.688	1.364	0.938
Eximbank (Romania)	1.124	1.364	1.533
Českomoravská záruční a rozvojová banka (CMZRB - Czech Republic)	0.462	1.364	0.63
Landwirtschaftliche Rentenbank (Germany)	0.764	1.364	1.042
KfW (Germany)	0.732	1.364	0.999
Instituto de Crédito Oficial (Spain)	0.652	1.364	0.889
Hrvatska Banka (HBOR - Croatia)	0.722	1.364	0.985
Cassa Depositi e Prestiti (Italy)	0.713	1.364	0.973
Societe Nationale de Credit et d'Investissement (Luxembourg)	1	1.364	1.364
MFB Hungarian Development Bank (Hungary)	0.587	1.364	0.8
OeEB (Austria)	0.763	1.364	1.041
Bank Gospodarstwa Krajowego (Poland)	0.635	1.364	0.866
SID Bank (Slovenia)	0.701	1.364	0.956
Slovenská záručná a rozvojová banka (Slovakia)	0.67	1.364	0.914
Municipality Finance (Finland)	0.769	1.364	1.049
Finnvera (Finland)	0.691	1.364	0.942
KredEx (Estonia)	1.291	1.364	1.76
BNG Bank (Netherlands)	0.713	1.364	0.973
4-year average	**0.74**	**1.364**	**1.009**

Source: author, based on DEAP software computations

The decomposition of Malmquist Total Factor Productivity Change index, computed as 4-year average, into technological change and technical efficiency change shows that the dominant source of productivity growth has been represented by technological change.

The results synthesized in Table 6 suggest that European NPBs experienced, on average, productivity stagnation, computed as 4-year average. The 4-year average of the catching-up effect indicates a decline with 26 percent for the entire period, suggesting that the production process encountered difficulties in converting inputs into outputs and reaching the efficient frontier, meanwhile the impact of implementing new technologies contributed to an increase with 36.4 percent of the technological change level, being evidence of technological progress.

REFERENCES

Andries, A. M. (2011). The Determinants of Bank Efficiency and Productivity Growth in the Central and Eastern European Banking Systems. *Eastern European Economics*, *49*(6), 2011. doi:10.2753/EEE0012-8775490603

Angelidis, D., Lyroudi, K., & Koulakiotis, A. (2005, December). Productivity Measuring in the Czech Banking Industry, *International Business &. Economic Research Journal*, *4*(12).

Banerjee B. (2012). *Banking Sector Efficiency in New EU Member States: A Survey*. Banka Slovenije, no. 3/2012.

Banker, R. D., Chanes, A., & Cooper, W. (1984). Some Model for Estimating Technical and Scale Inefficiencies in Data Envelopment Analysis. *Management Science*, *30*(9), 1078–1092. doi:10.1287/mnsc.30.9.1078

Barr, R. S., & Siems, T. F. (1996). *Bank failure prediction using DEA to measure management quality. In Financial Industry Studies*. Federal Reserve Bank of Dallas.

Berger, A. N. (2003). The economic effects of technological progress: Evidence from the banking industry. *Journal of Money, Credit and Banking*, *35*(2), 2003. doi:10.1353/mcb.2003.0009

Boitan, I. (2015). Measuring social responsible banks' efficiency and productivity – a nonparametric approach. *Journal of Applied Quantitative Methods*, *10*(2), 14 – 26.

Casu, B., Girardone, C., & Molyneux, P. (2004). Productivity change in European banking: A comparison of parametric and non-parametric approaches. *Journal of Banking & Finance*, 28(10), 2521–254. doi:10.1016/j.jbankfin.2003.10.014

Caves, D., Cristensen, L., & Diewert, W. (1982). The economic theory of index numbers and measurement of input, output and productivity. *Econometrica*, 50(6), 1393–1414. doi:10.2307/1913388

Charnes, A., Cooper, W. W., & Rhodes, E. (1978). Measuring the Efficiency of Decision Making Units. *European Journal of Operational Research*, 2(6), 429–444. doi:10.1016/0377-2217(78)90138-8

Coelli, T. (1996). *A guide to DEAP version 2.1. A data envelopment analysis computer program*. Centre for Efficiency and Productivity Analysis Working Paper 96/08, Department of Econometrics, University of New England.

De Luna-Martínez, J., & Vicente, C. L. (2012). *Global Survey of Development Banks*. World Bank Policy Research Working Paper No.5969.

Fare, R., & Grosskopf, S. S. (1994). Productivity Growth, technical Progress, and Efficiency Change in Industrialized Countries. American Economic Review, 84(1), 66–83.

Ferreira, C. (2011). *Efficiency and integration in European banking markets*. School of Economics and Management, Working Paper WP 08/2011/DE/UECE, 2011.

Frame, W. S., & White, L. J. (2009). Technological Change, Financial Innovation, and Diffusion in Banking. In A. N. Berger, P. Molyneux, & J. O. S. Wilson (Eds.), *The Oxford Handbook of Banking. Oxford University Press*. doi:10.2139/ssrn.1434486

Gutierrez, E., Rudolph, H. P., Homa, T., & Beneit, E. B. (2011). *Development Banks, Role and Mechanisms to Increase their Efficiency*. World Bank Policy Research paper no. 5729.

Guzowska, M., Kisielewska, M., Nellis, J. G., & Zarzecki, D. (2004). *Efficiency of the polish banking sector-assessing the impact of transformation*. Szczecin University Mickiewicza.

Haas, D. A., & Murphy, F. H. (2003). Compensating for Non-Homogeneity in Decision-Making Units in Data Envelopment Analysis. *European Journal of Operational Research*, 144(3), 530–544. doi:10.1016/S0377-2217(02)00139-X

Ho, S. J., & Mallick, S. K. (2006). *The Impact of Information Technology on the Banking Industry: Theory and Empirics.* University of London.

International Monetary Fund. (2007). Financial Sector Assessment Program Update. In Switzerland Technical Note: The Swiss Banking System—Structure, Performance, and Medium-Term Challenges. Author.

Kirikal, L., Sõrg, M., & Vensel, V. (2004, December). Estonian Banking Sector Performance Analysis Using Malmquist Indexes And DuPont Financial Ratio Analysis. *International Business &. Economic Research Journal, 3*(12).

Micco, A., Panizza, U., & Yanez, M. (2007). Bank Ownership and Performance. Does Politics Matter? *Journal of Banking & Finance, 31*(1), 219–241. doi:10.1016/j.jbankfin.2006.02.007

Nenovsky, N., Chobanov, P., Mihaylova, G., & Koleva, D. (2008). *Efficiency of the Bulgarian Banking System: Traditional Approach and Data Envelopment Analysis.* Agency for Economic Analysis and Forecasting Working paper series no. 1/2008.

Řepková, I. (2014). Efficiency of the Czech banking sector employing the DEA window analysis approach. *Procedia Economics and Finance, 12,* 587–596. doi:10.1016/S2212-5671(14)00383-9

Rudolph, H.P. (2010). *State Financial Institutions: Can They Be Relied on to Kick-Start Lending?.* World Bank Crisis Response, Note no. 12.

Saeed, K.A., & Bampton, R. (2013). The Impact of Information and Communication Technology on the Performance of Libyan Banks. *Journal of WEI Business and Economics, 2*(3).

Schmit, M., Gheeraert, L., Denuit, T., & Warny, C. (2011). *Public Financial Institutions in Europe.* European Association of Public Banks.

Scippacercola, S., & Sepe, E. (2014, Winter). Principal Component Analysis to Ranking Technical Efficiencies through Stochastic Frontier Analysis and DEA. *Journal of Applied Quantitative Methods, 9*(4).

Sobreira, R., & Zendron, P. (2011). Implications of Basel II for National Development Banks. In *Credit, Money and Macroeconomic Policy: A Post-Keynesian Approach.* Cheltenham, UK: Edward Elgar Publishing. doi:10.4337/9781849808729.00018

Titko, J., & Jureviciene, D. (2014). DEA Application at Cross-Country Benchmarking: Latvian vs. Lithuanian banking sector. *Procedia: Social and Behavioral Sciences, 110*, 1124–1135. doi:10.1016/j.sbspro.2013.12.959

Toci, V. Z. (2009). *Efficiency of Banks in South-East Europe: With Special Reference to Kosovo*. Central Bank of the Republic of Kosovo, CBK Working Paper No. 4.

Varias, A. D., & Sofianopoulou, S. (2012). Efficiency evaluation of Greek commercial banks using data envelopment analysis. *Lecture Notes in Management Science, 4*, 254–261.

Chapter 5

Financial Business Models with Social Impact:
Potential Candidates for National Promotional Banks

INTRODUCTION

European organizations and decision makers are aware of the occurrence of a momentum for promotional banks' development and more active involvement in mediating and channeling funding from EU sources to local communities or national benefit. Recent debates are discussing the opportunity to expand the coverage of the promotional banks' main definition so as to include other types of non-banking financial institutions that could also exert a significant influence within the Investment Plan for Europe. In this respect, it can be mentioned the proposal advanced by the European Committee of the Regions (2016, p.3) which explains that, in practice, promotional institutions do not always take the form of banks but in some countries they act as investment agencies, companies or funds, often along the lines of venture capital funds.

This last chapter aims at elaborating several proposals regarding particular financial institutions that might act as potential candidates for performing a promotional bank activity. In other words, the chapter will investigate whether financial institutions that have already adopted and implemented a special business model, whose mission is subordinated to the active involvement in the local community's needs, by mitigating social and financial exclusion, by contributing to the human development (education, health, culture) and by financing ecological projects (renewable energy, organic farms) might

DOI: 10.4018/978-1-5225-1845-7.ch005

Copyright ©2017, IGI Global. Copying or distributing in print or electronic forms without written permission of IGI Global is prohibited.

mimic promotional activity and play an increasing, more visible role in the context of the new EU funding mechanisms.

It has been performed a comprehensive radiography of the diverse, coexisting typology of financial intermediaries that depict the potential for being considered NPBs, due to their commitment for making a valuable contribution for pursuing and achieving medium and long-term economic and social goals. To ensure that the selection comprises only those financial institutions that fulfill the NPBs features, it has been followed the directions expressed in EC's 2015 communication "Working together for jobs and growth: The role of National Promotional Banks (NPBs) in supporting the Investment Plan for Europe", namely:

- NPBs might be established in various forms and offer different products, but have to carry out development or promotional activities;
- Provide financing to different key sectors where market failures have been identified and which are underserved by commercial banks.

It has been adopted an in-depth documentation and data collection strategy, meant to cover all EU countries and a broad range of financial institutions that fall under the scope of NPBs flexible definition.

During the last decade the European financial industry has witnessed the emergence or development of different business models, belonging to alternative finance institutions that operate complementary to mainstream banking. All of them have in common the declared mission to catalyze sustainable development, by bringing together economic, financial, social and environmental values in a bottom-up approach, as well as the awareness of dealing with customers' money, to which they aim to exert a societal and environmental responsible dimension. Customer-centricity is a common feature of all these alternative business models. A socially-oriented business model is guided by "satisfying existing needs in the real economy and the society whilst simultaneously taking into account their social, cultural, ecological and economic sustainability. Furthering the common good by generating multiple returns with respect to these aspects is at its core" (Institute for Social Banking, 2011, p.1).

In spite of increased heterogeneity in terms of balance sheet size, their mission and focus (social, environmental or both), financial products and services, they all depict the same core mission, of putting people's needs first, profitability being a necessary condition for further going concern but not a purpose per se.

The European socially responsible (sustainable) financial industry has become a diverse, multifaceted place, characterized by a wide range of actors and business practices. In the viewpoint of Carboni (2011), the exact perimeter of this industry is difficult to be accurately assessed, as it stands at the crossroads between traditional banking and alternative finance, between profit-seeking financial institutions and not-for-profit or charitable entities, or between privately owned and public institutions.

Investing in a socially responsible manner consists in channelling finance towards those investment projects that might fulfil both financial and social concerns. According to Haigh and Hazelton (2004), the research on whether financial markets might act as a mechanism for social responsibility has been exploratory in nature and limited in scope. Cullis, Lewis, & Winnett (1992) argue that socially responsible financial behavior is limited by the ability of financial markets to transform the measure of moral commitments or duties into pecuniary returns.

Carroll (1979, 2000) classifies an institution's involvement in social responsibility in terms of four typologies: i) economic responsibilities, comprising concerns related to ensuring the going concern of the business, in order to provide jobs for employees, appropriate products and services for customers and obtain profit for shareholders; ii) legal responsibilities, related to the appropriate compliance with national and international regulations; iii) ethical responsibilities, in terms of conducting regular business morally, with fairness and honesty; iv) philanthropic responsibilities, consisting in voluntary contributions to society and environment.

Lantos (2002) broadly discusses the issue of altruistic or philanthropic social responsibility, by delineating between the form of capital ownership, namely public or private. He argues that, from the viewpoint of publicly held institutions, altruistic social responsibility impairs "shareholder property rights, unfairly confiscating stockholder wealth, and it spends money for the general welfare at the possible expense of those the firm should be caring for, notably employees and customers" (Lantos, 2002, p.2). At the opposite, the involvement of private institutions in social responsibility is perceived as beneficial. It is simpler to channel a fraction of institution's profits for alleviating local community needs as "the owners are accountable only to one another regarding the use of their earnings, and so they can frame the mission and goals of their organization to include societal as well as financial performance dimensions as long as consumers and employees are informed" (Lantos, 2002, p.19).

An interesting viewpoint has been launched by Semeniuk (2012, p.24), claiming that social responsibility practices don't always succeed in fulfilling both the market goals and the interests of society, as on the background of "the state retreat from the moral or social domain and the freedom that the voluntary regulation grants businesses, it is possible that certain social interests would be addressed by neither the state nor businesses".

The Typology of Social Impact Financial Business Models

For the purpose of this study it has been identified three types of business models that simultaneously coexist in the European financial industry, in parallel with the mainstream banking model, which comply with the EC's flexible definition of NPBs.

In the following it has been discussed the conceptual features of each of them, their definition, specific risks and the peculiarities of their financial statements. These financial intermediaries that might act as potential candidates for NPBs have been chosen due to their business models' specificity, which implies having specific knowledge on the economic and financial territorial realities.

Cooperative Banks

Traditionally, cooperative banks have played an important role in alleviating the needs of local communities and enhancing financial and social inclusion. Their core mission is to reconcile the interests of society with their own financial interests and in subsidiary to maintain their business going concern while complying with prudential regulations.

As they hold a high degree of awareness on the specific vulnerabilities and needs of the local communities in their country of residence, they have clearly defined a mission focused on supporting human and social development (social housing, health and education), on alleviating financial and social exclusion by funding low income or marginalized social groups as well as small and medium-sized enterprises, or on addressing environmental concerns. The European Association of Cooperative Banks (EACB) enumerates the key values which are specific to cooperative banks' business model, such as "trust between the bank and its members/clients, democratic and prudent governance, resilience to adverse market developments, close proximity to customers, social commitment and solidarity" (EACB, 2014, p.2).

According to Fonteyne (2007), cooperative banks are increasingly more viewed as a major catalyst of social cohesion and local economy development, due to their broad territorial coverage and their significant market share, in terms of deposits and credit in several European financial markets. Ferri,

Kalmi and Kerola (2014, pp. 195-196) argue that cooperative banks might be assigned to the category of stakeholder banks, due to several features: profit maximization is not their main aim; customer-centricity by maximizing customer satisfaction; customer proximity, as they are operating in a limited geographical area; relationship-lending oriented; the members of the cooperative banks and board members are typically local residents and in some cases entrepreneurs.

Some authors reveal the similarities between cooperative banks' business model and other ethical alternatives to mainstream banking. For instance, Sachs (2010) argues that cooperative banks' customer-oriented activity positions them within the European family of social, ethical finances. Fonteyne and Hardy (2011) point that although cooperative banks are not the only way in the pursuit of the banking ethical behavior, they are however an effective one.

Another strand of literature has concluded that cooperative banks do play also a positive role on maintaining financial stability (Köhler, 2014). In this respect, Cihák and Hesse (2007) and Groeneveld (2012) explain that cooperative banks have more access to soft information regarding their members or customers, which decreases the likelihood of making lending mistakes.

Fonteyne and Hardy (2011) identify two determinants of the widespread and long lasting success of the cooperative banking business model, namely their ability to solve problems of opportunistic behavior in the banking sector and attendant financial stability risks. Their engagement to financially supporting those investment projects or types of customers underserved by regular banks, and hence to address some market failures, is a common feature with the promotional bank's business model.

Cooperative banks are operating as a typical retail-oriented institution. Their main activity gravitates around providing loans to households and small and medium-sized enterprises and deposit-taking services. Their financial statements comprise on the liability side customer deposits, but an important share is hold also by debt securities issued, subordinated debt, derivative financial instruments and other trade liabilities. The asset side reconciles loans provided to customers, investments in financial assets to be held until maturity or for trading purposes, derivative financial instruments and interbank deposits.

According to the data provided by the European Association of Cooperative Banks, cooperative banks are currently operating in 19 European countries (see Figure 1).

Figure 1. Cooperative banks in Europe
Source: Author, based on data collected from the European Association of Cooperative Banks (EACB)

Social, Ethical or Alternative Banks

Despite their different denominations, these banks with ethical financial behaviour all share the same social connotations, a values-based vision and mission, as well as common intrinsic characteristics.

The Institute for Social Banking (2011, p.1) defined *social banking* as the process for provisioning "banking and financial services that consequently pursue, as their main objective, a positive contribution to the potential of all human beings to develop, today and in the future".

As Benedikter (2011) argues, social banking is often called "banking for social cohesion", being defined as banks with a conscience, as they always assess the societal and environmental impact of their financial decision making. According to Pehrson (2011), the definition of social banking comprises several criteria:

1. It is a form of classical banking combined with a vision of a sustainable society;
2. Is exclusively linked to the real economy, no speculation being allowed;
3. The focus is on maximizing sustainability and societal impact, not on maximizing profits;
4. Transparency of lending activity is essential.

The European Federation of Ethical and Alternative Banks - FEBEA (2012) claims that *ethical banks* represent a new generation of social banks which has been evolved from the original mutual or cooperative banks. Their goal is to finance economic initiatives meant to promote social inclusion, sustainable development and social entrepreneurship. On Carboni (2011, p.2) viewpoint, the ethical business model relies on social and environmental variables that are taken into account by investors' and savers' decisions.

Mettenheim and Butzbach (2011, p.7) outline the specificities of *alternative banks*, namely their non-profit-maximizing goals, their social or public mandates and their stakeholder model of corporate governance, whose mission consists of stimulating sustainable development, environmental sustainability, social inclusion, regional policies and social and cultural investments.

In defining their role and choosing the destination of the money collected from customers, ethical banks take into account the vulnerabilities and specific needs to be addressed in their country of residence. Some examples of such clearly stated missions are:

1. Social and human development (Banca Populare Etica, Italy);
2. Financing of the social and health sectors (Bank für Sozialwirtschaft, Germany);
3. Ecological projects (renewable energy, organic agriculture), social ones (social houses, rural tourism, health) and cultural ones (GLS Bank, Germany; La Nef, France; Merkur, Denmark; Ekobanken, Sweden);
4. Financing the charity sector (Charity Bank, UK);

5. Exclusive financing of ecological projects (Eko-Osuusraha, Finland);
6. Mitigating financial and social exclusion, by financing the low income or disadvantaged social groups (Oikocredit, Netherlands).

In a similar fashion, Barigozzi and Tedeschi (2012, p.3) concluded that ethical banking has been defined in the economic literature by reliance on two accepted characteristics:

1. Social profitability, understood as funding economic activities with social added value and as the absence in any case of investments in speculative projects or in those that fulfil negative social criteria;
2. Economic profitability, which means no negative profits, bank good management.

Ethical banks' balance sheet comprises basic financial products and services, such as deposits placed at the central bank and credit institutions, loans, bonds and shares acquired in companies and credit institutions in case of a strategic partnership, meant to be held in bank's portfolio, not sold (on the asset side) and debt to credit institutions and central banks, deposits collected (on the liability side). They do not invest in risky projects or financial assets or liabilities to be held for successive trading or obtaining speculative gains, nor in derivatives. Although the credit policy may vary among ethical banks, loans are preferably guaranteed by collateral, represented by mortgages, personal property and/or claims. The revenues are mainly represented by interest income and commission income. The increased transparency of these ethical business models builds on the on-going dialogue both with own customers and people directly affected by banks' actions. They closely monitor how the money lend is used by borrowers, what impact it exerts on local community and environment and inform their depositors on the manner their savings have been used. As FEBEA (2012) documents, some ethical banks give their customers the opportunity to decide the destination of part of their savings.

According to the data provided by the Institute for Social Banking and FEBEA, there are currently 35 ethical or social banks located in 13 European countries (see Figure 2). There are no aggregated figures on ethical banks' activity size; therefore, to obtain a picture on their financial structure and financial indicators one has to examine their annual financial reports.

Sustainable or socially responsible banks represent a niche of mainstream banks that have implemented some Corporate Social Responsibility policies or voluntarily joined a banking sustainability framework. The most known

Figure 2. Ethical/social banks in Europe
Source: Author, based on data collected from the Institute for Social Banking and FEBEA

and widespread international sustainable frameworks that financial institutions voluntarily adhered to are:

- *The United Nations Environment Program – Financial Initiative (UNEP FI)* launched in May, 1992 which aims at increasing the financial industry's awareness on the environmental agenda.

- *The United Nations Global Compact* launched in July, 2000 is the world's largest corporate citizenship and sustainability initiative. The signatory financial institutions have to fulfill several principles, in the areas of human rights, labor standards, the environment and anti-corruption.
- *The Equator Principles* launched in 2003 provide its members a framework for identifying, assessing and managing environmental and social risks associated with projects of more than USD 10 million, as well as principles related to climate change and human rights.
- *The Global Alliance for Banking on Values (GABV)* launched in 2009, aims at increasing the impact of values-based banking globally and promotes the transition to a more resilient, transparent and diverse banking landscape (Boitan, 2014).

The understanding attributed by international organizations to the sustainable (socially responsible) financial behaviour, the meaning assigned by individual banks and, last but not least, the meanings conveyed in the economic and academic literature have been briefly discussed in the following.

The International Financial Corporation, a division of the World Bank, has defined the financial institutions' sustainability through four complementing dimensions of good business performance:

1. The *financial sustainability* of the financial institution, so that it can continue to make a long-term contribution to development;
2. The *economic sustainability* of the projects and companies the financial institution finances, through their contribution to host economies;
3. *Environmental sustainability* through the preservation of natural resources;
4. *Social sustainability* through improved living standards, poverty reduction, concern for the welfare of communities and respect for key human rights" (Barbu, Boitan 2013, p.9).

In the acceptation of another international organization, called the Global Alliance for Banking on Values, sustainable banks are those that comply with a set of sustainable banking principles and have as objective to promote a positive, viable alternative to the current financial system. These financial institutions have to be committed to social banking and the triple bottom line of people, planet and profit, being aware of their responsibility for improving the quality of life for current and future generations (GABV, 2014).

Banktrack, a global network comprising worldwide civil society organizations, claims that a conventional bank cannot become a sustainable one without redefining its banking business strategy. The first step consists in choosing the societal and environmental issues the bank wishes to involve in, to assign priorities. Secondly, it has to assess which is the desired exposure on types of customers, economic sectors, country regions or cross border (Banktrack, 2006, p.7).

In early 2003 the civil society organizations which were members of Banktrack launched the Collevecchio Declaration, to express their vision related to a sustainable financial system and to provide a guiding benchmark for the banking sector, in its way toward fulfilling the sustainability best practices. According to the first principle, titled Commitment to sustainability,

financial institutions must expand their missions from ones that prioritize profit maximization to a vision of social and environmental sustainability. A commitment to sustainability would require financial institutions…to put sustainability objectives on an equal footing to maximization of shareholder value and client satisfaction, and to actively strive to finance transactions that promote sustainability (Collevecchio Declaration, 2003, p.3).

Further is a selection of major players on the sustainability field, each with its own approach toward putting their mission and expertise in the service of people.

According to BNP Paribas (2014) CSR policy, its responsible behaviour takes the form of four pillars: *economic* responsibility: financing the economy in an ethical manner; *social* responsibility: pursuing a committed and fair human resources policy; *civic* responsibility: combating exclusion, promoting education and culture; *environmental* responsibility: combating climate change.

In the viewpoint of Banco Santander (2013), being sustainable implies performing the mainstream banking business and, at the same time, contributing to the economic and social progress of the local communities in the countries of residence, without neglecting its environmental impact.

In a similar vein, Nordea (2014) aims at bringing together a strong balance sheet, high ratings and solid returns with conducting the banking business in a responsible and transparent way and managing its environmental impact in a sustainable way.

In its latest Sustainability report, ABN Amro (2013) reveals which the key issues, meant to achieve and secure its leadership position in sustainability, are: the pursue of sustainable and transparent business operations; putting customers' interests at the core of banking activity and building long term relationships; the use of financial expertise for the benefit of society; the provision of financial and investment services and advice in a sustainable manner.

ING (2013) perceives banking sustainability as a driver for long-term prosperity. It has designed its own sustainability framework, which builds on 5 pillars: enabling people and businesses to make informed financial decisions – customer centricity; provision of financial products and services that are inclusive and accessible; management of environmental footprint; positive contribution to local communities; providing support and engaging bank's employees.

Societe Generale's (2014) CSR policy has stated several strategic priorities: responsible finance, solidarity-based banking, and responsible employer by promoting diversity and employability, internal environmental impact and responsible sourcing, role in society.

At Unicredit (2014) sustainability is at the core of banking activity, being visible in three areas: commercial banking activities, corporate citizenship (financial inclusion, environment protection) and philanthropy (supporting initiatives outside of bank's traditional functions).

A notably contribution to the literature devoted to this field is the one of Kaeufer (2010, p.5), who identified the existence of five levels of socially responsible and green banking behaviours:

Level 1 Behaviour: *Unfocused corporate activities,* performed by most banks and consisting of sponsoring green events and undertaking public relations activities that are not related to the core business of the bank, but to societal or environmental challenges.

Level 2 Behaviour: *Isolated business projects or business practices.* Banks positioned at this level implement social or environmental criteria in some of their business lines or range of financial products. It is rather a superficial, isolated approach, than a more comprehensive, bank-wide application one.

Level 3 Behaviour: *Systemic business practices.* Most of a bank's business lines and products embed socially responsible principles and standards, to pursue a positive impact on people and environment.

Level 4: *Strategic eco-system innovation.* Banks already implementing strong social and environmental principles in their regular activity actively get involved in the spread of this behaviour to the broader financial system's participants. Several examples of this engagement are membership into professional networks or alliances and public conversations with all the interested parties: civil society representatives, investors, customers, financial institutions, regulators.

Level 5: *Intentional (purpose-driven) eco-system innovation.* A socially responsible bank included in this level of evolution is perceived to be a "hybrid" institution, as it commits that, on behalf its financial intermediation function, to mitigate and address the core contemporaneous challenges, by innovating at the level of the whole eco-system.

On the other hand, Carboni (2011) believes that conventional banks, even though they made several steps toward a responsible behaviour, are still far away from a coherent approach to sustainable finance. San-Jose, Retolaza, & Gutierrez (2009) have made a trenchant distinction between the goals that determine the adoption of sustainable behaviour by conventional financial institutions and the mission of ethical, social banks. In their opinion, traditional banks choose to develop their social side not from moral ethics but to use the involvement in the CSR sphere as competitive advantage, subordinated to the strengthening of economic profitability. In this context, Clerck (2010) raised the issue of business models that superficially address aspects of sustainability and their potential to cancel, on the long term, the fundamental focus of ethical banks or other alternative finance institutions.

By taking a look at sustainable banks' statements of financial position, one can observe that the asset side comprises various types of loans to customers (corporate finance, small and medium enterprises loans, retail loans, housing, project financing short-term loans) and to banks, but also large amounts of operations implying financial assets, such as financial assets held for trading, financial assets held for sale, financial investments or equity investments. On the liability side there are deposits attracted from banks and customers, but also financial liabilities held for trading, subordinated debt, issued debt. The items financial assets or financial liabilities held for trading represent the speculative component of responsible banks' balance sheet, a component that couldn't be found in the balance sheet of ethical banks. These financial instruments have been acquired with the purpose of selling or repurchasing them in the near term, with the aim of obtaining profits from short-term fluctuations recorded by their price. Also, these items include trading derivatives, excepting those derivatives that are designated as hedging instruments in the process of risks management.

To assess the spread of socially responsible or sustainable banks across Europe, it has been performed a country-by-country analysis, differentiated for each main international sustainability framework, namely: the United Nations Environment Program – Financial Initiative (UNEP FI), the United

Nations Global Compact, the Equator Principles and the Global Alliance for Banking on Values (GABV). The results have been illustrated in the form of several Europe maps (see Figures 3, 4, 5 and 6), to gain a comprehensive and clear insight.

A recent research conducted by Boitan (2014) has identified a sample of 13 European banks that voluntarily adhered to the same three sustainability standards, namely the Equator Principles, the UN Global Compact and the

Figure 3. Spread of UN global compact
Source: author, based on data collected from the sustainability frameworks' websites

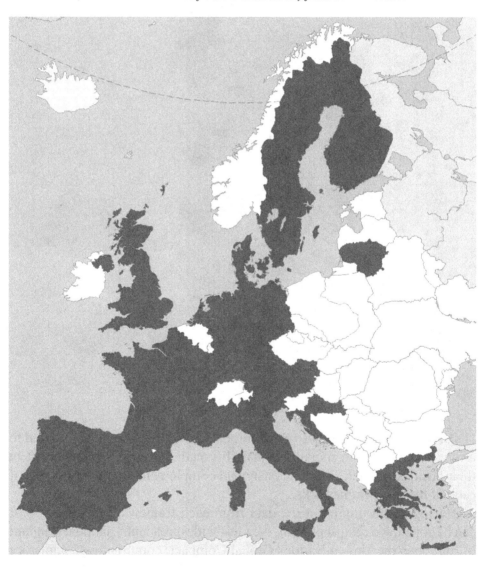

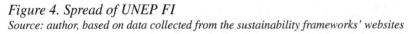

Figure 4. Spread of UNEP FI
Source: author, based on data collected from the sustainability frameworks' websites

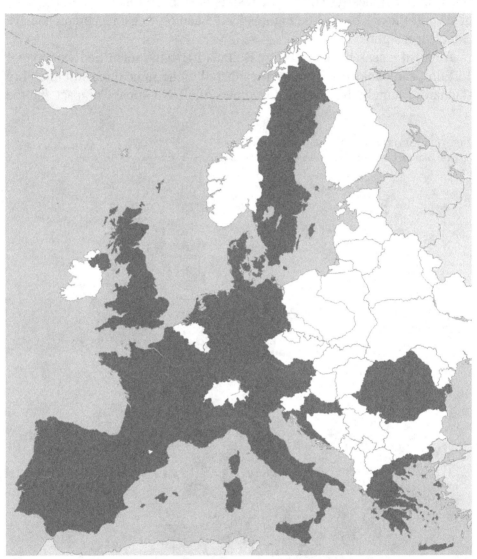

UNEP FI. It means that these conventional banks are strongly committed to a long-term, in-depth social responsibility path and wish to implement in their business model, simultaneously and complementary, the principles of each of the three frameworks.

Having as starting point the data from each framework membership, it can be concluded that, at present, the most widespread international standard in Europe is the United Nations Global Compact, comprising 42 signatory

Figure 5. Spread of Equator principles
Source: author, based on data collected from the sustainability frameworks' websites

banks in 14 countries. On the second place in the ranking is the Equator Principles which comprises 31 signatory banks from 10 countries, followed by the UNEP FI, with 29 banks from 13 countries. The most recently launched framework, represented by the GABV's sustainable banking principles, is currently joined by 5 banks in 5 European countries.

Figure 6. Spread of GABV principles
Source: author, based on data collected from the sustainability frameworks' websites

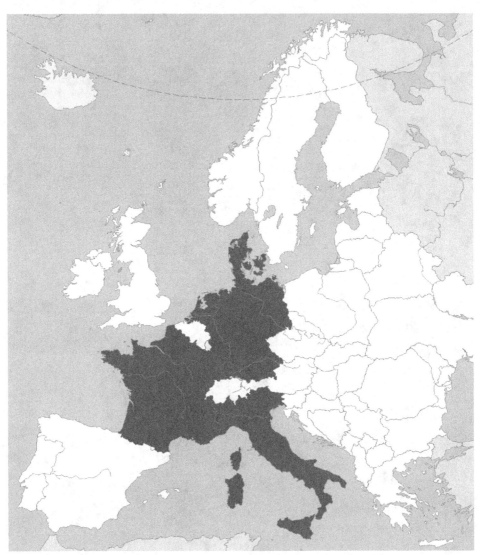

Social Impact Financial Institutions' Involvement in Providing EU Financing to End-Users

A matter of interest is whether the various types of European social impact financial institutions have applied for funding from EU financial instruments and, consequently, have been authorized to act as financial intermediaries on behalf of the European institutions (European Investment Fund and European

Investment Bank) and carry out lending activities or providing guarantees to customers in their country of residence. To perform this qualitative investigation, for each EU country it has been obtained the list of financial intermediaries registered with the European Investment Fund and it has been checked which of them is constituted as an ethical bank, as a cooperative bank or is a commercial bank that voluntarily joined a sustainability framework. The final results have been summarized in Table 1.

Table 1. Social impact financial institutions carrying out lending or guarantees from EU financial resources

Country	Financial intermediary name	Financial intermediary type	Type of financing provided	Investment focus	Sources of finance
Belgium	Credal societe cooperative	Cooperative bank	Micro-loans	Micro-enterprises including individuals	European Progress Microfinance Facility
Bulgaria	CIBANK	Socially responsible bank (UN Global Compact)	Loans	SMEs	COSME Loan Guarantee Facility, European Fund for Strategic Investments, JEREMIE - Joint European Resources for Micro to Medium Enterprises
France	La NEF	Ethical bank	Loans	Social enterprises	European Commission's Programme for Employment and Social Innovation ("EaSI")
	Banque Populaire et Caisse d'Epargne	Cooperative bank	Loans	Mobile master students	Erasmus+ Master Loan Guarantee Facility
			Loans	Innovative SMEs and small Mid-Caps	Competitiveness and Innovation Framework Programme (CIP)
	Société Générale	Socially responsible bank (Equator principles, UNEP-FI)	Loans	Small businesses	COSME Loan Guarantee Facility, European Fund for Strategic Investments
Germany	NRW Bank	Socially responsible bank (UNEP-FI)	Loans	SMEs and small mid-caps	European Fund for Strategic Investments, InnovFin SME Guarantee Facility

continued on following page

125

Table 1. Continued

Country	Financial intermediary name	Financial intermediary type	Type of financing provided	Investment focus	Sources of finance
Greece	Alpha Bank	Socially responsible bank (UNEP-FI)	Loans	SMEs	JEREMIE - Joint European Resources for Micro to Medium Enterprises
	EUROBANK ERGASIAS	Socially responsible bank (UNEP-FI)	Loans	SMEs	JEREMIE - Joint European Resources for Micro to Medium Enterprises
	Piraeus Bank	Socially responsible bank (UNEP-FI)	Loans	SMEs	JEREMIE - Joint European Resources for Micro to Medium Enterprises
	Cooperative Bank of Karditsa	Cooperative bank	Micro-loans	Micro-enterprises	European Commission's Programme for Employment and Social Innovation ("EaSI")
Italy	Banco Popolare	Cooperative bank	Loans	Innovative SMEs & Small Mid-Cap	European Fund for Strategic Investments, InnovFin SME Guarantee Facility
Netherlands	ABN AMRO	Socially responsible bank (Equator principles, UNEP-FI)	Loans	Innovative SMEs & Small Mid-Cap	Risk sharing instrument
	Robeco	Socially responsible bank (UNEP-FI)	Loans	SMEs & Small Mid-Cap	EIB Group Risk Enhancement Mandate (EREM)
Romania	Banca Comerciala Romana	Socially responsible bank (UNEP-FI)	Loans	SMEs	JEREMIE - Joint European Resources for Micro to Medium Enterprises
	Raifeissen Bank Romania	Socially responsible bank (UN Global Compact)	Loans	SMEs	JEREMIE - Joint European Resources for Micro to Medium Enterprises
Slovakia	Ceskoslovenska obchodna banka	Socially responsible bank (UN Global Compact)	Loans, micro-loans, guarantees	SMEs including micro-enterprises and individuals	Competitiveness and Innovation Framework Programme (CIP)

continued on following page

Table 1. Continued

Country	Financial intermediary name	Financial intermediary type	Type of financing provided	Investment focus	Sources of finance
Spain	Banco Santander	Socially responsible bank (Equator principles, UNEP-FI)	Loans	SMEs, Micro-enterprises including individuals based in Extremadura Region	JEREMIE - Joint European Resources for Micro to Medium Enterprises
	Banco Popular Español	Socially responsible bank (Equator principles, UN Global Compact)	Micro-loans	Micro-enterprises including individuals	European Commission's Programme for Employment and Social Innovation ("EaSI")
	Bankinter	Socially responsible bank (UN Global Compact)	Loans	Innovative SMEs and small Mid-Caps	Risk sharing instrument, InnovFin SME Guarantee Facility
Sweden	Swedbank AB	Socially responsible bank (UNEP-FI)	Loans	SMEs	COSME Loan Guarantee Facility, European Fund for Strategic Investments
UK	Barclays	Socially responsible bank (Equator Principles, UNEP-FI)	Loans	Innovative SMEs and small Mid-Caps	InnovFin SME Guarantee Facility, European Fund for Strategic Investments

Source: information and data collected and synthesized by the author, from www.eif.org

From the synthesis above it can be extracted several conclusions. First, the overwhelming majority of the EU financial resources is channeled by alternative finance institutions to SMEs and usually takes the form of loans or micro-loans. Secondly, most financial institutions that have applied until recently for obtaining EU financing are sustainable or socially responsible banks. This might be due to their more developed and territorially expanded network of branches, to a higher number of employees that can monitor and manage the financing attracted from EU, to a wider customer typology to which it is addressed (individuals, SMEs, large companies). Ethical and cooperative banks are concentrating their activity only in the areas where they hold branches, so that the number of clients they serve is lower compared with their sustainable peers.

Third, the most active social impact institutions, in terms of both the number of finance contracts signed with EU institutions (5 distinct facilities provided by European Commission) and the diversified range of projects financed operate in France, closely followed by those located in Greece and Spain.

The results of this qualitative investigation are encouraging, as they outline the existing involvement of alternative finance institutions in obtaining EU funding and then channeling it towards innovative projects or towards small and medium-size entrepreneurs. In addition, irrespective their legal form of organization, their mission and core activities are compatible with national promotional banks' flexible definition, creating prospects for an increasing contribution to the implementation of the Investment Plan for Europe.

REFERENCES

Amro, A. B. N. (2013). *Sustainability report*. available at http://www.abnamro. com/en/Sustainability/reports/index.html

Banco Santander. (2013). *Sustainability strategy*. Retrieved from http://www. santander.com/csgs/Satellite/CFWCSancomQP01/en_GB/Corporate/Sustainability/Santander-and-sustainability/Sustainability-strategy.html

Banktrack. (2006). *The do's and don'ts of sustainable banking – A Banktrack manual*. Retrieved from http://www.banktrack.org/manage/ems_files/download/the_dos_and_donts_of_sustainable_banking/061129_the_dos_and_donts_of_sustainable_banking_bt_manual.pdf

Barbu, T., & Boitan, I. (2013). The emergence of ethical banks – a way towards sustainable banking business. In Prospective Innovation at Ethical Banking and Finance. Taadler Publishing House.

Barigozzi, F., & Tedeschi, P. (2012). *Credit Markets with Ethical Banks and Motivated Borrowers*. AICCON Working papers No 99-2012. Retrieved from http://econpapers.repec.org/paper/risaiccon/2012_5f099.htm

Benedikter, R. (2011). *European Answers to the Financial Crisis: Social Banking and Social Finance*. Retrieved from http://iis-db.stanford.edu/docs/526/social_banking.pdf

Boitan, I. (2014). *The social responsibility stream in banking activity. A European assessment*. Paper presented at the SGEM multidisciplinary conference, Albena, Bulgaria.

Carboni, V. (2011). *Banking on ethics*. Retrieved from http://www.banktrack. org/manage/ems_files/download/banking_on_ethics/110418_crbmbanche_ alternativefinale18_aprile.pdf

Carroll, A. B. (1979). A three dimensional model of corporate performance. *Academy of Management Review, 4*, 497–505.

Carroll, A. B. (2000). The four faces of corporate citizenship. In Business Ethics 00/01. Dushkin/McGraw-Hill.

Cihák, M., & Hesse, H. (2007). *Cooperative Banks and Financial Stability.* IMF Working Papers 2. International Monetary Fund.

Collevecchio Declaration. (2003). *The role and responsibility of financial institutions*. Retrieved from http://www.banktrack.org/download/colleve-chio_declaration/030401_collevecchio_declaration_with_signatories.pdf

Cullis, J. G., Lewis, A., & Winnett, A. (1992). Paying To Be Good? UK Ethical Investments. *Kyklos, 45*(1), 3–23. doi:10.1111/j.1467-6435.1992.tb02104.x

de Clerck, F. (2010). Ethical banking. *Networking social finance.*

European Association of Cooperative Banks (2014). *Roadmap for Cooperative Banks - An Approach That Balances Regulation and Stimulation of Local Growth*. Author.

European Commission. (2015). Working together for jobs and growth: The role of National Promotional Banks (NPBs) in supporting the Investment Plan for Europe. Communication from the Commission to the European Parliament and the Council.

European Committee of the Regions. (2016). *Opinion - Working together for jobs and growth: The role of National and Regional Promotional Banks (NPBs) in supporting the Investment Plan for Europe*. Communication from the Commission to the European Parliament and the Council, COM (2015) 361 final, 117th plenary session.

FEBEA. (2012). *What really differentiates ethical banks from traditional banks?*. FEBEA.

Ferri, G., Kalmi, P., & Kerola, E. (2014). Does bank ownership affect lending behavior? Evidence from the Euro area. *Journal of Banking & Finance, 48*, 194–209. doi:10.1016/j.jbankfin.2014.05.007

Fonteyne, W. (2007). *Cooperative Banks in Europe – Policy Issues.* IMF Working Paper No. 07/159.

Fonteyne, W., & Hardy, D.C. (2011). Cooperative banking and ethics: past, present and future, *Ethical Perspectives, 4,* 491-514.

Global Alliance for Banking on Values. (2014). *Principles of sustainable finance and sustainable banking.* Retrieved from http://www.gabv.org/about-us/our-principles

Groeneveld, J. M. (2012). The cooperative banking model: performance and opportunities. In SUERF Study 2012/2. Larcier.

Haigh, M., & Hazelton, J. (2004). Financial Markets: A Tool for Social Responsibility? *Journal of Business Ethics, 52*(1), 59–71. doi:10.1023/B:BUSI.0000033107.22587.0b

ING. (2013). *Sustainability report.* Retrieved from http://www.ing.com/ING-in-Society/Sustainability/Sustainability-report-2013.htm

Institute for Social Banking. (2011). *Definition of Social Banking.* Retrieved from http://www.social-banking.org/the-institute/what-is-social-banking/

Kaeufer, K. (2010). *Banking as a Vehicle for Socio-economic Development and Change: Case Studies of Socially Responsible and Green Banks.* Retrieved from http://www.gabv.org/wp-content/uploads/SocialBanking.pdf

Köhler, M. (2014). Which banks are more risky? The impact of business models on bank stability. *Journal of Financial Stability.* doi:10.1016/j.jfs.2014.02.005

Lantos, G. P. (2002). The Ethicality of Altruistic Corporate Social Responsibility. *Journal of Consumer Marketing, 19*(3), 205–228. doi:10.1108/07363760210426049

Nordea. (2014). *CSR strategy and governance.* Retrieved from http://www.nordea.com/About+Nordea/Corporate+Social+Responsibility/CSR+strategy+and+governance/1513972.html

Paribas, B. N. P. (2014). *Being a Responsible Bank: the CSR policy of BNP Paribas.* Retrieved from http://www.bnpparibas.com/en/responsible-bank/our-corporate-social-responsibility/economic-responsibility

Pehrson, L. (2011). Banking with a Differenc.*5th African Microfinance Conference, Addis Abeba.*

Sachs, K. (2010). Common Tools, Common Goals, Concrete Solutions., *Networking Social Finance.*

San-Jose, L., Retolaza, J. L., & Gutierrez, J. (2009). *Ethical banks: An Alternative in the Financial Crisis.* Available at: http://ssrn.com/abstract=1416757

Semeniuk, J. (2012). The Alignment of Morality and Profitability in Corporate Social Responsibility. *Erasmus Student:The Journal of Philosophy*, (2).

Societe Generale. (2014). *CSR strategy and governance.* Retrieved from https://www.societegenerale.com/en/measuring-our-performance/csr/CSR-strategy-and-governance

Unicredit. (2014). *Our approach as a sustainable bank.* Retrieved from https://www.unicreditgroup.eu/en/sustainability/our-vision-of-sustainable-bank.html

von Mettenheim, K., & Butzbach, O. (2011). *Alternative Banking: Competitive Advantage and Social Inclusion.* Paper presented at the Society for the Advancement of Social Economics 23rd Annual Conference Universidad Autónoma de Madrid.

Conclusion

The renewed interest on the role national promotional banks have to play in the coming years is widely ascertained at European level. The developmental goals established several years ago, represented by the Europe 2020 strategy, launched in 2010 by the European Commission, and the complementing Investment Plan for Europe greatly match the mission assumed by NPBs and cannot be achieved solely by relying on competing commercial banks in a country. The three mutually reinforcing national and European priorities for growth envisaged by the Europe 2020 strategy are in line with their promotional mandate, namely:

1. Smart growth, which emphasizes the need to boost knowledge, research, innovation, education and the use of internet;
2. Sustainable growth, which focuses on increasing industry's competitiveness, stimulating entrepreneurship incentives and fighting against natural resources' waste;
3. Inclusive growth, which targets labour markets and the people wellbeing, by enhancing job creation, skills acquisition, mitigating poverty and social exclusion.

As emphasized by Europe 2020 strategy, the European trend is to focus on smart, green and inclusive development which implies the identification and fostering of new sources of growth, innovation and competitiveness that have their roots in knowledge intensive activities, productivity and environmental sustainability. Bassanini, Pennisi and Reviglio (2015) explain that economic development is reinforced by development finance, the latter being defined as "long term finance coupled with the capacity to provide technical assistance to the borrower and to evaluate financial and social returns as well as to assess the opportunities and the risks inherent in development projects and programs and to formulate supporting policy measures" (pp. 13-14). Another trend concerning the NPB's activity has been signaled by Volberding (2016) which claims that in recent years national governments have adapted NPBs so as to indirectly implement national economic policies by means of market-based mechanisms. The author draws also attention on the challenge imposed by the creation of new NPBs, namely they channel domestic and European financial resources to national SMEs and projects, undermining the goal of European financial integration.

KfW Group, a leading NPB in Europe, enumerates several major challenges faced by world's economies which have to be addressed through the specific activity performed by NPBs, namely climate and environmental protection, globalization, technical progress and demographic change (ageing, migration etc.).

In terms of policy recommendations, one should start with the European Commission (2015) communication which clearly states that the establishment of a national promotional bank isn't a substitute for government's structural policies and reform, in terms of improving legal and fiscal systems, administrative procedures, reducing the costs of doing business.

Practitioners and economic literature agree that macro-economic policies and large scale investment projects are directly influencing each other, the former being sometimes the subject of modifications in order to facilitate the investment environment. In addition, Bassanini, Pennisi and Reviglio (2015, p. 16) argue that environmental, social inclusion and information communications technology issues must not be treated as a distinct set of policies and measures to complement macroeconomic development policies but must merge with them, be included in the overall macroeconomic strategy of a country.

The book aims to increase knowledge on promotional banks' business by reconciling various dimensions (conceptual, qualitative analyses, statistical and mathematical analyses) with recent and past developments, as well as prospects for further emergence of new entities.

The first chapter explains the context that triggered the revival of national and European authorities' interest regarding promotional banks and creates the conceptual framework for understanding the specificity of promotional banks' business model, its intrinsic governance and management features. It examines each specific feature, and then identifies European NPBs depicting those features. The main discrepancies appear in terms of classifying NPBs in deposit taking and non-deposit taking institutions, or according to their lending models (first and second tier lending).

The second chapter has followed a three-fold structure, to better discriminate between the standpoints shared by decision makers and academia / research centers and the historical record perspectives related to European national promotional banks' economic and social involvement

An important finding comes from synthesizing the European national promotional banks that have applied for EU funding from the newly launched

EC's financial instruments. It has been found out that 11 out of 18 NPBs have applied for obtaining this type of funding. HBOR from Croatia is the most active NPB, in terms of the number of finance contracts recently signed with EU institutions and also the most diversified range of projects financed, and followed by NPBs from Czech Republic, France, Germany and Italy.

The last part of the chapter has assessed and explained the patterns of the relationship between promotional banks' size, expressed in terms of total assets, and several macroeconomic fundamentals such as GDP, debt-to-GDP ratio, GDP per capita, production in construction index, exports/GDP, employment rate, research and development expenditure as share in GDP and electricity generated from renewable sources.

Chapter 3 aims at classifying NPBs in homogenous clusters, based on the level of similarity or proximity computed for a given set of attributes. It has been applied a data mining technique called cluster analysis in order to perform an agglomerative hierarchical clustering of the 18 NPBs in the sample. The first set of attributes is related to the overall activity performed by a NPB, namely: total assets, return on equity and tier 1 capital ratio. The first classification of banks into smaller clusters proved moderate fragmentation in respect of the total number of clusters generated and almost unchanged composition one year from another. Some NPBs distinguish themselves as they recorded the highest level of ROE (it is the case of Municipality Finance) and respectively the highest level of tier 1 ratio (Eximbank). Interestingly, NPBs with mixed ownership structure, which do not attract deposits from customers and rely solely on second-tier lending, were always included in the same cluster during each year considered.

The second set of attributes relates to NPBs balance sheet structure, namely: the share of loans in total assets, the share of financial assets to total assets and total liabilities. The new classification performed indicated increased fragmentation in the number of clusters, changing composition one year from another as well as the appearance of more outlier banks, that hold their unique cluster and hence greater dissimilarity compared to the remaining ones. NPBs from Czech Republic, Estonia, Hungary, Poland, Romania and Spain were always outliers suggesting increased persistence of dissimilarities during the entire time span and far apart features compared to the remaining banks. For instance, in 3 out of 4 years Eximbank from Romania recorded the highest share of financial assets in total assets.

Chapter 4 makes significant contribution to existing literature in the field of efficiency and productivity, as it is the first study to comprehensively investigate the two concepts in relationship with a different financial institution type, namely European NPBs. The first sub-chapter applied the

Data Envelopment Analysis technique in order to quantify the performance depicted by each promotional bank in the sample, expressed as the degree of relative efficiency, for each year in the time span 2011 – 2014 and to build an efficient frontier represented by the combination of the most efficient banks in the initial sample.

The relative efficiency scores have indicated that three national promotional banks always positioned on the efficient frontier (HBOR from Croatia, KfW from Germany, Societe Nationale de Credit et d'Investissement from Luxembourg) while Cassa Depositi e Prestiti from Italy acted efficiently only in 2011 and 2012, while in the subsequent two years its level of inefficiency is negligible (between 0.4% and 3%). Consequently, these best practice NPBs become benchmarks or peers for the remaining inefficient ones. It can be observed that during each of the four years of study HBOR from Croatia has been attributed most times as peer promotional bank for inefficient NPBs, meaning that its business model shows the most balanced mix between the amounts of financial resources collected and the financing provided in the form of loans.

The ranking of NPBs according to the technical efficiency scores obtained in each year illustrated several constant presences within the top-5 hierarchy, namely HBOR (Croatia), KfW (Germany), Societe Nationale de Credit et d'Investissement (Luxembourg), Cassa Depositi e Prestiti (Italy), Finnvera (Finland), BNG Bank (Netherlands) and Landwirtschaftliche Rentenbank (Germany), meaning that these banks depict the greatest potential for optimizing their lending ability by relying on currently existing liabilities' level. By correlating this finding with the one ascertaining that most efficiency scores lie in the range 0.75-1, it seems that the inefficiency level is between 0.25-0 for most NPBs and thus they are not far away from the best practice standard.

The second sub-chapter employs a DEA-type Malmquist index of total factor productivity to measure the productivity changes over time for each NPB in the sample and to investigate the sources of productivity change during the time span 2011-2014.

Eximbank (Romania) has constantly witnessed one of the highest productivity growth during each year considered. Four NPBs always exhibited a productivity decline pattern, more or less pronounced: Českomoravská záruční a rozvojová banka (CMZRB - Czech Republic), Cassa Depositi e Prestiti (Italy), Bank Gospodarstwa Krajowego (Poland) and SID Bank (Slovenia). However, most banks in the sample show mixed evidence of productivity developments one year from another.

By decomposing total productivity into its two components, namely changes in technical efficiency, due to a catch-up effect and changes in technology, due to frontier movement it has been identified that the component which contributed most to Malmquist indexes path over time has been the catch-up effect during 2011-2012 and the frontier shift effect during 2013-2014. In other words, during the first two years NPBs strived to converge as much as possible to the efficient frontier by improving their efficiency scores, while during the latter two years they incorporated several technology developments and innovations that shifted the efficient frontier itself.

By correlating the empirical findings in chapters 3 and 4, it can be observed that the four fully efficient NPBs depict the most balanced financial structure and are the closest to the genuine features of promotional business model. Specifically, they record the highest levels of loans to total assets ratio and values fluctuating around the sample's average for the share of financial assets in total assets, return on equity and the asset and liability size.

Chapter 5 provides a comprehensive, topical outlook on the diverse typology of business models with social impact operating across European financial industry, which depicts the potential for acting as candidates for performing a promotional bank activity.

The novelty of the chapter resides in unifying the different financial alternatives to mainstream banking, represented by cooperative banks, ethical banks and sustainable banks, by providing a snapshot into their business models' mission and specificities and their current spread across European Union member states. It has been performed also a visual analysis, depicted in the form of several European geographical maps, to reveal the territorial spread of each type of financial institution operating according to the principles of NPBs. The conclusion is that the most spread are cooperative banks (19 countries in the map), followed by socially responsible banks signatories of the UN Global Compact (14 countries in the map), socially responsible banks signatories of the UNEP FI and ethical banks (13 countries in the map) and socially responsible banks signatories of the Equator principles (10 countries).

Further, the chapter has identified those financial institutions that have applied for obtaining European funding from EU or the European Investment Bank, by indicating the name of the EC's facility under which they received financing and the main beneficiaries of the financing. The findings indicated that although 12 EU countries out of 28 hold at least one social impact financial institution that had applied for EU financing, the most active institutions, in terms of the number of finance contracts signed with EU are located in France, Greece and Spain.

Last but not least, the chapter indirectly aimed at outlining the fundamental role financial institutions, in general, have to play, to support the achievement of contemporaneous ambitious desiderate for enhancing employment and growth within EU. In order to become a reliable tool for improving the quality of life, money collected and managed by financial institutions should acquire a socially responsible dimension.

Also, banking customers and investors could contribute to the profound transformation of banking business behaviour by renunciation to the passive, neutral attitude toward where their money is invested. They have to actively get involved in requiring the financial institutions' improvement of transparency and communication with the public, the channelling of investments for financing green, environment-friendly projects or development of human capital, for diminishing adverse impacts on the natural environment and population, for helping develop the communities in which they conduct business.

However, it will take some time until a critical mass of mainstream financial institutions will internalize the socially responsible values and will behave accordingly. Promotional banks have their distinct positioning in this respect, but have to become more visible, more active, to increase collaboration with European institutions and convert themselves into a benchmark of best practices.

The subject of the book has focused exclusively on NPBs developed and operating in Europe the more so as this topic is on the agenda of European decision-makers. However, further research might be devoted to qualitative and quantitative comparative analyses in order to discriminate whether there is a difference between national promotional banks operating in advanced countries and their peers operating in developing countries, as well as at European or international level, in terms of fundamental mission and objectives, operational tools and activities performed.

REFERENCES

Bassanini, F., Pennisi, G., & Reviglio, E. (2015). *The Development/Promotional Banks: From the Financial and Economic Crisis to Sustainable and Inclusive Development*. Retrieved from http://www.bassanini.it/wp-content/uploads/2015/02/Bassanini_Pennisi_Reviglio_CDP-developmentbanks-FINALE-n.-207-numero-142014.pdf

European Commission. (2015). Working together for jobs and growth: The role of National Promotional Banks (NPBs) in supporting the Investment Plan for Europe. Communication from the Commission to the European Parliament and the Council.

Volberding, P. (2016). *National development banks and the rise of market-based protectionism in Europe*. Paper presented at CEEISA-ISA 2016 Conference, Ljubljana, Slovenia.

Appendix

APPENDIX 1: Graphical Agglomeration Schedules for the First Cluster Analysis Model

Figure 1. Dendogram using single linkage
Source: extracted from SPSS output, Cluster analysis performed for 2011 year-end data

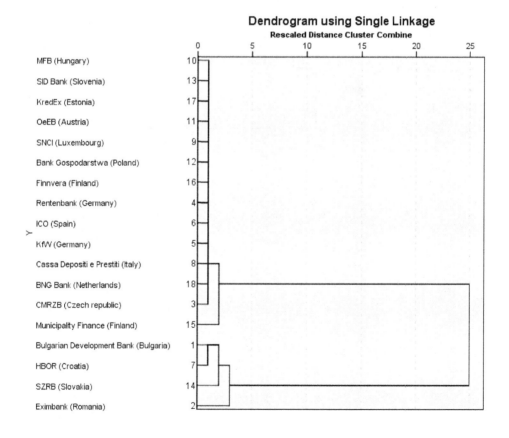

Figure 2. Dendogram using complete linkage
Source: extracted from SPSS output, Cluster analysis performed for 2011 year-end data

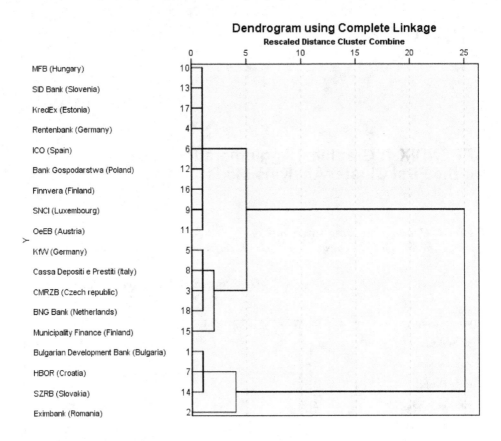

Dendrogram using Complete Linkage

Figure 3. Dendogram using Ward linkage
Source: extracted from SPSS output, Cluster analysis performed for 2011 year-end data

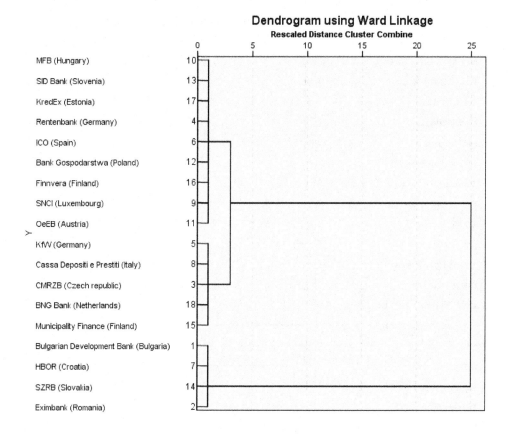

Figure 4. Dendogram using single linkage: Rescaled cluster combine
Source: extracted from SPSS output, Cluster analysis performed for 2012 year-end data

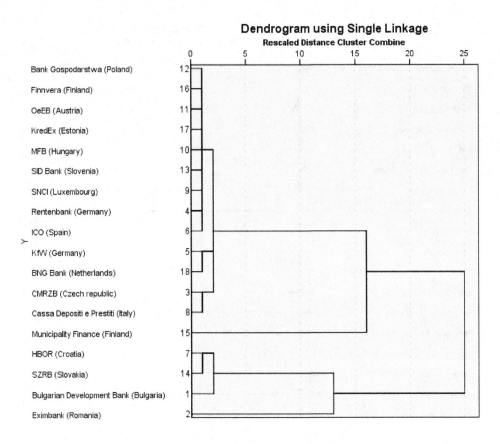

Figure 5. Dendogram using complete linkage: Rescaled distance cluster combine
Source: extracted from SPSS output, Cluster analysis performed for 2012 year-end data

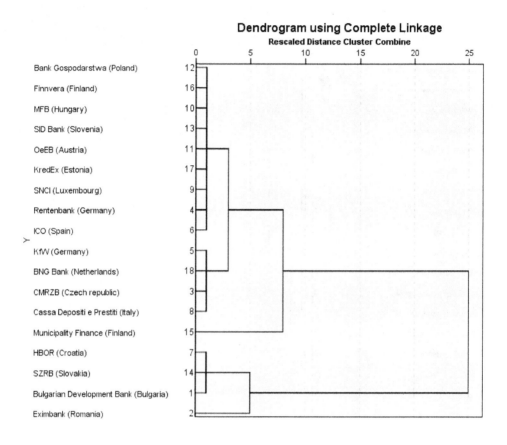

Figure 6. Dendogram using Ward linkage: Rescaled distance cluster combine
Source: extracted from SPSS output, Cluster analysis performed for 2012 year-end data

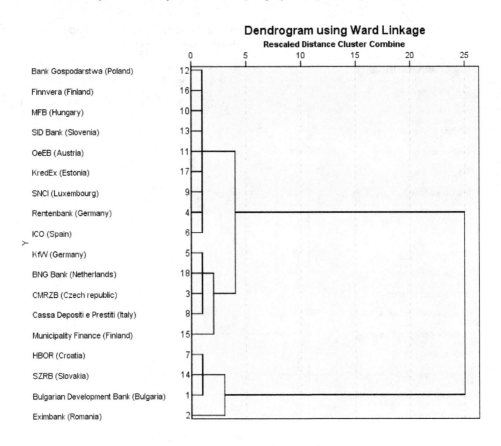

144

Figure 7. Dendogram using single linkage: Rescaled distance cluster combine
Source: extracted from SPSS output, Cluster analysis performed for 2013 year-end data

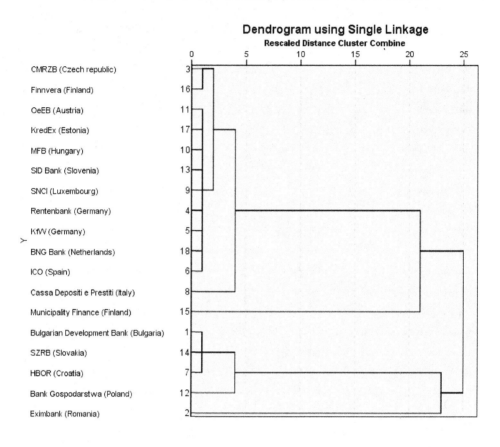

Figure 8. Dendogram using complete linkage: Rescaled distance cluster combine
Source: extracted from SPSS output, Cluster analysis performed for 2013 year-end data

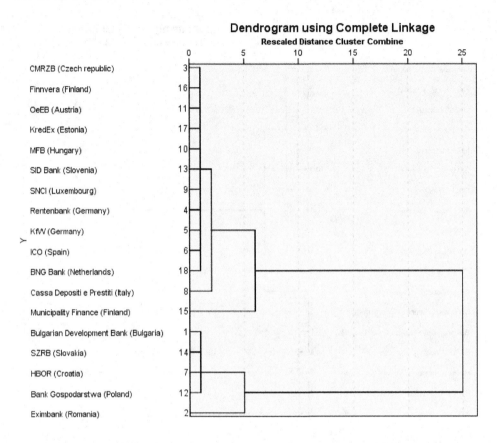

Figure 9. Dendogram using Ward linkage: Rescaled distance cluster combine
Source: extracted from SPSS output, Cluster analysis performed for 2013 year-end data

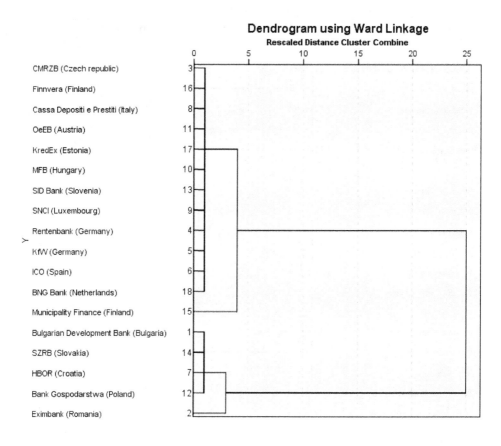

Figure 10. Dendogram using Single linkage: Rescaled distance cluster combine
Source: extracted from SPSS output, Cluster analysis performed for 2014 year-end data

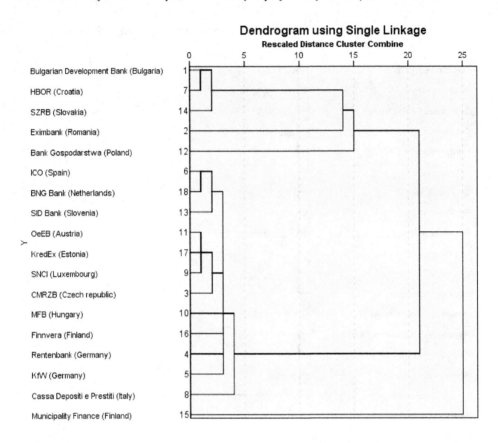

Figure 11. Dendogram using Complete linkage: Rescaled distance cluster combine
Source: extracted from SPSS output, Cluster analysis performed for 2014 year-end data

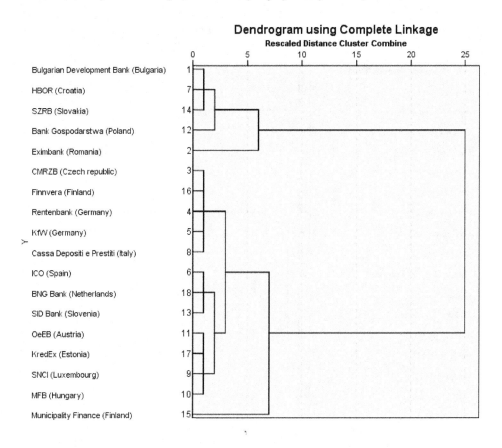

Figure 12. Dendogram using Ward linkage: Rescaled distance cluster combine
Source: extracted from SPSS output, Cluster analysis performed for 2014 year-end data

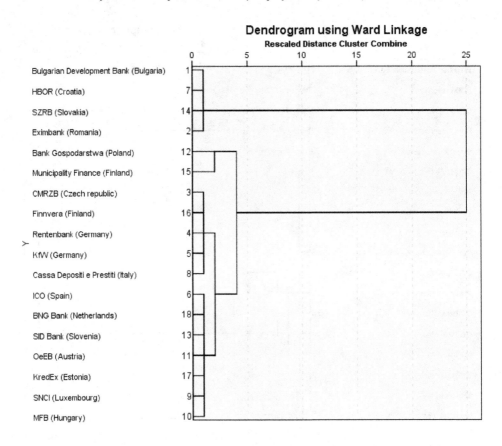

APPENDIX 2: Graphical Agglomeration Schedules for the Second Cluster Analysis Model

Figure 13. Dendogram using single linkage: Rescaled distance cluster combine
Source: extracted from SPSS output, Cluster analysis performed for 2011 year-end data

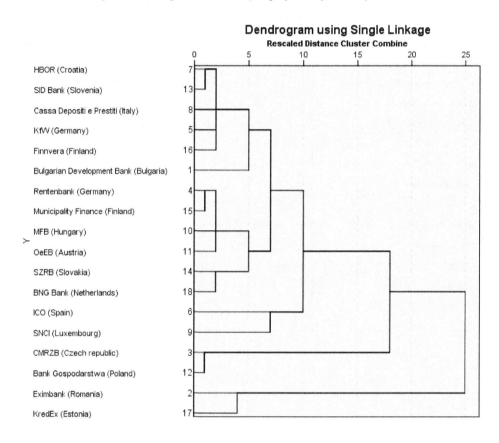

Figure 14. Dendogram using complete linkage: Rescaled distance cluster combine
Source: extracted from SPSS output, Cluster analysis performed for 2011 year-end data

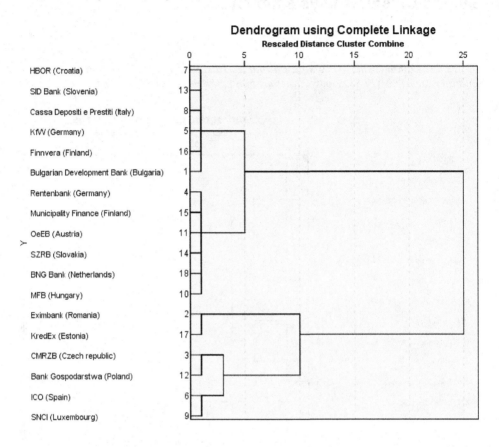

Figure 15. Dendogram using Ward linkage: Rescaled distance cluster combine
Source: extracted from SPSS output, Cluster analysis performed for 2011 year-end data

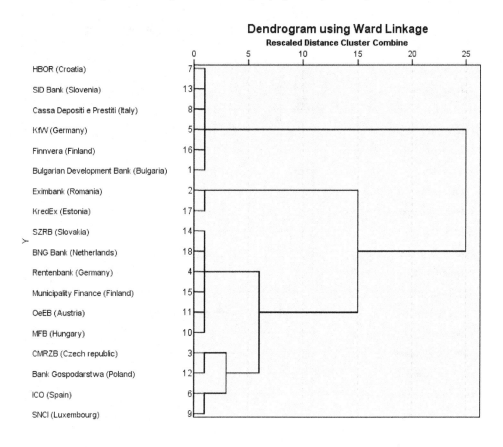

Figure 16. Dendogram using single linkage: Rescaled distance cluster combine
Source: extracted from SPSS output, Cluster analysis performed for 2012 year-end data

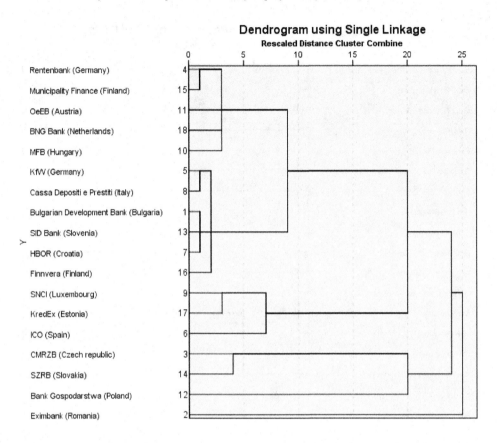

Dendrogram using Single Linkage
Rescaled Distance Cluster Combine

Figure 17. Dendogram using complete linkage: Rescaled distance cluster combine
Source: extracted from SPSS output, Cluster analysis performed for 2012 year-end data

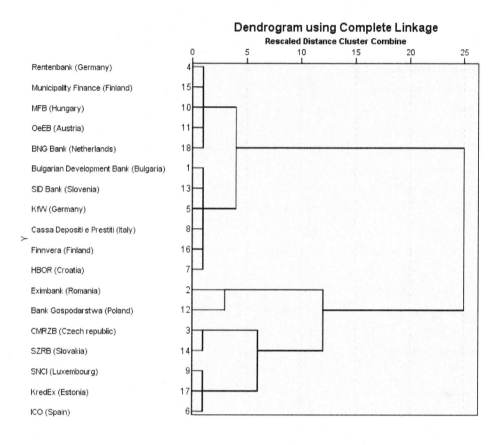

Figure 18. Dendogram using Ward linkage: Rescaled distance cluster combine
Source: extracted from SPSS output, Cluster analysis performed for 2012 year-end data

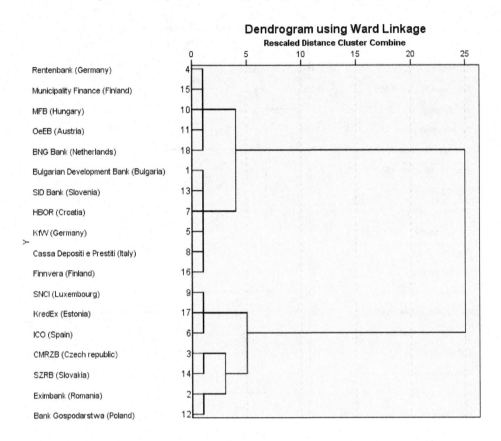

Figure 19. Dendogram using single linkage: Rescaled distance cluster combine
Source: extracted from SPSS output, Cluster analysis performed for 2013 year-end data

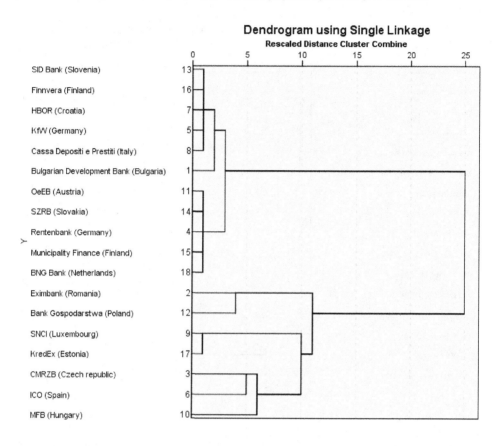

Figure 20. Dendogram using complete linkage: Rescaled distance cluster combine
Source: extracted from SPSS output, Cluster analysis performed for 2013 year-end data

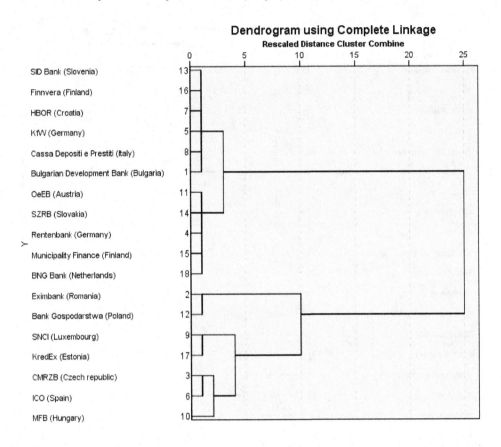

Figure 21. Dendogram using Ward linkage: Rescaled distance cluster combine
Source: extracted from SPSS output, Cluster analysis performed for 2013 year-end data

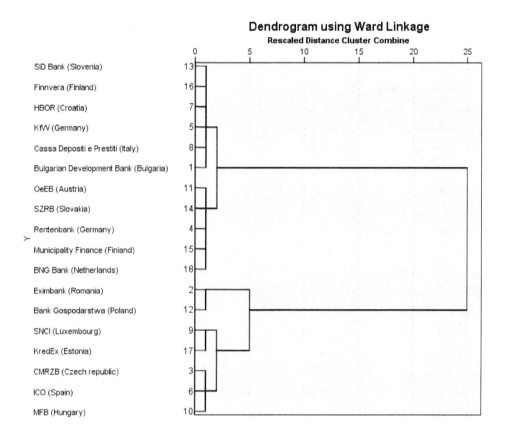

Figure 22. Dendogram using single linkage: Rescaled distance cluster combine
Source: extracted from SPSS output, Cluster analysis performed for 2014 year-end data

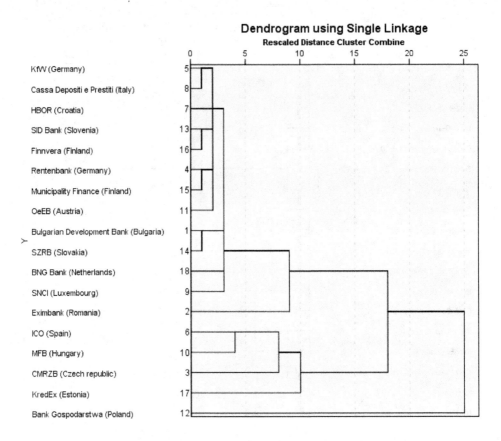

Figure 23. Dendogram using complete linkage: Rescaled distance cluster combine
Source: extracted from SPSS output, Cluster analysis performed for 2014 year-end data

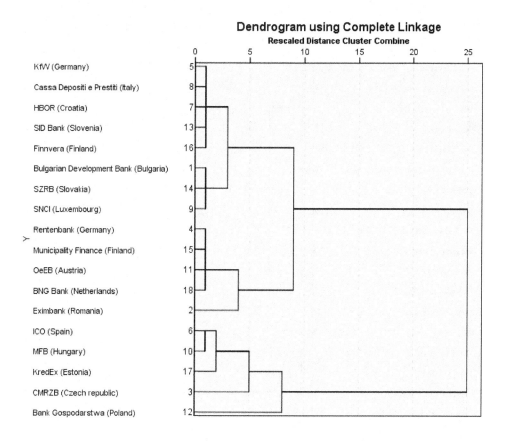

Figure 24. Dendogram using Ward linkage: Rescaled distance cluster combine
Source: extracted from SPSS output, Cluster analysis performed for 2014 year-end data

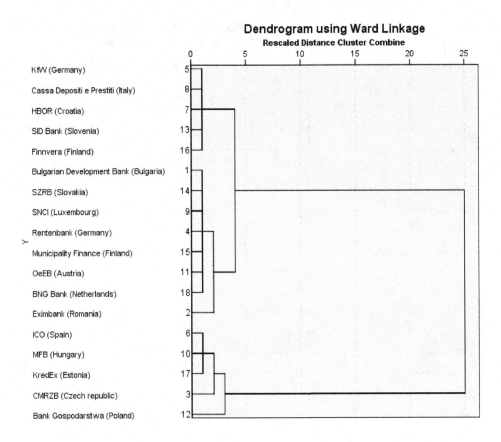

Related Readings

To continue IGI Global's long-standing tradition of advancing innovation through emerging research, please find below a compiled list of recommended IGI Global book chapters and journal articles in the areas of banking, finance, and economics. These related readings will provide additional information and guidance to further enrich your knowledge and assist you with your own research.

Abdin, J. (2015). Foreign Direct Investment (FDI) in Bangladesh: Trends, Challenges, and Recommendations. *International Journal of Sustainable Economies Management*, *4*(2), 36–45. doi:10.4018/IJSEM.2015040104

Agwu, E. M., & Murray, P. J. (2015). Empirical Study of Barriers to Electronic Commerce Uptake by SMEs in Developing Economies. *International Journal of Innovation in the Digital Economy*, *6*(2), 1–19. doi:10.4018/ijide.2015040101

Al-Hasan, S., Thomas, B., & Mansour, A. (2016). Internet Adoption and International Marketing in the Jordanian Banking Sector. *International Journal of Online Marketing*, *6*(2), 34–48. doi:10.4018/IJOM.2016040103

Alemu, T., Bandyopadhyay, T., & Negash, S. (2015). Electronic Payment Adoption in the Banking Sector of Low-Income Countries. *International Journal of Information Systems in the Service Sector*, *7*(4), 27–47. doi:10.4018/IJISSS.2015100102

Alganer, Y., & Yılmaz, G. (2015). Fiscal Integration and Harmonization: European Union Integration from Fiscal Perspectives – Objectives, Means, Obstacles, and Politics. In E. Sorhun, Ü. Hacıoğlu, & H. Dinçer (Eds.), *Regional Economic Integration and the Global Financial System* (pp. 49–58). Hershey, PA: Business Science Reference. doi:10.4018/978-1-4666-7308-3.ch005

Alt, R., Eckert, C., & Puschmann, T. (2015). Network Management and Service Systems: The Case of German and Swiss Banks. *Information Resources Management Journal*, *28*(1), 38–56. doi:10.4018/irmj.2015010103

Anthopoulos, L. G., & Siozos, P. (2015). Can IT Innovation become a Tool against Fiscal Crisis?: Findings from Europe. *International Journal of Public Administration in the Digital Age*, *2*(1), 39–55. doi:10.4018/ijpada.2015010103

Artienwicz, N. (2016). Behavioral Stream in Polish Accounting: Its Relation to Behavioral Finance and the Perspectives for Neuroaccounting Development in Poland. In B. Christiansen & E. Lechman (Eds.), *Neuroeconomics and the Decision-Making Process* (pp. 246–261). Hershey, PA: Business Science Reference. doi:10.4018/978-1-4666-9989-2.ch013

Asongu, S. A., & Nguena, C. L. (2015). Equitable and Sustainable Development of Foreign Land Acquisitions: Lessons, Policies, and Implications. In E. Osabuohien (Ed.), *Handbook of Research on In-Country Determinants and Implications of Foreign Land Acquisitions* (pp. 1–20). Hershey, PA: Business Science Reference. doi:10.4018/978-1-4666-7405-9.ch001

Aybars, A. (2014). The Relationship Between Institutional Investment and Earnings Management: Empirical Evidence from Turkey. *International Journal of Corporate Finance and Accounting*, *1*(1), 1–21. doi:10.4018/ijcfa.2014010101

Baber, H. (2016). Risk Mitigation Practices in Banking: A Study of HDFC Bank. *International Journal of Risk and Contingency Management*, *5*(3), 18–32. doi:10.4018/IJRCM.2016070102

Bachrane, M., Khaled, A., El Alami, J., & Hanoune, M. (2016). Investment Location Selection based on Economic Intelligence and Macbeth Decision Aid Model. *Journal of Information Technology Research*, *9*(3), 37–48. doi:10.4018/JITR.2016070103

Backović, N., Milićević, V., & Sofronijevic, A. (2016). Strategic Directions in European Sustainable City Management. In M. Erdoğdu, T. Arun, & I. Ahmad (Eds.), *Handbook of Research on Green Economic Development Initiatives and Strategies* (pp. 147–168). Hershey, PA: Business Science Reference. doi:10.4018/978-1-5225-0440-5.ch008

Ballas, A., Sykianakis, N., Tzovas, C., & Vassilakopoulos, C. (2014). An Investigation of Greek Firms Compliance to IFRS Mandatory Disclosure Requirements. *International Journal of Corporate Finance and Accounting*, *1*(1), 22–39. doi:10.4018/ijcfa.2014010102

Banerji, D., & Das, R. (2014). Critical Review of Curriculum in Legal Financial Studies in Turkey: Perspectives and Prospects. In N. Baporikar (Ed.), *Handbook of Research on Higher Education in the MENA Region: Policy and Practice* (pp. 102–118). Hershey, PA: IGI Global. doi:10.4018/978-1-4666-6198-1.ch006

Baranowska-Prokop, E., & Sikora, T. (2017). Competitiveness of Polish International New Ventures from Managerial Perspective. In A. Vlachvei, O. Notta, K. Karantininis, & N. Tsounis (Eds.), *Factors Affecting Firm Competitiveness and Performance in the Modern Business World* (pp. 83–107). Hershey, PA: Business Science Reference. doi:10.4018/978-1-5225-0843-4.ch003

Barat, S. (2016). Importance of Customer Satisfaction in a Community Bank. *International Journal of Innovation in the Digital Economy*, 7(4), 56–73. doi:10.4018/IJIDE.2016100104

Batrancea, L., Nichita, A., Batrancea, I., & Kirchler, E. (2016). Tax Compliance Behavior: An Upshot of Trust in and Power of Authorities across Europe and MENA. In M. Erdoğdu & B. Christiansen (Eds.), *Handbook of Research on Public Finance in Europe and the MENA Region* (pp. 248–267). Hershey, PA: Business Science Reference. doi:10.4018/978-1-5225-0053-7.ch012

Bihari, S. C. (2014). When Citi was Found Sleeping. In V. Jham & S. Puri (Eds.), *Cases on Consumer-Centric Marketing Management* (pp. 258–277). Hershey, PA: IGI Global. doi:10.4018/978-1-4666-4357-4.ch021

Bird, R. M. (2016). Transparency, Technology and Taxation. In M. Erdoğdu & B. Christiansen (Eds.), *Handbook of Research on Public Finance in Europe and the MENA Region* (pp. 11–29). Hershey, PA: Business Science Reference. doi:10.4018/978-1-5225-0053-7.ch002

Bodea, C., Stelian, S., & Mogos, R. (2017). E-Learning Solution for Enhancing Entrepreneurship Competencies in the Service Sector. In I. Hosu & I. Iancu (Eds.), *Digital Entrepreneurship and Global Innovation* (pp. 225–244). Hershey, PA: Business Science Reference. doi:10.4018/978-1-5225-0953-0.ch011

Boitan, I. A. (2016). Early Warning Tools for Financial System Distress: Current Drawbacks and Future Challenges. In Q. Munir (Ed.), *Handbook of Research on Financial and Banking Crisis Prediction through Early Warning Systems* (pp. 97–114). Hershey, PA: IGI Global. doi:10.4018/978-1-4666-9484-2.ch005

Buggea, E., Castiglione, R., Cerquitelli, T., Grosso, L., Rontini, G., Scolari, A., & Xiang, L. (2014). Internationalization Services for Small and Medium Enterprises: A Case Study. In C. Machado & P. Melo (Eds.), *Effective Human Resources Management in Small and Medium Enterprises: Global Perspectives* (pp. 393–414). Hershey, PA: IGI Global. doi:10.4018/978-1-4666-4731-2.ch019

Cabanda, E., & Domingo, E. C. (2014). A Production Approach to Performance of Banks with Microfinance Operations. *International Journal of Information Systems in the Service Sector*, 6(2), 18–35. doi:10.4018/ijisss.2014040102

Çavuşoğlu, T., & Önal, D. K. (2016). A Panel VAR Analysis of the Shadow Economy in Europe and MENA. In M. Erdoğdu & B. Christiansen (Eds.), *Handbook of Research on Public Finance in Europe and the MENA Region* (pp. 201–220). Hershey, PA: IGI Global. doi:10.4018/978-1-5225-0053-7.ch010

Celik, I. E., Dinçer, H., & Hacioğlu, Ü. (2014). Investment and Development Banks and Strategies in Turkey. In Ü. Hacioğlu & H. Dinçer (Eds.), *Globalization and Governance in the International Political Economy* (pp. 131–140). Hershey, PA: IGI Global. doi:10.4018/978-1-4666-4639-1.ch010

Cheng, P. (2016). Fragile by Design: The Political Origins of Banking Crises and Scarce Credit. *International Journal of Applied Behavioral Economics*, 5(1), 48–52. doi:10.4018/ijabe.2016010103

Choudhury, M. A. (2014). Productivity Analysis in Ethically Induced Financing Environment: A Case Study of Indonesian Islamic Banks. In *Socio-Cybernetic Study of God and the World-System* (pp. 192–218). Hershey, PA: IGI Global. doi:10.4018/978-1-4666-4643-8.ch007

Chytis, E., Filos, J., Tagkas, P., & Rodosthenous, M. (2016). Audit Firms, Deferred Taxation and Financial Reporting: The Case of The Athens Stock Exchange. *International Journal of Corporate Finance and Accounting*, 3(1), 1–21. doi:10.4018/IJCFA.2016010101

Chytis, E., Koumanakos, E., & Goumas, S. (2015). Deferred Tax Positions under the Prism of Financial Crisis and the Effects of a Corporate Tax Reform. *International Journal of Corporate Finance and Accounting*, 2(2), 21–58. doi:10.4018/IJCFA.2015070102

Cinelli, S. A. (2017). The World's Oldest Profession - Now and Then: Disruption of the Commercial Banking Model. In W. Vassallo (Ed.), *Crowdfunding for Sustainable Entrepreneurship and Innovation* (pp. 78–89). Hershey, PA: IGI Global. doi:10.4018/978-1-5225-0568-6.ch005

Ciocoiu, C. N., & Cicea, C. (2015). Development of the Green Economy in Romania: Dimensions, Strengths and Weaknesses. In A. Jean-Vasile, I. Andreea, & T. Adrian (Eds.), *Green Economic Structures in Modern Business and Society* (pp. 161–179). Hershey, PA: IGI Global. doi:10.4018/978-1-4666-8219-1.ch009

Cipolla-Ficarra, F. V., & Alma, J. (2014). Banking Online: Design for a New Credibility. In F. Cipolla-Ficarra (Ed.), *Advanced Research and Trends in New Technologies, Software, Human-Computer Interaction, and Communicability* (pp. 71–82). Hershey, PA: Information Science Reference. doi:10.4018/978-1-4666-4490-8.ch007

Cossiavelou, V. (2017). ACTA as Media Gatekeeping Factor: The EU Role as Global Negotiator. *International Journal of Interdisciplinary Telecommunications and Networking*, 9(1), 26–37. doi:10.4018/IJITN.2017010103

Cura, S. (2015). The Impact of Sovereign Debt Crisis on the EU Economy: Is This the End of the Dream? In E. Sorhun, Ü. Hacıoğlu, & H. Dinçer (Eds.), *Regional Economic Integration and the Global Financial System* (pp. 1–11). Hershey, PA: Business Science Reference. doi:10.4018/978-1-4666-7308-3.ch001

da Silva, A., Pletsch, C. S., Klann, R. C., Fasolin, L. B., & Scarpin, J. E. (2015). Influence of International Accounting Convergence on the Level of Earnings Management in both Brazilian and Chilean Companies. In I. Lourenço & M. Major (Eds.), *Standardization of Financial Reporting and Accounting in Latin American Countries* (pp. 195–218). Hershey, PA: Business Science Reference. doi:10.4018/978-1-4666-8453-9.ch009

Dapontas, D. K. (2016). Developing EWS Models for Contemporary Crises Using Extreme Value Binary Models: The Cases of Eurozone and Argentinian Peso (2014). In Q. Munir (Ed.), *Handbook of Research on Financial and Banking Crisis Prediction through Early Warning Systems* (pp. 332–352). Hershey, PA: Business Science Reference. doi:10.4018/978-1-4666-9484-2.ch016

Datta, N. (2015). Growth and Knowledge Management Strategy of Indian Commercial Banks: A Non-Parametric Approach. *International Journal of Measurement Technologies and Instrumentation Engineering*, 5(1), 28–45. doi:10.4018/IJMTIE.2015010103

Dima, I. C. (2015). Considerations on the Current State of Strategic Management. In I. Dima (Ed.), *Systemic Approaches to Strategic Management: Examples from the Automotive Industry* (pp. 166–218). Hershey, PA: Business Science Reference. doi:10.4018/978-1-4666-6481-4.ch008

Dinçer, H., & Hacıoğlu, Ü. (2014). The Competitiveness and Strategies in Global Financial System. In H. Dinçer & Ü. Hacioğlu (Eds.), *Global Strategies in Banking and Finance* (pp. 1–13). Hershey, PA: IGI Global. doi:10.4018/978-1-4666-4635-3.ch001

Ebenezer, E. E., Shi, W., & Mackie, W. E. (2015). Chinese Investments in Africa: Implications for Entrepreneurship. In J. Ofori-Dankwa & K. Omane-Antwi (Eds.), *Comparative Case Studies on Entrepreneurship in Developed and Developing Countries* (pp. 99–109). Hershey, PA: Business Science Reference. doi:10.4018/978-1-4666-7533-9.ch006

Edwards, J., & Newton, S. (2016). Enhancing Regulatory, Financial, Fiscal Investment Incentives as a Means of Promoting Foreign Direct Investment. In M. Ojo (Ed.), *Analyzing the Relationship between Corporate Social Responsibility and Foreign Direct Investment* (pp. 191–201). Hershey, PA: Business Science Reference. doi:10.4018/978-1-5225-0305-7.ch013

Eken, M. H., & Kale, S. (2014). Bank Branch Efficiency with DEA. In I. Osman, A. Anouze, & A. Emrouznejad (Eds.), *Handbook of Research on Strategic Performance Management and Measurement Using Data Envelopment Analysis* (pp. 626–667). Hershey, PA: IGI Global. doi:10.4018/978-1-4666-4474-8.ch022

Eken, M. H., Kale, S., & Selimler, H. (2014). Analyzing the Efficiency of European Banks: A DEA-Based Risk and Profitability Approach. In H. Dinçer & Ü. Hacioğlu (Eds.), *Global Strategies in Banking and Finance* (pp. 28–55). Hershey, PA: Business Science Reference. doi:10.4018/978-1-4666-4635-3.ch003

El Dessouky, N. F. (2016). Corporate Social Responsibility of Public Banking Sector for Sustainable Development: A Comparative Study between Malaysia and Egypt. In M. Al-Shammari & H. Masri (Eds.), *Ethical and Social Perspectives on Global Business Interaction in Emerging Markets* (pp. 52–73). Hershey, PA: IGI Global. doi:10.4018/978-1-4666-9864-2.ch004

El-Firjani, E. R., & Faraj, S. M. (2016). International Accounting Standards: Adoption, Implementation and Challenges. In E. Uchenna, M. Nnadi, S. Tanna, & F. Iyoha (Eds.), *Economics and Political Implications of International Financial Reporting Standards* (pp. 231–250). Hershey, PA: Business Science Reference. doi:10.4018/978-1-4666-9876-5.ch011

Encinas-Ferrer, C. (2017). Currency Parity and Competitiveness: The Case of Greece. In A. Vlachvei, O. Notta, K. Karantininis, & N. Tsounis (Eds.), *Factors Affecting Firm Competitiveness and Performance in the Modern Business World* (pp. 282–299). Hershey, PA: Business Science Reference. doi:10.4018/978-1-5225-0843-4.ch010

Engwanda, M. N. (2015). Mobile Banking Adoption in the United States: A Structural Equation Modeling Analysis. *International Journal of E-Services and Mobile Applications*, 7(3), 18–30. doi:10.4018/IJESMA.2015070102

Epler, P., & Ross, R. (2015). Spending Options for Service Delivery Models. In *Models for Effective Service Delivery in Special Education Programs* (pp. 91–112). Hershey, PA: Information Science Reference. doi:10.4018/978-1-4666-7397-7.ch005

Ertürk, E., Yılmaz, D., & Çetin, I. (2016). Optimum Currency Area Theory and Business Cycle Convergence in EMU: Considering the Sovereign Debt Crisis. In R. Das (Ed.), *Handbook of Research on Global Indicators of Economic and Political Convergence* (pp. 67–91). Hershey, PA: Business Science Reference. doi:10.4018/978-1-5225-0215-9.ch004

Eryigit, S. B. (2016). Does Trust Matter for Foreign Direct Investment Decisions? In M. Al-Shammari & H. Masri (Eds.), *Ethical and Social Perspectives on Global Business Interaction in Emerging Markets* (pp. 224–239). Hershey, PA: Business Science Reference. doi:10.4018/978-1-4666-9864-2.ch013

Eshraghi, A. (2014). Fund Manager Overconfidence and Investment Narratives. In R. Hart (Ed.), *Communication and Language Analysis in the Corporate World* (pp. 1–20). Hershey, PA: IGI Global. doi:10.4018/978-1-4666-4999-6.ch001

Espagne, E., & Aglietta, M. (2016). Financing Energy and Low-Carbon Investment in Europe: Public Guarantees and the ECB. In M. Erdoğdu, T. Arun, & I. Ahmad (Eds.), *Handbook of Research on Green Economic Development Initiatives and Strategies* (pp. 132–146). Hershey, PA: Business Science Reference. doi:10.4018/978-1-5225-0440-5.ch007

Even, A., Parmet, Y., & Erez, L. (2015). Factors that Affect Customers Readiness for Internet-based BI Services. *International Journal of Business Intelligence Research*, 6(1), 30–48. doi:10.4018/IJBIR.2015010103

Feldman, R., Govindaraj, S., Liu, S., & Livnat, J. (2014). Optimal Portfolio Construction Using Qualitative and Quantitative Signals. In R. Hart (Ed.), *Communication and Language Analysis in the Corporate World* (pp. 140–161). Hershey, PA: Information Science Reference. doi:10.4018/978-1-4666-4999-6.ch009

Fiodendji, K., Kamgnia, B. D., & Tanimoune, N. A. (2014). Inflation and Economic Performance in the CFA Franc Zone: Transmission Channels and Threshold Effects. In P. Schaeffer & E. Kouassi (Eds.), *Econometric Methods for Analyzing Economic Development* (pp. 10–29). Hershey, PA: Business Science Reference. doi:10.4018/978-1-4666-4329-1.ch002

Gáspár-Szilágyi, S. (2017). Human Rights Conditionality in the EU's Newly Concluded Association Agreements with the Eastern Partners. In C. Akrivopoulou (Ed.), *Defending Human Rights and Democracy in the Era of Globalization* (pp. 50–79). Hershey, PA: Information Science Reference. doi:10.4018/978-1-5225-0723-9.ch003

Gedikli, A., Erdoğan, S., & Yıldırım, D. Ç. (2015). After The Global Crisis, Is It Globalization or Globalonelization? In Ö. Olgu, H. Dinçer, & Ü. Hacıoğlu (Eds.), *Handbook of Research on Strategic Developments and Regulatory Practice in Global Finance* (pp. 287–307). Hershey, PA: Business Science Reference. doi:10.4018/978-1-4666-7288-8.ch018

Ghobakhloo, M., Hong, T. S., & Standing, C. (2015). B2B E-Commerce Success among Small and Medium-Sized Enterprises: A Business Network Perspective. *Journal of Organizational and End User Computing*, 27(1), 1–32. doi:10.4018/joeuc.2015010101

Goel, S. (2014). Fraud Detection and Corporate Filings. In R. Hart (Ed.), *Communication and Language Analysis in the Corporate World* (pp. 315–332). Hershey, PA: IGI Global. doi:10.4018/978-1-4666-4999-6.ch018

Gordini, N. (2014). Genetic Algorithms for Small Enterprises Default Prediction: Empirical Evidence from Italy. In P. Vasant (Ed.), *Handbook of Research on Novel Soft Computing Intelligent Algorithms: Theory and Practical Applications* (pp. 258–293). Hershey, PA: IGI Global. doi:10.4018/978-1-4666-4450-2.ch009

Guillet de Monthoux, P., & Statler, M. (2014). Theory U: Rethinking Business as Practical European Philosophy. In O. Gunnlaugson, C. Baron, & M. Cayer (Eds.), *Perspectives on Theory U: Insights from the Field* (pp. 234–243). Hershey, PA: Business Science Reference. doi:10.4018/978-1-4666-4793-0.ch015

Günaydin, D., Cavlak, H., & Cavlak, N. (2015). Social Exclusion and Poverty: EU 2020 Objectives and Turkey. In Z. Copur (Ed.), *Handbook of Research on Behavioral Finance and Investment Strategies: Decision Making in the Financial Industry* (pp. 170–186). Hershey, PA: Business Science Reference. doi:10.4018/978-1-4666-7484-4.ch010

Gürcü, M., & Tengilimoğlu, D. (2017). Health Tourism-Based Destination Marketing. In A. Bayraktar & C. Uslay (Eds.), *Strategic Place Branding Methodologies and Theory for Tourist Attraction* (pp. 308–331). Hershey, PA: Business Science Reference. doi:10.4018/978-1-5225-0579-2.ch015

Hackney, D. D., McPherson, M. Q., Friesner, D., & Correia, C. (2014). On the Social Costs of Bankruptcy: Can the Bankruptcy Abuse Prevention and Consumer Protection Act (BAPCPA) of 2005 be an Effective Policy? *International Journal of Social Ecology and Sustainable Development*, 5(1), 58–91. doi:10.4018/ijsesd.2014010106

Hasan, I., & Pasiouras, F. (2015). Stress Testing and Bank Efficiency: Evidence from Europe. *International Journal of Corporate Finance and Accounting*, 2(2), 1–20. doi:10.4018/IJCFA.2015070101

Henry, E., & Leone, A. J. (2014). Measuring the Tone of Accounting and Financial Narrative. In R. Hart (Ed.), *Communication and Language Analysis in the Corporate World* (pp. 36–47). Hershey, PA: IGI Global. doi:10.4018/978-1-4666-4999-6.ch003

Hocaoğlu, D. (2017). Challenges in Promoting Cities through Culture within the New Global Economy. In A. Bayraktar & C. Uslay (Eds.), *Global Place Branding Campaigns across Cities, Regions, and Nations* (pp. 229–250). Hershey, PA: Business Science Reference. doi:10.4018/978-1-5225-0576-1.ch011

Homata, A., Mihiotis, A., & Tzortzaki, A. M. (2017). Franchise Management and the Greek Franchise Industry. In A. Vlachvei, O. Notta, K. Karantininis, & N. Tsounis (Eds.), *Factors Affecting Firm Competitiveness and Performance in the Modern Business World* (pp. 251–281). Hershey, PA: Business Science Reference. doi:10.4018/978-1-5225-0843-4.ch009

Hu, J., Marques, J., Holt, S., & Camillo, A. A. (2014). Marketing Channels and Supply Chain Management in Contemporary Globalism: E-Commerce Development in China and its Implication for Business. In B. Christiansen, S. Yıldız, & E. Yıldız (Eds.), *Handbook of Research on Effective Marketing in Contemporary Globalism* (pp. 325–334). Hershey, PA: IGI Global. doi:10.4018/978-1-4666-6220-9.ch018

James, S. (2016). The Difficulties of Achieving Successful Tax Reform. In M. Erdoğdu & B. Christiansen (Eds.), *Handbook of Research on Public Finance in Europe and the MENA Region* (pp. 30–47). Hershey, PA: Business Science Reference. doi:10.4018/978-1-5225-0053-7.ch003

Jean-Vasile, A., & Alecu, A. (2016). Trends and Transformations in European Agricultural Economy, Rural Communities and Food Sustainability in Context of New Common Agricultural Policy (CAP) Reforms. In A. Jean-Vasile (Ed.), *Food Science, Production, and Engineering in Contemporary Economies* (pp. 1–24). Hershey, PA: Information Science Reference. doi:10.4018/978-1-5225-0341-5.ch001

Jeločnik, M., Zubovic, J., & Djukic, M. (2016). Implications of Globalization on Growing External Debt in Eight Transition Economies. In V. Erokhin (Ed.), *Global Perspectives on Trade Integration and Economies in Transition* (pp. 80–104). Hershey, PA: Business Science Reference. doi:10.4018/978-1-5225-0451-1.ch005

Jindrichovska, I., & Kubickova, D. (2016). Economic and Political Implications of IFRS Adoption in the Czech Republic. In E. Uchenna, M. Nnadi, S. Tanna, & F. Iyoha (Eds.), *Economics and Political Implications of International Financial Reporting Standards* (pp. 105–133). Hershey, PA: Business Science Reference. doi:10.4018/978-1-4666-9876-5.ch006

Kablan, A. (2014). Financial Control and Ratio Analysis in Local Governments. In H. Dinçer & Ü. Hacioğlu (Eds.), *Global Strategies in Banking and Finance* (pp. 410–422). Hershey, PA: Business Science Reference. doi:10.4018/978-1-4666-4635-3.ch027

Karaca, C. (2016). The Comparison of the Shadow Economy in Turkey and European Countries. In B. Christiansen & M. Erdoğdu (Eds.), *Comparative Economics and Regional Development in Turkey* (pp. 73–105). Hershey, PA: IGI Global. doi:10.4018/978-1-4666-8729-5.ch004

Karaibrahimoglu, Y. Z., & Tunç, G. (2014). Financial Statement Analysis under IFRS. In N. Ray & K. Chakraborty (Eds.), *Handbook of Research on Strategic Business Infrastructure Development and Contemporary Issues in Finance* (pp. 238–255). Hershey, PA: IGI Global. doi:10.4018/978-1-4666-5154-8.ch017

Kasemsap, K. (2015). The Role of E-Business Adoption in the Business World. In N. Ray, D. Das, S. Chaudhuri, & A. Ghosh (Eds.), *Strategic Infrastructure Development for Economic Growth and Social Change* (pp. 51–63). Hershey, PA: IGI Global. doi:10.4018/978-1-4666-7470-7.ch005

Kasemsap, K. (2015). The Role of Electronic Commerce in the Global Business Environments. In F. Cipolla-Ficarra (Ed.), *Handbook of Research on Interactive Information Quality in Expanding Social Network Communications* (pp. 304–324). Hershey, PA: IGI Global. doi:10.4018/978-1-4666-7377-9.ch019

Katou, A. A., & Katsouli, E. F. (2017). Empirical Evidence on Convergence of Travel and Tourism Competitiveness and Global Competitiveness Across the BRIC Countries. In M. Dhiman (Ed.), *Opportunities and Challenges for Tourism and Hospitality in the BRIC Nations* (pp. 1–14). Hershey, PA: Business Science Reference. doi:10.4018/978-1-5225-0708-6.ch001

Korres, G. M., & Kokkinou, A. (2014). Public Spending Efficiency: The Missing Factor through Financial Crisis. *International Journal of Social Ecology and Sustainable Development*, 5(4), 1–10. doi:10.4018/ijsesd.2014100101

Kushwaha, G. S., & Agrawal, S. R. (2015). Customer Management Practices: Multiple Case Studies in Stock Broking Services. *International Journal of Customer Relationship Marketing and Management*, 6(2), 1–14. doi:10.4018/IJCRMM.2015040101

Lara-Rubio, J., Martínez-Fiestas, M., & Cortés-Romero, A. M. (2014). Drop-Out Risk Measurement of E-Banking Customers. In F. Liébana-Cabanillas, F. Muñoz-Leiva, J. Sánchez-Fernández, & M. Martínez-Fiestas (Eds.), *Electronic Payment Systems for Competitive Advantage in E-Commerce* (pp. 143–162). Hershey, PA: IGI Global. doi:10.4018/978-1-4666-5190-6.ch009

LaRocca, R. N. (2014). Assessing the Political and Socio-Economic Impact of Corruption among Nations. *International Journal of Information Systems and Social Change*, 5(4), 18–40. doi:10.4018/ijissc.2014100102

Li, S. (2014). Pre-GFC Bank Behaviour Change and Basel Accords. In *Emerging Trends in Smart Banking: Risk Management Under Basel II and III* (pp. 35–56). Hershey, PA: IGI Global. doi:10.4018/978-1-4666-5950-6.ch003

Liu, L. (2014). Micro-Analysis of the Bank of China. In *International Cross-Listing of Chinese Firms* (pp. 226–233). Hershey, PA: IGI Global. doi:10.4018/978-1-4666-5047-3.ch007

Lokuwaduge, C. S. (2016). Exploring the New Public Management (NPM)-Based Reforms in the Public Sector Accounting: A Sri Lankan Study. In A. Ferreira, G. Azevedo, J. Oliveira, & R. Marques (Eds.), *Global Perspectives on Risk Management and Accounting in the Public Sector* (pp. 49–67). Hershey, PA: Information Science Reference. doi:10.4018/978-1-4666-9803-1.ch003

Long, P., & Vy, P. D. (2016). Internet Banking Service Quality, Customer Satisfaction and Customer Loyalty: The Case of Vietnam. *International Journal of Strategic Decision Sciences*, 7(1), 1–17. doi:10.4018/IJSDS.2016010101

Lopes, F. C., Morais, M. P., & Sasvari, P. (2014). Comparative Analysis on the Usage of Business Information Systems among Portuguese and Hungarian Small and Medium-Sized Enterprises. In H. Rahman & R. de Sousa (Eds.), *Information Systems and Technology for Organizational Agility, Intelligence, and Resilience* (pp. 265–296). Hershey, PA: IGI Global. doi:10.4018/978-1-4666-5970-4.ch013

Lopez-Iturriaga, F., & Pastor-Sanz, I. (2016). Using Self Organizing Maps for Banking Oversight: The Case of Spanish Savings Banks. In Q. Munir (Ed.), *Handbook of Research on Financial and Banking Crisis Prediction through Early Warning Systems* (pp. 116–140). Hershey, PA: Business Science Reference. doi:10.4018/978-1-4666-9484-2.ch006

Lu, Y. (2016). Public Financial Information Management for Benefits Maximization: Insights from Organization Theories. *International Journal of Organizational and Collective Intelligence*, 6(3), 50–74. doi:10.4018/IJOCI.2016070104

Man, M. (2015). Budgeting Technique of Strategic Management. In I. Dima (Ed.), *Systemic Approaches to Strategic Management: Examples from the Automotive Industry* (pp. 328–362). Hershey, PA: Business Science Reference. doi:10.4018/978-1-4666-6481-4.ch012

Marois, T. (2016). State-Owned Banks and Development: Dispelling Mainstream Myths. In M. Erdoğdu & B. Christiansen (Eds.), *Handbook of Research on Comparative Economic Development Perspectives on Europe and the MENA Region* (pp. 52–73). Hershey, PA: IGI Global. doi:10.4018/978-1-4666-9548-1.ch004

Marwah, G. S., & Ladhani, V. (2016). Financial Sector in Afghanistan: Regulatory Challenges in Financial Sector of Afghanistan. In A. Kashyap & A. Tomar (Eds.), *Financial Market Regulations and Legal Challenges in South Asia* (pp. 224–262). Hershey, PA: IGI Global. doi:10.4018/978-1-5225-0004-9.ch011

Medda, F. R., Partridge, C., & Carbonaro, G. (2015). Energy Investment in Smart Cities Unlocking Financial Instruments in Europe. In A. Vesco & F. Ferrero (Eds.), *Handbook of Research on Social, Economic, and Environmental Sustainability in the Development of Smart Cities* (pp. 408–433). Hershey, PA: Information Science Reference. doi:10.4018/978-1-4666-8282-5.ch019

Mertzanis, C. (2015). Marketing Financial Services and Products in Different Cultural Environments. In B. Rishi (Ed.), *Islamic Perspectives on Marketing and Consumer Behavior: Planning, Implementation, and Control* (pp. 232–267). Hershey, PA: Business Science Reference. doi:10.4018/978-1-4666-8139-2.ch011

Michael, O. B. (2015). Performance Measurement Systems and Firms' Characteristics: Empirical Evidences from Nigerian Banks. *International Journal of Business Analytics*, *2*(3), 67–83. doi:10.4018/IJBAN.2015070105

Milgram-Baleix, J., Parravano, M., & Pedauga, L. E. (2014). The Role of B2B E-Commerce in Market Share: Evidence from Spanish Manufacturing Firms. In F. Liébana-Cabanillas, F. Muñoz-Leiva, J. Sánchez-Fernández, & M. Martínez-Fiestas (Eds.), *Electronic Payment Systems for Competitive Advantage in E-Commerce* (pp. 1–14). Hershey, PA: IGI Global. doi:10.4018/978-1-4666-5190-6.ch001

Mion, L., Georgakopoulos, G., Kalantonis, P., & Eriotis, N. (2014). The Value Relevance of Accounting Information in Times of Crisis: An Empirical Study. *International Journal of Corporate Finance and Accounting*, *1*(2), 44–67. doi:10.4018/ijcfa.2014070104

Montero-Romero, T., & Cordobés-Madueño, M. (2014). Enterprise Resource Planning System (ERP) and Other Free Software for Accounting and Financial Management of Non-Profit Entities. In J. Ariza-Montes & A. Lucia-Casademunt (Eds.), *ICT Management in Non-Profit Organizations* (pp. 73–89). Hershey, PA: IGI Global. doi:10.4018/978-1-4666-5974-2.ch005

Mukherjee, S., & Chakraborty, D. (2016). Does Fiscal Policy Influence Per Capita CO2 Emission?: A Cross Country Empirical Analysis. In S. Dinda (Ed.), *Handbook of Research on Climate Change Impact on Health and Environmental Sustainability* (pp. 568–592). Hershey, PA: Information Science Reference. doi:10.4018/978-1-4666-8814-8.ch028

Munir, Q., & Kok, S. C. (2016). Early Warning System for Banking Crisis: Causes and Impacts. In Q. Munir (Ed.), *Handbook of Research on Financial and Banking Crisis Prediction through Early Warning Systems* (pp. 1–21). Hershey, PA: Business Science Reference. doi:10.4018/978-1-4666-9484-2.ch001

Nisha, N. (2016). Exploring the Dimensions of Mobile Banking Service Quality: Implications for the Banking Sector. *International Journal of Business Analytics*, *3*(3), 60–76. doi:10.4018/IJBAN.2016070104

Okon, E. E. (2016). Multinational Enterprises and African Economy. In M. Khan (Ed.), *Multinational Enterprise Management Strategies in Developing Countries* (pp. 351–381). Hershey, PA: IGI Global. doi:10.4018/978-1-5225-0276-0.ch018

Olgu, Ö., & Yılmaz, E. (2014). Foreign Ownership and Bank Efficiency: Evidence from Turkey. In H. Dinçer & Ü. Hacioğlu (Eds.), *Global Strategies in Banking and Finance* (pp. 75–100). Hershey, PA: Business Science Reference. doi:10.4018/978-1-4666-4635-3.ch006

Özer, A. C., & Gürel, H. (2017). Internet Banking Usage Level of Bankers: A Research on Sampling of Turkey. In S. Aljawarneh (Ed.), *Online Banking Security Measures and Data Protection* (pp. 27–39). Hershey, PA: IGI Global. doi:10.4018/978-1-5225-0864-9.ch002

Öztayşi, B., & Kahraman, C. (2014). Quantification of Corporate Performance Using Fuzzy Analytic Network Process: The Case of E-Commerce. In P. Vasant (Ed.), *Handbook of Research on Novel Soft Computing Intelligent Algorithms: Theory and Practical Applications* (pp. 385–413). Hershey, PA: IGI Global. doi:10.4018/978-1-4666-4450-2.ch013

Pan, B., Wei, S., Xu, X., & Hong, W. (2014). The Impact of Defense Investment on Economic Growth in the Perspective of Time Series: A Case Study of China. *International Journal of Applied Evolutionary Computation*, *5*(4), 44–58. doi:10.4018/IJAEC.2014100104

Patro, C. S., & Raghunath, K. M. (2016). Corporate Social Responsibility: A Manifestation in FDI. In M. Ojo (Ed.), *Analyzing the Relationship between Corporate Social Responsibility and Foreign Direct Investment* (pp. 202–227). Hershey, PA: Business Science Reference. doi:10.4018/978-1-5225-0305-7.ch014

Peng, E. Y., Shon, J., & Tan, C. (2014). Market Reactions to XBRL-Formatted Financial Information: Empirical Evidence from China. *International Journal of E-Business Research*, *10*(3), 1–17. doi:10.4018/ijebr.2014070101

Plaza i Font, J. P. (2016). The European Union as a Chaotic System. In Ş. Erçetin & H. Bağcı (Eds.), *Handbook of Research on Chaos and Complexity Theory in the Social Sciences* (pp. 33–42). Hershey, PA: Information Science Reference. doi:10.4018/978-1-5225-0148-0.ch003

Popescu, G. H. (2015). The Reform of EU Economic Governance. In G. Popescu & A. Jean-Vasile (Eds.), *Agricultural Management Strategies in a Changing Economy* (pp. 100–118). Hershey, PA: Business Science Reference. doi:10.4018/978-1-4666-7521-6.ch005

Puia, G. M., Affholter, J. A., & Potts, M. D. (2015). Factors Stimulating Entrepreneurship: A Comparison of Developed (U.S. and Europe) and Developing (West African) Countries. In J. Ofori-Dankwa & K. Omane-Antwi (Eds.), *Comparative Case Studies on Entrepreneurship in Developed and Developing Countries* (pp. 1–18). Hershey, PA: Business Science Reference. doi:10.4018/978-1-4666-7533-9.ch001

Rahimi, R., Nadda, V., & Hamid, M. (2016). HRM Practices in Banking Sector of Pakistan: Case of National Bank of Pakistan. *International Journal of Asian Business and Information Management*, *7*(2), 25–50. doi:10.4018/IJABIM.2016040103

Raina, V. K. (2014). Overview of Mobile Payment: Technologies and Security. In F. Liébana-Cabanillas, F. Muñoz-Leiva, J. Sánchez-Fernández, & M. Martínez-Fiestas (Eds.), *Electronic Payment Systems for Competitive Advantage in E-Commerce* (pp. 186–222). Hershey, PA: IGI Global. doi:10.4018/978-1-4666-5190-6.ch011

Ramos de Luna, I., Montoro-Ríos, F., & Liébana-Cabanillas, F. J. (2014). New Perspectives on Payment Systems: Near Field Communication (NFC) Payments through Mobile Phones. In F. Liébana-Cabanillas, F. Muñoz-Leiva, J. Sánchez-Fernández, & M. Martínez-Fiestas (Eds.), *Electronic Payment Systems for Competitive Advantage in E-Commerce* (pp. 260–278). Hershey, PA: IGI Global. doi:10.4018/978-1-4666-5190-6.ch013

Rana, P., & Pandey, D. (2016). Challenges and Issues in E-Banking Services and Operations in Developing Countries. In S. Joshi & R. Joshi (Eds.), *Designing and Implementing Global Supply Chain Management* (pp. 237–281). Hershey, PA: IGI Global. doi:10.4018/978-1-4666-9720-1.ch013

Raymond, M., & Rowe, F. (2016). IS Design Considerations for an Innovative Service BPO: Insights from a Banking Case Study. *International Journal of Information Technologies and Systems Approach*, 9(2), 39–56. doi:10.4018/IJITSA.2016070103

Rossetti di Valdalbero, D., & Birnbaum, B. (2017). Towards a New Economy: Co-Creation and Open Innovation in a Trustworthy Europe. In W. Vassallo (Ed.), *Crowdfunding for Sustainable Entrepreneurship and Innovation* (pp. 20–36). Hershey, PA: Business Science Reference. doi:10.4018/978-1-5225-0568-6.ch002

Rouhani, S., & Savoji, S. R. (2016). A Success Assessment Model for BI Tools Implementation: An Empirical Study of Banking Industry. *International Journal of Business Intelligence Research*, 7(1), 25–44. doi:10.4018/IJBIR.2016010103

Rundshagen, V. (2014). Business Schools: Internationalization towards a New European Perspective. In A. Dima (Ed.), *Handbook of Research on Trends in European Higher Education Convergence* (pp. 124–149). Hershey, PA: Information Science Reference. doi:10.4018/978-1-4666-5998-8.ch007

Rusko, R., & Pekkala, J. (2014). About the Challenges to Start E-Commerce Activity in SMEs: Push-Pull Effects. In F. Musso & E. Druica (Eds.), *Handbook of Research on Retailer-Consumer Relationship Development* (pp. 490–508). Hershey, PA: IGI Global. doi:10.4018/978-1-4666-6074-8.ch026

Saiz-Alvarez, J. M. (2016). Socioeconomics of Solidarity: A Multilateral Perspective from the European Union. In J. Saiz-Álvarez (Ed.), *Handbook of Research on Social Entrepreneurship and Solidarity Economics* (pp. 192–215). Hershey, PA: Business Science Reference. doi:10.4018/978-1-5225-0097-1.ch011

Samoilenko, S., & Osei-Bryson, K. (2014). Investigation of Determinants of Total Factor Productivity: An Analysis of the Impact of Investments in Telecoms on Economic Growth in Productivity in the Context of Transition Economies. *International Journal of Technology Diffusion*, *5*(1), 26–42. doi:10.4018/ijtd.2014010103

Sarigianni, C., Thalmann, S., & Manhart, M. (2015). Knowledge Risks of Social Media in the Financial Industry. *International Journal of Knowledge Management*, *11*(4), 19–34. doi:10.4018/IJKM.2015100102

Scheepers, M. D., & Kerr, D. V. (2014). Managerial Orientations and Digital Commerce Adoption in SMEs. In P. Ordóñez de Pablos (Ed.), *International Business Strategy and Entrepreneurship: An Information Technology Perspective* (pp. 185–201). Hershey, PA: IGI Global. doi:10.4018/978-1-4666-4753-4.ch012

Sen, S., & Sen, R. L. (2014). Impact of NPAs on Bank Profitability: An Empirical Study. In N. Ray & K. Chakraborty (Eds.), *Handbook of Research on Strategic Business Infrastructure Development and Contemporary Issues in Finance* (pp. 124–134). Hershey, PA: IGI Global. doi:10.4018/978-1-4666-5154-8.ch010

Sen, S., & Sen, R. L. (2015). An Empirical Analysis of FII Movement and Currency Value in India. In N. Ray, D. Das, S. Chaudhuri, & A. Ghosh (Eds.), *Strategic Infrastructure Development for Economic Growth and Social Change* (pp. 207–217). Hershey, PA: Business Science Reference. doi:10.4018/978-1-4666-7470-7.ch014

Shaikh, A. A., & Karjaluoto, H. (2016). On Some Misconceptions Concerning Digital Banking and Alternative Delivery Channels. *International Journal of E-Business Research*, *12*(3), 1–16. doi:10.4018/IJEBR.2016070101

Shalan, M. A. (2017). Considering Middle Circles in Mobile Cloud Computing: Ethics and Risk Governance. In K. Munir (Ed.), *Security Management in Mobile Cloud Computing* (pp. 43–72). Hershey, PA: Information Science Reference. doi:10.4018/978-1-5225-0602-7.ch003

Sindwani, R., & Goel, M. (2016). The Relationship between Service Quality Dimensions, Customer Satisfaction and Loyalty in Technology based Self Service Banking. *International Journal of E-Services and Mobile Applications*, *8*(2), 54–70. doi:10.4018/IJESMA.2016040104

Şiriner, İ., & Shaiymbetova, K. (2016). Impacts of Global Financial Crisis and Changes in Monetary Policy of Central Banks: An Analysis of Central Bank of the Republic of Turkey (CBRT) and Bank of Israel (BOI). In M. Erdoğdu & B. Christiansen (Eds.), *Handbook of Research on Public Finance in Europe and the MENA Region* (pp. 474–504). Hershey, PA: IGI Global. doi:10.4018/978-1-5225-0053-7.ch021

Sonmez, Y. (2015). The European Union: Another Round of Enlargement? In E. Sorhun, Ü. Hacıoğlu, & H. Dinçer (Eds.), *Regional Economic Integration and the Global Financial System* (pp. 73–87). Hershey, PA: Business Science Reference. doi:10.4018/978-1-4666-7308-3.ch007

Trimble, T. E. (2014). Party Rhetoric in Federal Budget Communications. In R. Hart (Ed.), *Communication and Language Analysis in the Public Sphere* (pp. 17–35). Hershey, PA: Information Science Reference. doi:10.4018/978-1-4666-5003-9.ch002

Tudor, C. L., & Vega, C. (2014). A Review of Textual Analysis in Economics and Finance. In R. Hart (Ed.), *Communication and Language Analysis in the Corporate World* (pp. 122–139). Hershey, PA: IGI Global. doi:10.4018/978-1-4666-4999-6.ch008

Uğurlu, M. (2016). Firm-Level Determinants of Foreign Investment and M&A Activity: Evidence from Turkey. In M. Erdoğdu & B. Christiansen (Eds.), *Handbook of Research on Comparative Economic Development Perspectives on Europe and the MENA Region* (pp. 265–292). Hershey, PA: Business Science Reference. doi:10.4018/978-1-4666-9548-1.ch013

Ushakov, D., & Chich-Jen, S. (2015). Global Economy Urbanization and Urban Economy Globalization: Forms, Factors, Results. In D. Ushakov (Ed.), *Urbanization and Migration as Factors Affecting Global Economic Development* (pp. 148–170). Hershey, PA: IGI Global. doi:10.4018/978-1-4666-7328-1.ch009

Uysal, Ü. E. (2017). A Brief History of City Branding in Istanbul. In A. Bayraktar & C. Uslay (Eds.), *Global Place Branding Campaigns across Cities, Regions, and Nations* (pp. 117–131). Hershey, PA: Business Science Reference. doi:10.4018/978-1-5225-0576-1.ch006

Valek, L. (2016). Open Ways for Time Banking Research: Project Management and Beyond. *International Journal of Human Capital and Information Technology Professionals*, *7*(1), 35–47. doi:10.4018/IJHCITP.2016010103

Vardar, G., Aydoğan, B., & Acar, E. E. (2014). International Portfolio Diversification Benefits among Developed and Emerging Markets within the Context of the Recent Global Financial Crisis. In N. Ray & K. Chakraborty (Eds.), *Handbook of Research on Strategic Business Infrastructure Development and Contemporary Issues in Finance* (pp. 162–185). Hershey, PA: IGI Global. doi:10.4018/978-1-4666-5154-8.ch013

Vasudeva, S., & Singh, G. (2017). Impact of E-Core Service Quality Dimensions on Perceived Value of M-Banking in Case of Three Socio-Economic Variables. *International Journal of Technology and Human Interaction*, *13*(1), 1–20. doi:10.4018/IJTHI.2017010101

Voica, M. C., & Mirela, P. (2014). Investment Development Path in the European Union in the Context of Financial Crisis. *International Journal of Sustainable Economies Management*, *3*(4), 33–44. doi:10.4018/ijsem.2014100104

Wang, M., & Lin, C. (2014). Impact of Bank Operational Efficiency Using a Three-Stage DEA Model. *International Journal of Risk and Contingency Management*, *3*(4), 32–50. doi:10.4018/ijrcm.2014100103

Wang, Y., Shanmugam, M., Hajli, N., & Bugshan, H. (2015). Customer Attitudes towards Internet Banking and Social Media on Internet Banking in the UK. In N. Hajli (Ed.), *Handbook of Research on Integrating Social Media into Strategic Marketing* (pp. 287–302). Hershey, PA: Business Science Reference. doi:10.4018/978-1-4666-8353-2.ch017

Warf, B. (2016). Digital Money in the Age of Globalization. In I. Lee (Ed.), *Encyclopedia of E-Commerce Development, Implementation, and Management* (pp. 177–183). Hershey, PA: Business Science Reference. doi:10.4018/978-1-4666-9787-4.ch014

Yıldırım, D. Ç., Erdoğan, S., & Gedikli, A. (2015). Fiscal Harmonization or Fiscal Union in Eurozone? In Ö. Olgu, H. Dinçer, & Ü. Hacıoğlu (Eds.), *Handbook of Research on Strategic Developments and Regulatory Practice in Global Finance* (pp. 94–104). Hershey, PA: Business Science Reference. doi:10.4018/978-1-4666-7288-8.ch007

Youssef, M. A. (2015). Electronic Commerce and Change in Management Accounting Practices in an Egyptian Organization. In M. Khosrow-Pour (Ed.), *Strategic E-Commerce Systems and Tools for Competing in the Digital Marketplace* (pp. 189–205). Hershey, PA: IGI Global. doi:10.4018/978-1-4666-8133-0.ch010

Zhang, L. Z. (2015). Investment Strategies for Implementing Cloud Systems in Supply Chains. In F. Soliman (Ed.), *Business Transformation and Sustainability through Cloud System Implementation* (pp. 32–43). Hershey, PA: Business Science Reference. doi:10.4018/978-1-4666-6445-6.ch003

About the Author

Iustina Alina Boitan is Assoc. professor, Ph.D. at the Faculty of Finance and Banking from the Bucharest University of Economic Studies (Romania). She is member of several professional bodies, such as the Center of Financial and Monetary Research, within the Bucharest University of Economic Studies, Romania (since 2008) and the Monetary Research Center within the University of National and World Economy, Bulgaria (research fellow since 2015). She has been granted the Georgescu Roegen award for excellence in scientific research, concretized in papers published in journals indexed Thomson Reuters (Bucharest University of Economic Studies, 2014). Her research interests focus on banking systems' efficiency and competition, assessment of banking systems' distress, quantitative supervisory tools (such as the development of early warning systems), ethical or socially responsible banks. She holds in-depth expertise in quantitative methods applied to financial system.

Index

Purchase Print + Free E-Book or E-Book Only*

Purchase a print book through the IGI Global Online Bookstore and receive the e-book for free or purchase the e-book only! Shipping fees apply.

www.igi-global.com

Recommended Reference Books

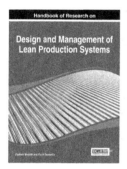

ISBN: 978-1-4666-5039-8
© 2014; 487 pp.
List Price: $260

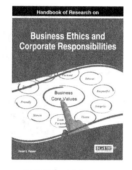

ISBN: 978-1-4666-7476-9
© 2015; 508 pp.
List Price: $212

ISBN: 978-1-4666-6182-0
© 2014; 325 pp.
List Price: $180

ISBN: 978-1-4666-4474-8
© 2014; 735 pp.
List Price: $276

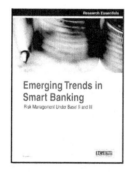

ISBN: 978-1-4666-5950-6
© 2014; 290 pp.
List Price: $156

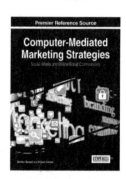

ISBN: 978-1-4666-6595-8
© 2015; 406 pp.
List Price: $156

*IGI Global now offers the exclusive opportunity to receive a free e-book with the purchase of the publication in print, or purchase any e-book publication only. You choose the format that best suits your needs. This offer is only valid on purchases made directly through IGI Global's Online Bookstore and not intended for use by book distributors or wholesalers. Shipping fees will be applied for hardcover purchases during checkout if this option is selected.

Should a new edition of any given publication become available, access will not be extended on the new edition and will only be available for the purchased publication. If a new edition becomes available, you will not lose access, but you would no longer receive new content for that publication (i.e. updates). The free e-book is only available to single institutions that purchase printed publications through IGI Global. Sharing the free e-book is prohibited and will result in the termination of e-access.

Publishing Information Science and Technology Research Since 1988

www.igi-global.com   Sign up at www.igi-global.com/newsletters   facebook.com/igiglobal   twitter.com/igiglobal

Stay Current on the Latest Emerging Research Developments

Become an IGI Global Reviewer for Authored Book Projects

The overall success of an authored book project is dependent on quality and timely reviews.

In this competitive age of scholarly publishing, constructive and timely feedback significantly decreases the turnaround time of manuscripts from submission to acceptance, allowing the publication and discovery of progressive research at a much more expeditious rate. Several IGI Global authored book projects are currently seeking highly qualified experts in the field to fill vacancies on their respective editorial review boards:

Applications may be sent to:
development@igi-global.com

Applicants must have a doctorate (or an equivalent degree) as well as publishing and reviewing experience. Reviewers are asked to write reviews in a timely, collegial, and constructive manner. All reviewers will begin their role on an ad-hoc basis for a period of one year, and upon successful completion of this term can be considered for full editorial review board status, with the potential for a subsequent promotion to Associate Editor.

If you have a colleague that may be interested in this opportunity,
we encourage you to share this information with them.

www.igi-global.com

InfoSci®-Books

A Database for Progressive Information Science and Technology Research

Maximize Your Library's Book Collection!

Invest in IGI Global's InfoSci®-Books database and gain access to
hundreds of reference books at a fraction of their individual list price.

The InfoSci®-Books database offers unlimited simultaneous users the
ability to precisely return search results through more than 75,000 full-text
chapters from nearly 3,400 reference books in the following academic research areas:

Business & Management Information Science & Technology • Computer Science & Information Technology
Educational Science & Technology • Engineering Science & Technology • Environmental Science & Technology
Government Science & Technology • Library Information Science & Technology • Media & Communication Science & Technology
Medical, Healthcare & Life Science & Technology • Security & Forensic Science & Technology • Social Sciences & Online Behavior

Peer-Reviewed Content:
• Cutting-edge research
• No embargoes
• Scholarly and professional
• Interdisciplinary

Award-Winning Platform:
• Unlimited simultaneous users
• Full-text in XML and PDF
• Advanced search engine
• No DRM

Librarian-Friendly:
• Free MARC records
• Discovery services
• COUNTER4/SUSHI compliant
• Training available

To find out more or request a free trial, visit:
www.igi-global.com/eresources

IGI Global
Proudly Partners with

eContent Pro

---

eContent Pro specializes in the following areas:

Academic Copy Editing
Our expert copy editors will conduct a full copy editing procedure on your manuscript and will also address your preferred reference style to make sure your paper meets the standards of the style of your choice.

Expert Translation
Our expert translators will work to ensure a clear cut and accurate translation of your document, ensuring that your research is flawlessly communicated to your audience.

Professional Proofreading
Our editors will conduct a comprehensive assessment of your content and address all shortcomings of the paper in terms of grammar, language structures, spelling, and formatting.

IGI Global Authors, Save 10% on eContent Pro's Services!

Scan the QR Code to Receive Your 10% Discount

The 10% discount is applied directly to your eContent Pro shopping cart when placing an order through IGI Global's referral link. Use the QR code to access this referral link. eContent Pro has the right to end or modify any promotion at any time.

Email: customerservice@econtentpro.com

econtentpro.com

Become an IRMA Member

Members of the **Information Resources Management Association (IRMA)** understand the importance of community within their field of study. The Information Resources Management Association is an ideal venue through which professionals, students, and academicians can convene and share the latest industry innovations and scholarly research that is changing the field of information science and technology. Become a member today and enjoy the benefits of membership as well as the opportunity to collaborate and network with fellow experts in the field.

IRMA Membership Benefits:

- **One FREE Journal Subscription**

- **30% Off Additional Journal Subscriptions**

- **20% Off Book Purchases**

- Updates on the latest events and research on Information Resources Management through the IRMA-L listserv.

- Updates on new open access and downloadable content added to Research IRM.

- A copy of the Information Technology Management Newsletter twice a year.

- A certificate of membership.

IRMA Membership $195

Scan code or visit **irma-international.org** and begin by selecting your free journal subscription.

Membership is good for one full year.

Encyclopedia of Information Science and Technology, Third Edition (10 Vols.)

Mehdi Khosrow-Pour, D.B.A. (Information Resources Management Association, USA)
ISBN: 978-1-4666-5888-2; **EISBN:** 978-1-4666-5889-9; © 2015; 10,384 pages.

The **Encyclopedia of Information Science and Technology, Third Edition** is a 10-volume compilation of authoritative, previously unpublished research-based articles contributed by thousands of researchers and experts from all over the world. This discipline-defining encyclopedia will serve research needs in numerous fields that are affected by the rapid pace and substantial impact of technological change. With an emphasis on modern issues and the presentation of potential opportunities, prospective solutions, and future directions in the field, it is a relevant and essential addition to any academic library's reference collection.

Take An Extra

30% Off[1]

[1] 30% discount offer cannot be combined with any other discount and is only valid on purchases made directly through IGI Global's Online Bookstore (www.igi-global.com/books), not intended for use by distributors or wholesalers. Offer expires December 31, 2016.

Free Lifetime E-Access with Print Purchase

Take 30% Off Retail Price:

Hardcover with Free E-Access:[2] **$2,765**
~~List Price: $3,950~~

E-Access with Free Hardcover:[2] **$2,765**
~~List Price: $3,950~~

E-Subscription Price:

One (1) Year E-Subscription: $1,288
~~List Price: $1,840~~

Two (2) Year E-Subscription: $2,177
~~List Price: $3,110~~

Recommend this Title to Your Institution's Library: www.igi-global.com/books

[2] IGI Global now offers the exclusive opportunity to receive free lifetime e-access with the purchase of the publication in print, or purchase any e-access publication and receive a free print copy of the publication. You choose the format that best suits your needs. This offer is only valid on purchases made directly through IGI Global's Online Bookstore and not intended for use by book distributors or wholesalers. Shipping fees will be applied for hardcover purchases during checkout if this option is selected.

The lifetime of a publication refers to its status as the current edition. Should a new edition of any given publication become available, access will not be extended on the new edition and will only be available for the purchased publication. If a new edition becomes available, you will not lose access, but you would no longer receive new content for that publication (i.e. updates). Free Lifetime E-Access is only available to single institutions that purchase printed publications through IGI Global. Sharing the Free Lifetime E-Access is prohibited and will result in the termination of e-access.

www.igi-global.com/infosci-ondemand

InfoSci®-OnDemand

Continuously updated with new material on a weekly basis, InfoSci®-OnDemand offers the ability to search through thousands of quality full-text research papers. Users can narrow each search by identifying key topic areas of interest, then display a complete listing of relevant papers, and purchase materials specific to their research needs.

Comprehensive Service
- Over 81,600+ journal articles, book chapters, and case studies.
- All content is downloadable in PDF format and can be stored locally for future use.

No Subscription Fees
- One time fee of $37.50 per PDF download.

Instant Access
- Receive a download link immediately after order completion!

Database Platform Features:
- Comprehensive Pay-Per-View Service
- Written by Prominent International Experts/Scholars
- Precise Search and Retrieval
- Updated With New Material on a Weekly Basis
- Immediate Access to Full-Text PDFs
- No Subscription Needed
- Purchased Research Can Be Stored Locally for Future Use

"It really provides an excellent entry into the research literature of the field. It presents a manageable number of highly relevant sources on topics of interest to a wide range of researchers. The sources are scholarly, but also accessible to 'practitioners'."
- Lisa Stimatz, MLS, University of North Carolina at Chapel Hill, USA

"It is an excellent and well designed database which will facilitate research, publication and teaching. It is a very very useful tool to have."
- George Ditsa, PhD, University of Wollongong, Australia

"I have accessed the database and find it to be a valuable tool to the IT/IS community. I found valuable articles meeting my search criteria 95% of the time."
- Lynda Louis, Xavier University of Louisiana, USA

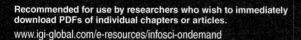
Recommended for use by researchers who wish to immediately download PDFs of individual chapters or articles.
www.igi-global.com/e-resources/infosci-ondemand

Printed in the United States
By Bookmasters